P9-CEI-939

The Special Taste Of Florida

The Special Taste Of Florida

G. Dean Foster

Seagate Publishing Company

Naples, Florida 34103

The Special Taste of Florida -
A Unique Look at America's Most Exciting Cuisine
Copyright ©1995, ©1996 By G. Dean Foster

First printing, November 1995
Second printing, June 1996

All rights reserved. No part of this book may be used
or reproduced in any manner whatsoever without writ-
ten permission, except in the case of brief quotations
embodied in critical articles and reviews.

For information, address:
Seagate Publishing Co.
4077 Tamiami Trail North, D201
P. O. Box 11911
Naples, Florida 34101-1911
(941) 261-9693

Printed and bound in the United States of America.

Library of Congress Catalog Card Number
94-74944

The Special Taste of Florida -
A Unique Look at America's Most Exciting Cuisine
G. Dean Foster
Seagate Publishing Company, Inc.

ISBN   0-9644572-7-X

To Marge, John & Robby

Acknowledgments

My sincere thanks to the many individuals who knowingly and unknowingly helped make The Special Taste of Florida such an enjoyable project.

My greatest admiration and appreciation to the individual chefs, restaurants owners and hotel management people who generously provided their energy and respective talents to create this publication. You were all selected to be a part of The Special Taste of Florida because you are so very good at what you do.

Additional thanks to William Kreuser, Douglas Speirn-Smith, Patricia Carpenter and Doris Reynolds for their unselfish gift of time and advice. To Timothy Kling, Mary McCulley and Sharron Fisher for a tasteful collaboration of cover design and photography.

TABLE OF CONTENTS

CENTRAL FLORIDA

THE GULF COAST

Charcoal Grilled Turkey Burgers

Oven Roasted Pork Loin with Peppercorn Port Wine Glaze & Fresh Raspberries
Veal Tenderloin with Wild Mushroom Sauce
Yellowtail Snapper with Herb Tomato Caper Butter
Fried Apples & Strawberries in White Wine Dough, Tossed in Cinnamon Sugar
Char-Broiled Dolphin á la Timbers West
Snapper Almondine
Absolut® Citrus Tuna au Poivre
Timbers' Pineapple Salsa
Pecan Pralines
The Veranda Bourbon Street Filet
Portobello Mushrooms
Cashew Encrusted Grouper Meunière
Chardonnay's Scallop Pancake
Escargot with Angel Hair Pasta
Chocolate Truffles Chardonnay
Skillet Roasted Mussels
Bronzed Swordfish Caesar Salad
Sun Dried Tomato Encrusted Chicken with Shiitake Mushrooms
Corsican Summer Salad
Onion Soup with Brie Cheese Gratine
Smoked Breast of Duck with Orange Walnut Vinaigrette
Cornish Game Hen and Florida Lobster with Cognac & Green Peppercorn Sauce
Seafood Mixed Grill with Florida Beurre Blanc
Roasted Oriental Duckling
Sautéed Red Snapper with Lobster Succotash
Roasted Colorado Rack of Lamb with Sunflower Seeds, Opal Basil & Garlic Crust
Red Tomato Vinaigrette
Baked Wild Mushrooms & Yucca Root Strudel with Pinot Noir Sauce
Chicken Roulade with Granny Smith Apple Vinaigrette
Sautéed Salmon with Absolut Citron®
Grilled Portobello Mushroom & Eggplant with Tomato Basil Vinaigrette
Hazelnut Crusted Grouper with Raspberry Beurre Blanc
Osso Bucco Braised in Port Wine Sauce
Jumbo Lump Crab Cakes with Red Pepper Coulis
Grilled Marinated Lamb Loin with Marsala Sauce
Farfalle "Bowtie" Pasta with Chicken & Gorgonzola Cheese
Chicken Ali-Oli
Capellini with Shrimp & Lobster
Roast Quail with Apple, Walnuts, Sausage, Cheese & Wild Mushroom Risotto

THE ATLANTIC COAST

Introduction

From the very start, our goal with the first edition of *The Special Taste of Florida* was to create a cookbook filled with exciting and delicious recipes that capture the essence and personality of Florida's very special cuisine. Additionally, we wanted to feature recipes that are very "do-able" in normal home kitchens by amateur cooks at all levels. These same goals were foremost in our minds with this revised edition.

The revised edition of *The Special Taste of Florida* arrives only seven months after the first edition was printed. It contains eleven new restaurant selections and forty-five new recipes. With the enthusiastic response to the first edition, many asked us why would we go to the trouble to revise it. Our response is simple and is based on the nature of the culinary industry. With new and exciting recipes and techniques brought to the market almost daily, why wait?

The determining factor in our decision to revise the book was ultimately the outstanding recipes we received from highly regarded Florida restaurants that were not featured in our first edition, including: *The Grill* at The Ritz-Carlton on Amelia Island, honored as the second AAA Five- Diamond restaurant in Florida...*Chef Allen's*, featuring Allen Susser - arguably Florida's most recognized chef and restaurant owner... Florida's finest natural food restaurant, *Unicorn Village* in Aventura... Darrel & Oliver's exciting new *East City Grill* in Ft. Lauderdale...*Damiano's at the Tarrimore House* in Delray Beach...*The Restaurant* at the elegant Ritz-Carlton in Palm Beach...the award winning *Turnberry Isle Resort & Club*...Key West's venerable *Pier House Restaurant*...*Marchand's Bar & Grill* in St. Petersburg's stunning Renaissance Vinoy Resort...Sanibel Island's *Greenhouse Grill*...and *Maxwell's on the Bay* in Naples.

While we were especially pleased *The Special Taste of Florida* became the best-selling cookbook in Florida, we were surprised at the number of books ordered by chefs and restaurant owners from other parts of the country. There is evidently a great deal of communication among those with culinary interests. We are proud to say that many of these people felt Florida has become the hotbed for the America's most talented young chefs and the country's most exciting cuisine.

As with the first edition, we gave our selected chefs and restaurants substantial latitude to create delicious recipes that are fun to make and accurately reflect their respective culinary styles. Many recipes featured are their personal favorites. We are extremely pleased with the new recipes added to our revised edition, as well as those selected a few months ago. We hope they will provide you with many wonderful meals.

BUD & ALLEY'S

Route C30-A • Santa Rosa Beach, Florida 33245 • (904) 231-5900

Bud & Alley's has been a warm, friendly gathering place in the Panhandle town of Seaside for close to 10 years. The popular eatery is legendary for its consistently superb regional cuisine and comfortable beach setting. Seasonal menus provide a unique combination of the rustic cooking styles of Tuscany, the coastal Mediterranean and the coastal south. An on premise culinary herb garden builds the foundation for cuisine utilizing the region's finest and freshest in locally available seafood. The Roof-Top Bar is a favorite spot to hang out with friends for Tapas, cocktails and spectacular sunsets.

Bud & Alley's is rated by Florida Trend Magazine as one of the finest restaurants in the state and has been featured on CNN's "On The Menu" numerous times. Additional awards include The Wine Spectator Magazine's Award of Excellence.

YELLOWTAIL SNAPPER
WITH FIRE ROASTED TOMATO TARRAGON SAUCE

Serves 4

4 6-oz. yellowtail snapper filets, skin on
4 Tbsp. peanut oil
1 Tbsp. butter
1 cup flour
1 Tbsp. sea salt
1 tsp. fresh ground pepper
4 shallots, rough chopped
3 cloves of garlic, rough chopped

¹/₄ cup fresh tarragon leaves rough chopped
¹/₃ cup of dry sauvignon blanc
¹/₃ cup of light fish stock
4 oven roast plum tomatoes, rough chopped
4 Tbsp. butter

Take the four boneless filets and dust them in the dusting mixture of flour, salt and pepper. Sauté the fish in peanut oil over high heat.

Add the tablespoon of butter to oil shortly after placing fish in oil (the butter helps achieve the desired crispness for sautéed fish). Sauté first side until it is golden brown then turn it over and cook until you are just able to flake fish. Remove immediately and place fish on paper towels to drain.

Remove excess oil from pan, reserving natural browning and fish drippings. Immediately place pan over medium high heat and add tarragon, garlic and shallots, tossing briefly (the tarragon aroma will be intense at this point).

Add sauvignon blanc to deglaze pan then add fish stock and roasted tomatoes. Reduce sauce by ²/₃. Lower heat to medium setting and whisk in 4 tablespoons of cold butter, bit by bit until butter is just dissolved, taking care not to let butter break. Add salt and pepper to sauce to taste. Pour sauce over fish and serve. Garnish with sprigs of fresh tarragon.

FISH STOCK PREPARATION

It's amazing what a good fish stock can do for a seafood sauce; Bud & Alley's offers the following:

In an 8-quart sauce pan place:

4 fish bones, heads on
2 bay leaves
2 crushed garlic cloves
2 stalks of celery, course chopped
1 medium onion, chopped

a few sprigs of parsley and reserved
  tarragon stems
6 peppercorns
2 qt. of water
1 Tbsp. salt

Over medium high heat, add all the ingredients except the water and sweat the vegetables until the onions become translucent. Add the water and bring to a boil.

Simmer for 20 minutes, skimming the foam and scum. Strain through a fine sieve and cheese cloth.

SEAFOOD STEW WITH ROUILLE SAUCE

A bouillabaise with a Southern accent.
Serves 2

2 Tbsp. canola oil
10 little neck clams
6 large shrimp, peeled and deveined
8 large raw oysters
4 oz. grouper filet, diced
2 Roma tomatoes, sliced in rounds
2 quartered new potatoes, blanched
2 green onions, chopped

1 tsp. fresh oregano
1 tsp. chopped garlic
⅝ cup white wine
¼ tsp. cracked black pepper
4 Tbsp. unsalted butter, diced
4 oz. light fish stock
1 lemon, juice only

In a medium sized sauté pan, heat the canola oil then add the clams, grouper, shrimp, garlic and sautè until slightly cooked. Add white wine, cover and let steam until the clams have opened. Next add oysters, potatoes, oregano, green onions, and tomatoes. Let simmer for 30 seconds, then add the lemon juice and fish stock. Whisk in cold butter bit by bit until butter has dissolved. Season with salt and pepper.

Serve in large soup or pasta bowl and drizzle with extra virgin olive oil. Garnish with a tablespoon of rouille sauce and serve with a wedge of warm grilled French bread.

Rouille Sauce

Yield 2 cups

2 egg yolks
1 Tbsp. garlic
^{1}/$_4$ cup roasted, peeled and seeded red
   pepper
1 lemon, juice only

^{1}/$_3$ cup fresh bread crumbs
^{1}/$_4$ cup chopped parsley
2^1/$_2$ cups olive oil
^{1}/$_2$ Tbsp. Louisiana hot sauce
salt and pepper to taste

This will store in your refrigerator in a tightly-wrapped container for 2 weeks. In a food processor, add the egg yolks, garlic, roast peppers, parsley, lemon juice and hot sauce. While processing these ingredients, slowly add the oil until it thickens. If the mixture becomes too thick, thin slightly with a little warm water. (Consistency should be slightly thinner than mayonnaise.) Continue until the oil is fully incorporated.

Next blend in bread crumbs and season with salt and pepper. Place one tablespoon on top of the finished seafood stew.

Grilled Swordfish on Portobello Mushroom
with Country Ham Tapenade & Roasted Red Pepper Coulis

An excellent dish - perfect for grilled swordfish.
Serves 2

2 5-oz. swordfish tournedos, 2^1/$_2$-inches
   high by 2-inches wide
2 Portobello mushrooms

1 cup extra virgin olive oil
salt and pepper

Portobello Mushroom

Preheat oven to 350°F. Remove stems from the mushrooms and brush with the olive oil until very well oiled (the mushrooms should be well absorbed with olive oil). Season with salt and pepper and grill until slightly tender. Place the mushrooms on a small sheet pan and place in the oven and bake until thoroughly tender and slightly shriveled.

Grilled Swordfish

Brush with olive oil and place over "white hot" coals or a wood burning grill. Grill the swordfish for one minute then turn it 90° for one minute to achieve cross angled grill marks. Repeat the same procedure for the other side of the fish.

Next place the fish in the preheated oven for about 8 to 10 minutes to finish the cooking procedure. (Test doneness by pressing lightly with index finger until fish starts to separate.)

COUNTRY HAM TAPENADE

8 oz. "Virginia Ham" or good quality
   Prosciutto ham, finely diced
4 anchovie filets, chopped
4 oz. pitted kalamata olives (sliced)
¹/₄ cup chopped chives
¹/₄ cup chopped Italian parsley

2 Tbsp. chopped garlic
1 cup extra virgin olive oil
1 Tbsp. freshly squeezed lemon juice
2 tsp. cracked black pepper

    In a medium sized stainless mixing bowl, combine above ingredients and mix thoroughly until combined. Cover and refrigerate for 24 hours. Mix thoroughly again before serving.

    Note: "Tapenade" is a staple condiment in Mediterranean cooking. It is widely used as an accompaniment for grilled or roasted vegetables such as eggplant, zucchini, tomatoes, onions, etc… or simply rubbed on grilled bread and served with assorted cheeses such as fresh mozzarella, goat cheese or Pecorino Romano, etc. It is traditionally made by combining black olives, capers, garlic, anchovy, parsley and olive oil. In an airtight container, the tapenade can be stored up to a month.

ROASTED RED PEPPER COULIS

6 large red peppers (sweet)
1 cup extra virgin olive oil
salt and pepper

¹/₂ cup dry white wine
1 Tbsp. garlic

    Over hot coals, grill the peppers until lightly charred and blistered. Remove from the grill and place in a stainless steel bowl and cover with plastic wrap. This will allow the peppers to steam while they cool. This helps the peeling process.

    Once cooled, peel the charred skins away from the peppers and discard any seeds. Place the peppers in a food processor along with the garlic and white wine. Process until smooth and add the olive oil slowly until incorporated. Season to taste with salt and pepper.

CRIOLLA'S

130 East Highway 30-A • Grayton Beach, Florida 32459 • (904) 267-1267

Nestled in the village of Grayton Beach in Florida's Panhandle is Criolla's - winner of Florida Trend's Golden Spoon Award since 1991 as one of Florida's top twenty restaurants. Criolla's beautiful Caribbean architecture is the perfect setting for Chef/Owner Johnny Earles' cuisine, a fusion of the Creole styles of his native Louisiana, together with the various Creole influences of the Caribbean. The wine list of Criolla's is impressive, with over 180 bottle selections and 25 by the glass.

Criolla's is the perfect example of the many excellent restaurants in the Panhandle which are now receiving regional and national recognition. In fact, during our initial conversation with Chef Earles, Southern Living Magazine was in the restaurant for a photo shoot.

KISS YO' MAMA SOUP

If yo' mama makes this soup, you will indeed kiss her. It is marvelous.
Makes 3 quarts

7 cups fresh corn, cut off the cob (substitute frozen only, not canned)
¹/₂ cup roasted, peeled, chopped poblano chiles (substitute canned green chiles)
2 medium sized chiptole chiles, chopped (substitute canned chiptoles, if necessary)
1 cup chopped yellow onion

¹/₄ lb. unsalted butter
1 cup rich chicken stock
3 cups milk
8 oz. sour cream at room temperature
¹/₄ cup fresh goat cheese, such as Chevre
¹/₂ lb. Louisiana crawfish tails
2 Tbsp. fresh chives, chopped
salt to taste

In a non aluminum pot, sauté the onion, corn, chiptoles and poblanos in the butter over medium heat for 5 minutes. Add the chicken stock, cover and simmer for 5 minutes. Remove from the heat and cool for 15 minutes.

Purée the mixture in a blender or a food processor and strain through a medium sieve, using a rubber spatula to retrieve as much as possible. Discard the remaining pulp. Add the milk and return the mixture to the original pot and bring slowly to a boil. Reduce the heat to a simmer for 5 minutes, stirring frequently.

Remove from the heat and stir in the sour cream and crawfish tails. Salt to taste and serve. Garnish the bowls with goat cheese and chopped chives.

Soft Shell Po' Boy

with Chayote Choux Choux

For crab lovers, it is hard to fathom a better tasting sandwich than Johnny Earl's po' boy creation.

Soft Shell Crab

1 cleaned, fresh, soft blue crab
Kosher salt
chili powder, such as Chimayo or Ancho
2 Tbsp. peanut oil

Heat a skillet to medium high heat, lightly dust bottom side of crab with chili powder and salt.

Sauté bottom side down in 2 Tbsp. peanut oil for 1 and ¹/₂ minutes, turn, sauté for 1 and ¹/₂ minutes more and remove.

To serve, place 2 Tbsp. Choux Choux on sour dough toast and crab on top.

Chayote Choux Choux

1 cup red cabbage, finely chopped
³/₄ cup chayote squash, peeled, seeded, diced
¹/₂ cup green onions, chopped
¹/₂ cup green bell pepper, diced
¹/₄ cup red bell pepper, diced
¹/₄ cup green tomatoes, chopped
¹/₄ carrot, julienne
1 Tbsp. jalapeño pepper, minced

1 Tbsp. salt
²/₃ cup distilled white vinegar
3 Tbsp. sugar
¹/₂ tsp. celery seed
¹/₂ tsp. dry mustard
¹/₄ tsp. turmeric
¹/₈ tsp. dry ground ginger

Combine cabbage, chayote, onion, bell peppers, tomatoes, carrot and jalapeño in a bowl; toss with salt and let stand 5 to 6 hours (or overnight) at room temperature. Drain vegetables.

In large non-aluminum pan, combine vinegar, sugar, celery seed, mustard, turmeric and ginger; simmer, covered, for 10 minutes. Add vegetables; cover and simmer, stirring occasionally, until vegetables are tender-crisp, approximately 15 to 20 minutes.

Cool choux-choux, then store tightly covered in the refrigerator up to 1 month.

KEY LIME CHEESECAKE

This cheesecake has a very special crust made with ground, roasted Macadamia nuts, which are then covered with melted semi-sweet chocolate. The results are heavenly.
One 10-inch Cake

FILLING

3 lb. cream cheese, softened
3 cups granulated sugar
9 whole eggs
1 Tbsp. vanilla extract
1 cup key lime juice
2 cups unsweetened coconut, toasted
    (health food or gourmet stores)

CRUST

1½ cups ground, roasted Macadamia nuts
    (substitute crushed graham crackers)
¼ cup granulated sugar
4 Tbsp. unsalted butter
2 oz. semi-sweet chocolate

Grease inside and paper line the bottom of a 10-inch springform pan. Slowly melt the chocolate over low heat in a double boiler. Keep warm but do not over heat. Using an electric mixer, combine ground nuts or graham cracker crumbs with the sugar and melted butter. Press mixture into bottom of pan using back of a large metal spoon. Spread a thin layer of melted chocolate over the crust, using a pastry brush. Set pan in refrigerator so chocolate hardens.

Break up cream cheese and place in mixer bowl. Using mixer paddle attachment, beat cream cheese until smooth and creamy. Scrape down your bowl with rubber spatula. Continue mixing, gradually adding sugar. In a separate bowl, add vanilla to the eggs. Slowly add egg mixture, one egg at a time to the creamy mixture. When eggs are incorporated, scrape your bowl and continue mixing until smooth. Stir in the key-lime juice. Pour mixture into springform pan, leaving about ⅛-inch space from the top. Place cake in a roasting pan and fill the pan with enough water so that it comes halfway up the side of the cake pan. Bake in pre-heated 400° F. oven for 25-30 minutes. Reduce temperature to 350°F. and turn roasting pan and bake for 40-45 minutes. Turn the pan one final time and continue baking for another 40 minutes. Take cake out of the oven and allow to cool. Leave cake in springform pan, cover with plastic wrap and refrigerate overnight. The next day, unmold the cake and garnish sides of cake with toasted, unsweetened coconut. Yields 12 servings. Cake must be refrigerated

ELEPHANT WALK RESTAURANT

Sandestin Resort
9300 Highway 98 West • Destin, Florida 32541 • (904) 267-4800

John Wiley wandered the world for 30 years after a herd of elephants trampled his father's tea plantation in Ceylon in 1890. When he discovered the white sand beaches of Sandestin, he knew he had found his home and erected the Elephant Walk Restaurant. Today, the Elephant Walk is the signature restaurant for the beautiful Sandestin Resort, located on the Gulf of Mexico in Florida's panhandle, and another example of the fine cuisine served in this region of the state.

Elephant Walk commemorates the treasures Wiley found during his journey to Sandestin, with dishes like Tahitianese Duck, Shrimp and Lobster Ragout, and Tamarind Tango Tuna, all in a unique jungle setting. The culinary delights range from seafood favorites to traditional dishes, and have earned Elephant Walk recognition as one of Florida's top 200 restaurants, and winner of the Emerald Coast Chefs' Challenge.

ELEPHANT WALK POPPYSEED VINAIGRETTE

This vinaigrette is also outstanding with grilled chicken.

2 cups water
1/3 cup sugar
1/3 cup lemon juice **
1/8 cup lime juice **
3 Tbsp. plus 2 tsp. orange juice**
1 tsp. orange juice concentrate
1/2 shallot, finely diced

3 raspberries, smashed
1/2 cup plus 1 Tbsp. vegetable oil
1 tsp. grenadine
2 tsp. red wine vinegar
3 Tbsp. poppy seeds
salt and pepper to taste

**all juices should be fresh squeezed.

Boil water with sugar and allow to cool. Combine all ingredients except vegetable oil and poppy seeds. Add oil slowly while blending to emulsify. Add poppy seeds at the time of serving. This may be served with any kind of green or fruit salad.

GRILLED CHICKEN BREAST
WITH STONE GROUND MUSTARD & HERBS

2 5-oz. boneless chicken breasts, skin on
1/4 cup white wine
1/2 cup whipping cream
4 Tbsp. stone ground mustard

1/2 tsp. fresh thyme, chopped
1/4 tsp. fresh tarragon, chopped
salt and pepper
2 Tbsp. salad oil

Season chicken skin with salt and pepper. Place 2 Tbsp. salad oil in sauté pan and place on heat until smoking. Place the chicken, skin side down, in pan and brown. When skin is brown, turn over and place in a 300°F. oven until chicken is done. When chicken is done, remove from pan and discard grease. Deglaze pan with white wine and reduce. Add whipping cream, mustard and herbs. Reduce to desired consistency. Salt and pepper to taste.

ELEPHANT WALK CRAB CAKES

Serves 2

3 Tbsp. mayonnaise
1 Tbsp. Dijon mustard
1 tsp. dry mustard
1 whole egg
1 egg yolk
1/4 tsp. celery seed
3 dashes Worcestershire®
2-3 dashes Tabasco® Sauce
1/2 lemon, juice only
2 Tbsp. Old Bay Seasoning®

3 Tbsp. chopped parsley
fine bread crumbs - enough to bind
    ingredients
small diced bread - enough to bind
    ingredients
4 Tbsp. pimento
3 Tbsp. scallions
1 lb. jumbo lump crab
1/2 lb. crab claw meat

Combine all ingredients except bread crumbs, crab meat and claw meat. Mix thoroughly. Gently add crab meat and claw meat, mix. Add bread crumbs and diced bread until mixture coheres well. Form into cakes and dust with fine bread crumbs. Sauté in butter or deep fry.

CHOCOLATE DECADENCE
WITH RASPBERRY SAUCE

The sauce is superb - a traditional accompaniment to chocolate cake.

3 2/3 lb. semi-sweet chocolate
1/4 cup flour
10 Tbsp. unsalted butter

10 Tbsp. lightly salted butter
1/4 cup sugar
14 eggs

Heat butter and chocolate over a water bath until melted. Sift flour into chocolate and incorporate until smooth. Combine the sugar with eggs. Add the egg mixture to the chocolate mixture. Mix on low speed for about 5 minutes. Bake at 250°F. for 10 minutes. *NOTE: Cake should bake to only 1 1/2 inches high.*

Raspberry Sauce

2 pts. fresh raspberries
4 Tbsp. corn syrup
$^1/_2$ lemon

Push berries through a fine sieve into a bowl. Discard the pulp and seeds. Warm corn syrup and lemon juice in a sauce pan to 110°F. Stir warm corn syrup into raspberry purée and mix well. Place in refrigerator until ready to use.

*"Life is so brief that we should not glance either too far backwards or forwards
... therefore study how to fix our happiness in our glass
and on our plate."*

Grimond de la Reynière

FLAMINGO CAFÉ

414 Highway 98 • Destin, Florida 32541 • (904) 837-0961

Destin's most exquisite waterfront restaurant since 1986, the immensely popular Flamingo Café blends the casual atmosphere of a café with the style and quality of a gourmet restaurant. The entire dining area and bar overlook the beautiful Destin Harbor, with additional seating available on the full length veranda.

As with a number of restaurants in the Florida Panhandle, there is a Cajun influence to the cuisine. At the Flamingo Café their culinary thrust is a mixture of Cajun, Continental and the style so often referred to as "Floribbean," an innovative, international island fare introducing fresh Florida products and seafood to a unique blend of tropical fruit and Caribbean flavors. This fusion of styles is handled with great skill and is an excellent example of the Florida Cuisine which is attracting so much interest across the country.

SHRIMP & CRAB EN CROUTE

Serves 2 as an appetizer

¹/₂ cup bechamel sauce (cold)
¹/₄ cup crabmeat

¹/₄ cup poached shrimp
2 sheets phyllo pastry dough

Combine bechamel, crab and shrimp in small mixing bowl. On a work space, fold 1 sheet phyllo in half lengthwise. Then cut phyllo in half, lengthwise. Place ¹/₂ phyllo on top of second half diagonally. Then place ¹/₂ crabmeat mixture in center of phyllo. Fold accordingly to seal. Repeat with second sheet of phyllo and remainder of crab/shrimp mixture. Brush sealed phyllo with melted butter.

Bake on ungreased baking sheet at 350°F. for approximately 5-8 minutes or until lightly golden brown and flaky.

BECHAMEL SAUCE

Yield: Approximately 2¹/₄ cups sauce

2 cups whipping cream
2 Tbsp. white wine
1¹/₂ Tbsp. chopped garlic

"gold dust" to taste (6:1 ratio, salt:white
pepper)
1 Tbsp. roux (50/50 ratio fat and flour)

Place heavy cream, white wine, garlic and gold dust in saucepan. Just before boiling point, add roux, just enough to thicken slightly thicker than creamed soup. Strain through a fine sieve and refrigerate until ready to use.

CORN & CRAB CHOWDER

A special Southern treat.
Serves 20

1 diced red bell pepper
1 diced green bell pepper
1 diced yellow bell pepper
1 medium diced onion
4 stalks diced celery
1 small can undrained cream style corn
1 small can undrained whole kernel corn
¹/₄ tsp. cayenne pepper

1¹/₂ tsp. black pepper
2 bay leaves
2 qt. chicken stock
1 qt. whipping cream
2 cups roux (50/50 ratio fat and flour)
³/₄ cup sugar
salt & pepper to taste
crabmeat (desired amount)

In a stock pot, sauté the first ten ingredients and sweat the vegetables. Add chicken stock and bring to a boil. Reduce heat to simmer. Add the roux and let simmer 10-15 minutes. Add heavy cream gradually, as you are stirring. Add sugar, salt and white pepper to taste. Gently add crabmeat upon serving.

HOUSE SMOKED SALMON SALAD

At the Flamingo Café, they cure and smoke their own salmon for this salad. We understand most people do not have cold smokers at home, so you will want to use sliced smoked salmon from your local specialty food store!

Ingredients for 1 salad:
2 oz. sliced smoked salmon
5 asparagus spears
1 Roma tomato, sliced

2 Tbsp. shaved red onion
1 Tbsp. julienne carrot
1 cup mixed baby greens
¹/₄ cup cilantro sour cream

In a mixing bowl, combine all ingredients except salmon and shaved onions. Toss with dressing and place on a chilled plate. Top with sliced salmon and red onions. Garnish with rye toast points and fresh lemon.

CILANTRO SOUR CREAM

¹/₂ cup sour cream
¹/₂ cup heavy cream
4 dashes Tabasco Sauce®

juice of ¹/₂ lemon
salt & pepper to taste
¹/₂ bunch cilantro, chopped

Combine all ingredients well. An excellent accompaniment to this are roasted peppers or capers.

SNAPPER DESTIN

Serves 4-6

1 cup all-purpose flour
2 Tbsp. Old Bay Seasoning®
2 Tbsp. paprika
1 Tbsp. black pepper
1 Tbsp. white pepper
1¹/₂ tsp. red pepper
1¹/₂ tsp. garlic powder
2 lb. red snapper filets, cut into 4 to 6
    pieces
¹/₂ cup butter or margarine melted
PAM® vegetable cooking spray
8 to 12 jumbo shrimp, peeled, deveined
    with tails on

1 lb. fresh lump crabmeat, drained and
    flaked
2 to 3 Tbsp. butter or margarine
¹/₂ to ³/₄ cup hollandaise sauce (recipe
    below)
¹/₂ to ³/₄ cup lemon meuniere sauce (recipe
    below)
¹/₂ to ³/₄ cup garlic beurre blanc sauce
    (recipe below)
carrot flowers (optional)
lemon wedges (optional)
onion fans (optional)

Combine first 7 ingredients, mixing well. Dredge filets in this flour mixture, then dip filets in ¹/₂ cup melted butter. Spray a fish basket with PAM; place fish in basket. Grill over medium-hot coals 10 minutes on each side or until fish flakes easily when tested with a fork.

Sauté shrimp and crabmeat in 2 to 3 Tbsp. butter. Spoon 2 Tbsp. of each sauce onto each plate; place filet on sauces. Top each with ¹/₄ cup crabmeat and 2 shrimp. If desired, garnish with carrot flowers, lemon wedges, and onion fans.

LEMON MEUNIÈRE SAUCE

Yield: 2 cups

3 Tbsp. lemon juice
2 Tbsp. white wine
1 Tbsp. white vinegar
1 shallot, chopped

¹/₄ cup plus 2 Tbsp. whipping cream
2 cups butter, softened
¹/₄ tsp. browning-and-seasoning sauce

Combine first 4 ingredients in a saucepan; bring mixture to a boil. Boil 2 minutes or until 95% of liquid evaporates. Add whipping cream and bring to a boil; boil 1 minute. Remove from heat. Cool 2 minutes. Return to low heat. Add butter, 2 Tbsp. at a time stirring with a whisk until butter is incorporated. Keep sauce temperature at 160°F. Stir in browning-and-seasoning sauce. Sauce will separate if reheated.

Garlic Beurre Blanc Sauce

Yield: 2 cups

2 Tbsp. white wine
1 Tbsp. white vinegar
6 cloves garlic, chopped

1 shallot, chopped
$^1/_2$ cup whipping cream
2 cups butter, softened

Combine first 4 ingredients in a saucepan and bring mixture to a boil. Boil 2 minutes or until 95% of liquid evaporates. Add whipping cream and bring to a boil for 1 minute, then remove from heat. Cool for 2 minutes, then return to low heat. Add butter, 2 Tbsp. at a time, stirring with a whisk until butter is incorporated. Keep sauce temperature at 160°F. Sauce will separate if reheated.

Hollandaise Sauce

Yield: 2 cups

6 egg yolks
1 Tbsp. dry white wine

2 Tbsp. lemon juice
$1^1/_2$ cups butter, melted

Combine egg yolks, wine and lemon juice in top of a double boiler. Place over boiling water, and cook, beating at medium speed of an electric mixer, 3 minutes or until thickened. Remove from heat. Add butter, 1 Tbsp. at a time, beating at medium speed of an electric mixer until thickened.

Mystery Pie

No mystery here; the praline sauce with ice cream makes this a memorable dessert.
Yield: 1 9-inch pie which serves 6-8

Preheat oven to 325°F. Prepare and roll out single-crust pastry. Line a 9-inch pie plate. Trim pastry to $^1/_2$-inch beyond edge of pie plate. Flute edge; do not prick pastry.

8 oz. cream cheese
2 eggs
$^1/_2$ cup granulated sugar
1 Tbsp. pure vanilla
3 eggs

1 cup granulated sugar
$^3/_4$ cup light corn syrup
$^1/_4$ cup melted lightly salted butter
$1^1/_2$ cups medium chopped pecans

Using a paddle in a mixing bowl, soften cream cheese until completely smooth. Make sure to periodically scrape bowl so you do not acquire any lumps. With mixer on low, add 2 eggs, one at a time, and incorporate thoroughly. Gradually add $^1/_2$ cup of sugar and pure vanilla and mix well for 3 minutes. Place mixture aside under refrigeration.

In separate bowl, whisk 3 eggs. Add 1 cup sugar, corn syrup and melted butter. Fold in pecans.

Remove cream cheese mixture from refrigerator and lightly fold into the pecan mixture, making a marbeling effect. Pour into prepared pastry shell. Place into preheated oven and bake 70-80 minutes or until a knife inserted in the center comes out clean. Cool completely, then store in refrigerator.

Serving Suggestion: Serve with a scoop of praline & cream ice cream on top, then drizzle praline sauce over the entire dessert.

PRALINE SAUCE

Yield: 1¼ cups sauce

¹/₂ **cup granulated sugar**
2 tsp. brown sugar
³/₄ **cup whipping cream, heated to just**
 below boiling point
1 tsp. pure vanilla

Heat granulated sugar over medium-high heat, stirring constantly, until it becomes caramelized. Remove from heat and add brown sugar, whisking until smooth. Gradually add heated cream until totally mixed through, then blend in vanilla.

When using strawberries, always wash before hulling to prevent excess moisture from being absorbed.

FLOUNDER'S CHOWDER & ALE HOUSE

800 Quietwater Beach Road • Pensacola Beach, Florida 32561 • (904) 932-2003

Flounder's Chowder & Ale House has, from small beginnings back in 1981, grown to be a top quality restaurant, listed among the top 200 restaurants in Florida, by Florida Trend Magazine, and also frequently runs away with the yearly "Best Seafood," "Best Place to Eat" and "Best Bar with Live Entertainment" awards by the Pensacola News Journal.

Admiral Flounder has not forgotten the varied history of the American people and not just from the seafaring community. The restaurant abounds with historical items drawn from all over America, mixed together with objects from our recent past. Also displayed are items from around the world which have made it to our shores in varied and interesting ways, including an actual raft which made it here from Cuba filled with refugees from Castro's regime.

"Chef Crab" or David Andrews, who hails from New York, has been with Flounder's for 10 years and is responsible for most of the exciting entrées and much of their special ambience. "To err is human, to flounder is divine," as Fred Flounder (the founder) would say.

BEER BOILED SHRIMP

There is something fundamentally special about good peel 'n eat shrimp!
Serves 4

4 lb. medium shrimp
2 bottles of dark beer (McGuires Ale)
$1/3$ cup of liquid Crab Boil
1 tsp. of cayenne pepper

$1/4$ cup of lemon juice
$1/2$ cup of Old Bay Seasoning®
1 tsp. of salt
2 fresh lemons, cut in halves

Fill large pot $3/4$ full of water and bring to a boil. Add all ingredients (except shrimp) and bring to a boil again. Add shrimp and cook for 5 minutes, stirring frequently until done. Strain and serve (shell optional) with cocktail sauce and fresh lemon wedges.

FLOUNDER'S FRIED FLOUNDER

The breading is perfect for fried fish filets.
Serves 6

BREADING

2 lb. self rising flour
4 Tbsp. of Old Bay Seasoning®
$2^1/4$ Tbsp. of black pepper

$1^1/3$ Tbsp. of salt
$1^1/3$ Tbsp. of granulated garlic
$1^1/3$ Tbsp. of paprika

Mix all dry ingredients together in a large bowl.

Egg Wash

4 whole eggs
1 cup whole milk

Mix eggs and milk; beat well.

Take flounder filets and drench heavily in egg wash and then in breading. Place in large pan with oil preheated to 350° to 375°F., ensuring flounder filets are completely covered. Cook until golden brown or to taste.

Mahi-Mahi
with Pecan, Butter and Frangelico Sauce

Serves 4

Pecan Sauce

1¹/₂ cups of pecan pieces
2 cups butter
¹/₄ cup of light brown sugar
¹/₂ cup of Frangelico Liqueur®

Mix pecan pieces and brown sugar and set aside. In a saucepan, melt the butter and add pecan and sugar mixture. Bring to a boil, add Frangelico and let flame. Serve over fish.

Grilled Mahi-Mahi

Brush 4 8-oz. filets with melted butter, then sprinkle with a seasoning mixture of 1 Tbsp. of lemon pepper, 1 Tbsp. of salt and 1 Tbsp. of granulated garlic. Grill fish until cooked to requirements, preferably over mesquite wood chips.

Thai Chicken

Serves 4

4 6-oz. chicken breasts, skinless, boneless
¹/₂ lb. peanut butter
2 Tbsp. of sesame seeds
1 Tbsp. sesame seed oil
1 tsp. of cayenne pepper - or to taste

Mix all ingredients and store at room temperature. When needed, warm and pour generously over chicken. Marinate the chicken breasts overnight in 1 cup each of brown sugar, Worcestershire Sauce and pineapple juice. Grill both sides until done. Then cover with Thai sauce.

JAMIE'S FRENCH RESTAURANT

424 East Zarragossa St. • Pensacola, Florida 32503 • (904) 434-2911

When Jamie's French Restaurant opened for business in 1980, Owner Gary Serafin wanted to share his love of fine food and wine with Pensacola. He did so with Elizabeth Dasher, graduate of the Culinary Institute of America, who created the special flavors which has distinguished Jamie's over the years.

Drawing its atmosphere from the historic Seville Square district of Pensacola, Jamie's steps back in time to provide an elegant dining experience, complete with fine linen, fireplaces and private dining rooms. Jamie's serves fresh Gulf seafood which is outstanding, but also offers such classics as fois gras, escargot and wild game dishes to provide something for every taste.

It is no wonder Jamie's has been recognized by Florida Trend Magazine for 10 consecutive years as one of Florida's finest restaurants and for the last two years has received the Wine Spectator Award of Excellence.

JAMIE'S HONEY MUSTARD DRESSING

$^3/_4$ cup honey
$^3/_4$ cup Dijon style mustard
$^1/_2$ cup lemon juice, preferably fresh
$1^1/_2$ cups salad oil
1 Tbsp. curry

1 Tbsp. celery seed
1 Tbsp. Colemans Dried Mustard®
1 Tbsp. fresh parsley
1 Tbsp. scallions, chopped

Pour into a large mixing bowl and blend. Refrigerate.

PISTACHIO CRUSTED TUNA
WITH TROPICAL FRUIT BEURRE BLANC

The combination of curry powder, pistachio nuts and the beurre blanc provide an exotic taste which is wonderful with tuna.
Serves 4

4 6-oz. tuna steaks
1 cup flour
$1^1/_2$ cups milk and 1 egg, mixed
1 cup shelled pistachio nuts (unsalted, uncolored)
1 cup bread crumbs

1 tsp. curry powder
$^1/_2$ tsp. powdered garlic
$^1/_2$ tsp. powdered onion
$^1/_2$ tsp. salt
$^1/_2$ tsp. black pepper

In a food processor, combine the nuts, bread crumbs and seasonings. Set up a breading station with three separate bowls: flour, egg wash and the nut mixture. Put the tuna steaks in the flour, then the egg wash, then the nut mixture. Sauté the tuna in 2 tablespoons olive oil over a high heat until brown on both sides. Finish cooking in a preheated 350°F. oven for approximately 5 minutes, or until desired doneness. Spoon the tropical fruit beurre blanc over the tuna and serve immediately.

TROPICAL FRUIT BEURRE BLANC

$^1/_2$ cup mango, diced
$^1/_4$ cup kiwi fruit, diced
$^1/_4$ cup pineapple, diced
2 Tbsp. Key lime juice

3 Tbsp. chopped shallots
$^1/_2$ cup white wine
$^1/_2$ lb. butter, cut into small pieces, at room temperature

For the beurre blanc, use a saucepan and reduce the shallots and the wine until almost dry. Remove from heat and swirl in the butter until a sauce forms. Fold the fruit into the sauce and spoon over the hot tuna.

CHILLED ZUCCHINI SOUP

Try this refreshing starter when the zucchini are in season and the weather is hot.
Serves 8

$^1/_4$ cup olive oil
1 medium onion, coarsely chopped
6-8 medium zucchini, trimmed, scrubbed
    and cut into $^1/_4$-inch slices

2 cloves garlic, minced
4 cups heavy cream
pinch of thyme
salt and freshly ground pepper to taste

Heat the oil in a large, heavy skillet over medium heat until rippling. Add onion and sauté, stirring occasionally, until softened. Add the zucchini and garlic, and reduce the heat to low. Simmer covered until browned. Remove from heat. Stir in 2 cups of the heavy cream and the thyme, and let cool slightly.

Place half the zucchini mixture in a blender or food processor and blend until smooth. Transfer to a large bowl and stir in 3 cups of the cream. Add the remaining zucchini to the blender and blend until smooth, adding to the existing mixture. Add the remaining cream and stir thoroughly. Force the mixture through a fine sieve, add salt and pepper to taste and refrigerate for several hours before serving. If coarser texture is desired, do not put mixture through the sieve.

MᶜGUIRE'S IRISH PUB AND BREWERY

600 E. Gregory St. • Pensacola, Florida 32501 • (904) 433-6789

McGuire's Irish Pub is a throwback to grand old turn-of-the-century saloons, Irish and otherwise. Winner of numerous Golden Spoon Awards as one of Florida's Top Restaurants, McGuire's offers a winning combination: fun with food, a sense of place and top quality fare at great value-for-the-money prices. The Pub also represents a rekindling of the American love affair with beef, serving the best burgers in North Florida, and peerless U.S. Prime steaks.

The owners, Molly and McGuire, have created a loyal following by serving the finest products available at the best possible prices. They pledge to provide warm and friendly service to each of their guests by professional, sincere employees who truly give a damn! McGuire's has covered all the bases - good food, good service and good fun.

SENATE BEAN SOUP

According to McGuire's, this is the same recipe as served in the U.S. Senate for 18¢ a bowl! Can you believe these are the same guys who spend $237.00 for an 18¢ aircraft bolt?
Serves 8 to 10

$1^1/_2$ lbs. (one bag) dried navy beans
2 large onions
3 stalks celery
2 carrots
1 cup diced ham

1 clove garlic
6 sprigs of fresh parsley
1 tsp. thyme
salt & pepper to taste

Rinse beans in cold water. Check carefully for rocks and pebbles, and cover with water. Soak at least 8 hours or overnight. Drain and return beans to the pot. Cover with 5 inches of water.

Finely chop the onions, celery, garlic and carrots and add to pot. Add ham and remaining ingredients.

Bring to boil, reduce heat and simmer until beans are tender. Watch this carefully and add water as needed or it will burn. Keep beans covered with water at all times and stir often.

Season to taste. This is really best prepared a day ahead of time and reheated, allowing the soup to thicken and the flavors to develop.

Serve hot with a bottle of Tabasco© and a bottle of McGuire's Irish Ale.

McGuire's Irish Stew

This is the real McCoy.

Serves 6

3 lb. inside round, cut into 1 inch cubes
2 cups beef broth or stock
4 large carrots, cut into 1 inch pieces
4 ribs of celery, cut into 1 inch pieces
2 med. onions, cut in half, then quartered
18 sm. new potatoes, left whole, skin on

2 cups fresh mushrooms, sliced
2 cups frozen green beans
1 Tbsp. granulated garlic
1 Tbsp. salt
1 Tbsp. pepper
1 cup frozen green peas, thawed

Heat a small amount of oil in a roasting pan or dutch oven. Add beef and cook until just brown. Add broth, garlic, salt and pepper and simmer over low heat until beef is tender.

In a separate pot, cover potatoes with water and cook until tender.

Add the carrots, celery and onion to beef and cook until almost done. Add potatoes and green beans and heat until the beans are hot. If needed, thicken juices with a browned roux. Add mushrooms. Spoon into bowls and garnish with peas.

Corned Beef & Cabbage

with Horseradish Sauce

Don't wait until St. Patrick's Day to try this.

Serves 4

1 lb. thinly sliced Hormel® corned beef
2 heads of green cabbage
2 slices of bacon

1 chicken bouillon cube
1 qt. water

Wash the cabbage, removing the tough outer leaves, and cut in half. Remove most of the core but do not completely core the cabbage or it will fall apart and be difficult to handle.

In a large pot, cook the bacon until almost crisp. Add water, chicken base and salt. Boil 15 to 20 minutes. Add the cabbage halves and cook until tender. Place the corned beef in a colander or steamer pan over the cabbage to heat through. While the cabbage is cooking, prepare the horseradish sauce. When done, remove from water immediately to prevent overcooking. Do not rinse.

Horseradish Sauce

1 Tbsp. butter or margarine
1 Tbsp. flour
2 cups milk

2 Tbsp. prepared horseradish
salt and pepper to taste

Over low heat, melt the butter, slowly stirring in the flour to make a roux. Do not brown. Slowly add milk, stirring constantly over medium heat until thick and creamy. Add horseradish and remove from heat. Cover to keep warm.

Place one piece of cabbage on a plate. Top with ¼ of the corned beef. Cover with sauce or serve the sauce on the side.

IRISH STEAK & MUSHROOM PIE

This is typical of the hearty fare at McGuire's.
Serves 4

¼ cup butter or margarine
2 lb. beef tenderloin cut into cubes
2 medium onion, chopped
3 cups sliced fresh mushrooms

½ cup burgundy or other dry red wine
3 cups brown gravy (see recipe below)
frozen puff pastry sheet
salt, pepper and granulated garlic to taste

Melt butter in a dutch oven or roasting pan. Add tenderloin pieces and cook until brown, do not over cook. Add onions and cook, stirring occasionally until they are transparent and tender. Remove from heat, pour cooking juices into a saucepan for the gravy.

Return beef and onion mixture to low heat. Add mushrooms, brown gravy and wine. Simmer until beef is tender.

Spoon into a casserole or individual oven proof dishes. Cover with puff pastry and seal to the edges of the casserole. Prick pastry with a fork or carve in a decorative design with the tip of a knife. Bake at 375°F. for 8 to 10 minutes or until the pastry is puffed and brown.

GRAVY

½ cup flour
2 - 3 cups beef bouillon or stock

Over low heat, slowly add flour to juices from beef to make a roux. Stir in bouillion or stock as needed to make 3 cups of gravy. Add salt and pepper to taste.

CAPTAIN ANDERSON'S

5551 N. Lagoon Drive • Panama City, Florida 32408 • (904) 234-2225

During a trip back to his homeland of Greece, Johnny Patronis enjoyed fish which was cooked over open charcoal grills. He brought the method back to Panama City, and through trial and error with the help of Chef Alonzo Keys, the perfect combination of local fish grilled over red hot coals became an instant success. It is easy to see the popularity of Captain Anderson's charcoal broiled delicacies, as the restaurant uses over 40,000 pounds of Kingsford charcoal every year!

As with all excellent seafood restaurants, the key to their success is the quality of ingredients used. At Captain Anderson's you will never find a piece of frozen fish. Every filet is cut by hand from whole fish, one fish at a time. During an average summer night, the restaurant grills over 500 servings of fresh fish, including snapper, grouper, amberjack, tuna, king mackerel and their favorite, the scamp.

CLASSIC BAKLAVA

With a name like Patronis, we felt good about this classic dish even before we tried the recipe.
We were not let down.

1 lb. very good quality unsalted butter
1/2 lb. margarine
10 cups coarsely chopped walnuts or
*   blanched almonds, or a mixture of*
*   both*

3 cups Zwieback® biscuit crumbs
2 lb. commercial phyllo or strudel pastry
*   whole cloves (optional)*

THE SYRUP

4 cups sugar
4 cups water
2 Tbsp. fresh lemon juice, strained

Clarify butter and margarine over a low heat. Remove pan from heat and cool for 3 minutes. With a spoon, skim the milky foam from the top of the mixture and discard. Pour the remaining clarified butter in a bowl and set aside.

Preheat oven to 400°F. and lightly butter a 15 x 18 x 3 inch baking pan.

In a large bowl, combine the nuts and the zwieback biscuit crumbs. Add 1/4 to 1/3 cup of the clarified butter-margarine mixture to the crumbs, enough to moisten it.

Layer 6 phyllo sheets on the bottom of the baking pan, one at a time, brushing each one generously with the butter mix. Sprinkle about 1/3 of the nut mixture over the sixth phyllo sheet and spread it evenly. Drizzle 1 to 2 teaspoons more of the butter mixture over the nuts.

Layer 4 phyllo sheets over the nuts, one at a time, again brushing each layer generously with the butter mixture. Spread another third of the nut mixture on top of the last phyllo sheet and drizzle with the butter mixture.

Top the pan with 5 to 6 sheets of phyllo, again brushing generously with the butter between each layer. Using your fingers, sprinkle the top phyllo sheet with water, then brush with the butter mixture.

Score into diamond shapes, first cutting gently with a sharp knife vertically, then horizontally, making sure the knife cuts all the way down through to the very bottom phyllo. Press a whole clove into each piece of baklava, if desired, prior to cooking.

Bake for 10 to 12 minutes at 400°F., or until the phyllo begins to crisp and brown slightly, then reduce heat to 325°F. and bake for 1½ to 2 hours, or until phyllo turns golden brown.

Five minutes before removing the baking pan from the oven, brush with one more ample dousing of butter and margarine.

To prepare the syrup, combine the sugar and water in a large saucepan and bring to a boil. Reduce the heat and simmer uncovered for 12 to 15 minutes until the syrup is heavy and thick. Remove the pot from the heat and immediately stir in the lemon juice.

Pour the hot syrup over the baklava. Place the baklava in the oven which has been turned off, but is still hot. Let stand until all the syrup is absorbed, about 20 minutes.

Cut the baklava in a diamond configuration and serve warm or at room temperature.

CAPTAIN ANDERSON'S FAMOUS FEUD CAKE

The desserts at Captain Anderson's are made fresh on a daily basis on the premises, and are well known along the Panhandle. We loved the popular Feud Cake, but we took home a peach pie.

3 cups fine ground pecans
6 eggs, separated
1½ cups granulated sugar
2½ Tbsp. all purpose flour

1 tsp. baking powder
1 pt. heavy cream, whipped
1 tsp. pure vanilla extract

Beat egg yolks by hand for 15 minutes, adding sugar gradually. Add the flour and baking powder, sifted. Add the pecan meal.

Beat the egg whites until stiff, and fold in to the pecan mixture. Bake in two layers in a 350°F. oven for thirty minutes.

Put the layers together and frost with the whipped cream flavored with 1 teaspoon vanilla extract. Sprinkle with ground pecans.

CHARCOAL GRILLED SCAMP IMPERIAL

The Scamp is often referred to as the "fisherman's fish." Years ago, local boat captains would go out on daily charters catching a variety of fish. The boat captains were known for calling the Scamp trashfish, usually finishing with the explanation, "I'll take it home and feed it to the cat." The captain was actually taking the most prized fish from the guy for himself, hence the title, "the fisherman's fish."

Serves 2

2 scamp filets, between 4 oz. and 6 oz.
   each
1 cup lump crab meat
2 tsp. olive oil
1 tsp. granulated garlic

1 tsp. Old Bay Seasoning®
$^1/_2$ tsp. coarse black pepper
$^1/_2$ tsp. oregano
2 Tbsp. butter

When you return from your local fish market, lightly coat the filets with olive oil and place in the refrigerator along with the crab meat. Coat the filets with the spices and grill over fiery hot coals. Scamp should flake on the grill, so grill for about 4 minutes on each side, until the meat is a solid white.

Sauté the crab meat for just a couple of minutes in some butter and place half directly on each filet. Top with a small splash of melted butter and serve with a wedge of fresh lemon.

SHE-CRAB SOUP

1 Tbsp. butter
1 tsp. grated onion
2 cups crab meat and coral eggs (crab roe)
$3^1/_2$ cups whole milk
1 tsp. Worcestershire Sauce®

1 Tbsp. flour
$^1/_2$ tsp. MSG or Accent®
pinch nutmeg
6 Tbsp. sherry

Put butter, onion, crab meat and eggs in top of a double boiler and simmer for 5 minutes.

In a separate bowl combine $^1/_2$ cup milk, Worcestershire Sauce, flour, nutmeg and some salt and pepper to taste and stir well. Heat the remaining milk and add to the milk & flour mixture. Add this to the crab meat mixture in the double boiler and slowly cook for 30 minutes. Pour into bowls and add 1 tablespoon of sherry to each bowl. If no coral eggs are available, grate yolks of 2 hard boiled eggs and add a teaspoon to each bowl.

CHEZ PIERRE

Restaurant • Patisserie
115 N. Adams Street • Tallahassee, Florida 32301 • (904) 222-0936

Located under the oaks in downtown Tallahassee, this charming restaurant has been enticing guests with traditional French cuisine since 1975.

Chez Pierre's menu reflects the provençal background of Chef Eric Favier. Lunch offers favorites such as Coq au Vin, Boeuf Bourguignon and Ratatouille. The dinner repertoire includes a Dilled Salmon Napoleon, Coquilles St. Jacques au Gratin, a Garlic-Studded Leg of Lamb smoked over fresh rosemary. The menu at Chez Pierre changes with the seasons, reflecting both the bounty of each season and the changing pleasures of the palate.

Chef Eric and his wife, Karen Cooley, have turned this downtown oasis into a two time Golden Spoon Award winner by offering the flavors of France served with Southern hospitality.

GIGOT D'AGNEAU PRINTANIER
(SPRINGTIME ROAST LEG OF LAMB)

The basics are covered here . . . and with a French flair.

1 leg of lamb	4 lg. onions, peeled & sliced
1 cup butter	6 lg. potatoes, peeled and thinly sliced
1 Tbsp. fresh thyme, chopped fine	2 bay leaves, crumbled
2 garlic cloves, slivered	salt & pepper
3 Tbsp. dry white wine	fresh parsley

Preheat oven to 450°F. Make incisions in the lamb and insert garlic. Rub the leg of lamb with butter and thyme. Bake for 30 minutes, then scrape the drippings from the bottom of the pan and mix with wine. Meanwhile, sauté the onions in butter for 5 minutes and pour into a large baking dish. Add the potatoes, salt, pepper, and bay leaves. Place the leg of lamb on top and pour cooking juices over all. Top with a small amount of salt and pepper. Bake for about 30 minutes. Garnish with fresh parsley just before serving.

POIRES AU VIN ROUGE
(PEARS IN RED WINE & LEMON JUICE)

6 lg. ripe, firm pears	2 Tbsp. fresh strawberry or raspberry
1 lemon, juice only	purée
2 cups strong red wine (Burgundy)	1 orange rind
1 cup sugar	sprigs of mint or handful of mint leaves

Peel and core pears. Zest orange and lemon. Simmer wine, sugar and rind for 5 minutes. Add pears and simmer covered for 35 to 45 minutes. Stir occasionally. (Pears should be tender but not mushy).

Remove pears. Add fruit purée to wine and simmer for 15 minutes. Stir in lemon juice and pour over pears. Serve cold with fresh mint leaves.

LEEK AND POTATO SOUP

Serves 6

3 large leeks, split, well cleaned and
    thickly sliced
1 head of romaine lettuce
4 large baking potatoes, peeled and cut
    into 1-inch cubes
2 cans chicken broth

3 cups water
1 Tbsp. thyme
1 Tbsp. sage
2 cloves garlic, chopped
1 cup whole milk
freshly ground pepper & salt

In a large saucepan, combine the leeks, potatoes, romaine, thyme, sage, garlic, chicken broth and 3 cups of water. Bring to a boil, lower the heat and simmer 20 to 25 minutes; or until the potatoes are very soft. Purée the soup in a food processor or blender until smooth. Return to the pan and stir in the milk until blended. Season with salt and pepper to taste. Reheat until hot before serving, or cover and refrigerate until chilled and serve cold.

FLORIDA POMPANO

WITH ORANGE MANGO BEURRE BLANC

This is sheer heaven - simple and elegant.
Serves 4

Dredge 4 8-oz. pompano filets in sifted flour and sauté in olive oil with a little bit of butter. Season with salt and pepper. Do not overcook. Pompano is at its best when it is lightly cooked. Top each freshly sautéed filet with orange mango beurre blanc and garnish with fresh orange and mango slices. This dish is wonderful accompanied by saffron rice and sautéed zucchini and tomatoes seasoned with thyme.

ORANGE MANGO BUERRE BLANC

2 tsp. chopped shallots
$^1/_2$ cup white wine vinegar
$^1/_2$ cup fish stock

$^1/_2$ cup softened butter
1 Tbsp. fresh orange juice
1 Tbsp. mango purée

Reduce mixture of shallots, vinegar, fish stock, orange juice, and mango purée to one-fourth of its original volume by boiling. Cool this mixture and add the butter a little at a time; beating constantly with a wire whisk until the sauce is creamy.

THE WHARF

4141 Apalachee Parkway • Tallahassee, Florida 32311 • (904) 656-2332

Early and Eva Duggar, the owners of the Wharf Seafood Restaurant, are no strangers to the seafood industry. Before opening the Wharf in 1986, they were in the wholesale seafood business for over 20 years, selling to markets world-wide. Their wealth of knowledge and experience with fresh seafood has transformed a small 75 seat restaurant into a 400-seat restaurant which is consistently listed as one of the top 100 restaurants in Florida.

With the help of their family and a management team hand-picked for their eye for detail and devotion to quality, they assure that everything they serve is absolutely perfect, from the smallest shrimp in their creole to the 15-pound lobster at their special lobster banquets. The Wharf is another example of an outstanding seafood restaurant which consistently serves top quality, fresh seafood to a dedicated following which has come to expect the best. The casual atmosphere and friendly staff only help to ensure a most pleasurable dining experience in Tallahassee.

BLACK BEAN SOUP
WITH SMOKED SHRIMP & JALAPEÑO CREAM

An excellent black bean soup - the addition of shrimp is a perfect touch.

1 lb. black beans
14 cups chicken stock
1¹/₂ lb. tomatoes (diced, chopped, seeded)
3 tsp. cumin
2 Tbsp. coriander leaves
¹/₂ cup red onions, chopped

¹/₂ cup diced tricolor bell peppers
1 jalapeño (minced)
2 tsp. minced garlic
salt and pepper
¹/₂ lb. med. shrimp, peeled & deveined

Soak black beans in water for 1 hour. Drain and put beans in pot with chicken stock. Simmer beans for 1 hour, uncovered. Stir in tomatoes, coriander leaves and cumin and simmer for another hour or until beans are soft. Sauté onions, bell peppers, jalapeño peppers and garlic in olive oil, then add to the soup.

JALAPEÑO CREAM

1 cup sour cream
2 minced jalapeños
2 Tbsp. coriander leaves

SMOKED SHRIMP

Bring a skillet to smoky hot, then add olive oil and sauté the number of pealed and deveined shrimp you desire for 25-35 seconds. Add to soup, serve with a dollop of jalapeño cream.

STUFFED GROUPER

An outstanding way to serve grouper.
Serves 6

6 fresh grouper filets (8-10 oz.) split for
  stuffing
2 cups bread crumbs
1/4 cup finely chopped bell pepper
1/4 cup finely chopped onion
1/4 cup finely chopped celery
1 tsp. grain mustard
1 tsp. oregano (or to taste)

1 Tbsp. chopped fresh parsley
2 Tbsp. lemon juice
1/4 tsp. salt & 1/4 tsp. pepper
3/4 cup sour cream
1/4 cup heavy cream
1 lb. sm. shrimp, peeled, deveined &
  boiled
1 1/2 lb. fresh blue crab meat

Combine bread crumbs, bell pepper, onion, celery, parsley, salt & pepper, toss to mix. Blend in sour cream, heavy cream, mustard and lemon. Add shrimp and crab meat, mix. Stuff grouper filets with the mixture and brush with butter, bake 20-25 minutes at 350°F. or until grouper flakes when pricked with fork.

DEVILED CRAB

1 lb. fresh blue crab meat
1/2 lb. saltines, crushed
1/2 bell pepper, chopped
1/2 onion, chopped
1/2 cup mayonnaise
1/2 cup ketchup

1/4 cup Worchestershire® sauce
1/4 cup French salad dressing
2 eggs, beaten
2 Tbsp. Old Bay Seafood seasoning
1/8 tsp. red and black pepper

Blend crab meat, crushed crackers, bell pepper and onion together, set aside. Mix remaining ingredients and add to the crab mixture. Shape into 3-4 oz. patties and place on a well-greased baking pan. Bake 10-15 minutes at 350°F. or until brown. Serve hot.

STUFFED SHRIMP

2 lbs. jumbo fresh shrimp
  (split for stuffing)

2 cups deviled crab mixture

Stuff shrimp with deviled crab. Place on greased baking dish and bake 8-12 minutes at 350°F., or until done. Serve with warm lemon butter.

Cinnamon Rice Pudding

Who doesn't love a good rice pudding? Well, here's a recipe for a GREAT rice pudding.

$^1/_4$ cup long grain rice
2 Tbsp. vanilla extract
4 cups milk
$^3/_4$ cup sugar
2 cinnamon sticks

$^3/_4$ tsp. salt
3 egg yolks
1 Tbsp. corn starch
1 Tbsp. butter
$^1/_4$ cup whipped cream

Blanch the rice for 5 minutes, then drain. In large pot combine rice and 3 cups of milk with sugar, salt and cinnamon sticks. Bring the mixture to a boil for 50 minutes (covered). In a separate sauce pan, combine 1 cup milk and 2 Tbsp. sugar. Add the milk mixture slowly to egg yolks. Add the corn starch and cook until thickened. Whisk in vanilla and butter. Stir the egg mixture into rice and refrigerate. After mixture is chilled, blend in whipped cream and serve.

To easily remove the peel and membrane that cling to oranges, place them in a bowl of boiling water and allow to stand for 3 minutes before peeling.

The Special Taste of Florida

THE AUGUSTINE GRILLE

The Marriott at Sawgrass
1000 TPC Blvd. • Ponte Vedra Beach, Florida 32082 • (904) 285-7777

Marriott at Sawgrass is recognized by many as the ultimate resort for those who play golf. After all, this lovely resort located on the Atlantic shore between Jacksonville and historic St. Augustine offers unparalleled play with 99 holes of world-renowned golf. It is appropriate that the resort's finest restaurant, The Augustine Grille, welcomes guests with a casual and inviting clubhouse atmosphere that is perfect for the Official Hotel of the Tournament Players Club (TPC) at Sawgrass.

Award-winning Chef Tony Pels, formerly of Spago in Los Angeles and Citronelle of Baltimore and Santa Barbara, prepares an exquisite array of delectable dishes. The cuisine varies according to season, allowing only the freshest of ingredients to be used at any time.

This is a restaurant where everything is excellent. Our general consensus is if you enjoy golf you will love the Marriott at Sawgrass, and if you enjoy fine dining you will love The Augustine Grille.

CHICKEN WRAPPED LOBSTER
SERVED WITH A YELLOW & PURPLE PEPPER RELISH

Serves 4

4 6-oz. chicken breast
4 3-oz. lobster tails, shelled
4 oz. sweet corn
$^1\!/_2$ red pepper, julienne

salt and pepper
1 qt. chicken stock
1 cup sherry

Pound the chicken breasts lightly to create even thickness. Place a lobster tail down the center of each chicken breast. Top with sweet corn and red pepper. Salt and pepper. Wrap the chicken breast around the lobster tail tightly. Wrap in plastic wrap and aluminum foil. Poke 6-7 holes with fork. Place in room temperature chicken stock and sherry. Bring to a simmer at approximately 170-180°F. for approximately 25-30 minutes. Internal temperature should be approximately 150-160°F. Slice and serve over relish.

RELISH

$^1\!/_2$ yellow pepper
$^1\!/_2$ purple pepper
$^1\!/_2$ cup corn
$^1\!/_2$ cup vinaigrette dressing

Dice peppers and mix ingredients. Season with salt and pepper.

GRILLED EGGPLANT AND RICOTTA ROLLATINI
WITH HOUSE DRIED TOMATO VINAIGRETTE

This dish is fun to make and is a treat for lunch or dinner. Great with garlic bread.
Serves 2

MARINADE

¹/₂ cup olive oil
¹/₂ cup dry white wine
3 Tbsp. salt
2 cloves garlic, chopped

4 tsp. oregano, fresh, chopped
2 small to medium eggplant, sliced length-
*   wise ¹/₄" thick*

FILLING

1 cup ricotta cheese
10 leaves basil, fresh, chopped
6 stems fresh oregano, chopped

2 cloves garlic, minced
2 tsp. olive oil
salt and cracked pepper to taste

Peel eggplant and slice ¹/₄-inch lengthwise. Rub with the 3 tablespoons of salt and place in the remaining marinade ingredients and let marinate for 2 hours. Grill over a medium flame. The eggplant should be cooked enough to be able to roll. Place the eggplant in the refrigerator to cool.

While the eggplant is cooling, mix all the filling ingredients well and also chill.

Lay out the sliced eggplant and spread filling over eggplant, totally covering it. Roll it up and cut it in half with a serrated knife, using a sawing motion. Stand the eggplant on end to display the spiral effect. Place 3 spirals on the center of the plate and place the tomato vinaigrette around the outside. Garnish with 8" long cheese stick and greens in the center of the rollatinis.

HOUSE DRIED TOMATO VINAIGRETTE

makes 1 cup of dressing

20 cherry tomatoes
¹/₂ cup extra virgin olive oil
¹/₄ cup balsamic vinegar
2 cloves garlic, chopped
8 leaves fresh basil, chopped

4 stems fresh oregano, chopped
2 plum tomatoes
¹/₂ teaspoon fresh parsley
salt and cracked black pepper to taste

Cut cherry tomatoes in half and place in a pan with the cut side up, season with kosher salt and place pan in the oven. Tomatoes should be dried but still tender with some moisture left, approximately 1¹/₂ hours in a 250°F. oven.

Peel and seed the plum tomatoes and purée. Mix remaining ingredients together, then add the dried tomatoes to the vinaigrette.

Aztec Tuna

Serves 2

1 12-oz. fresh tuna loin	1 Tbsp. coriander
1 cup dried black beans	1 Tbsp. dried oregano
2 cups chicken stock	1 Tbsp. salt
1 Bay leaf	1 Tbsp. fresh ground pepper
1 cinnamon stick	1 cup sour cream
¹/₂ roasted red bell pepper	4 Tbsp. sesame oil
¹/₂ roasted yellow bell pepper	2 Tbsp. wasabi powder
¹/₄ cup red wine vinegar	1 Tbsp. water
¹/₂ cup tomatoes, skinned, seeded, chopped	¹/₂ lemon, juice only
2 corn tortillas	4 tsp. chopped chives for garnish

Soak the beans overnight in water. Drain and cover with the chicken stock. Add 1 cinnamon stick and 1 bay leaf, and simmer the beans for 2 hours, or until well done. Continue to add chicken stock to avoid drying. Discard the cinnamon stick and bay leaf.

Seed the bell peppers, then roast them over a burner or grill until the skin darkens and blisters. Place the peppers in a plastic bag for 5 minutes. Remove the peppers from the bag and peel away the skin. Cut the peppers into a ¹/₄-inch dice. Combine the beans, peppers, 2 Tbsp. cumin and ¹/₄ cup red vinegar. Season to taste and reserve.

Moisten the wasabi with 1 Tbsp. water to create a paste. Combine this mixture with the sour cream, sesame oil and lemon juice. Thoroughly whisk together and reserve.

Cut the tortillas into thin strips. Fry at 350°F. until golden. Reserve.

Combine the ground coriander, oregano and 1 Tbsp. cumin, salt, pepper and oregano for a dry tuna rub. Cut the tuna loin into 4 pieces lengthwise. Dredge in the dry spice rub. Sear the tuna briefly on each side, or to preferred doneness.

Slice the tuna on the bias. Place half of the black beans on each plate. Arrange the tuna on top of the black beans. Arrange the tortilla strips in a pyramid on top of the tuna. Surround this with the wasabi sauce and garnish with chives and cut tomatoes.

If broiling a fish filet which tapers to a thin area at the tail, fold the end under so it doesn't overcook.

BEECH STREET GRILL

801 Beech Street • Fernandina Beach, Florida 32034 • (904) 277-3662

When the Beech Street Grill was opened 6 years ago in a restored 1889 Victorian home, it was a 40 seat restaurant. Within a short time, word had spread through the community and Jacksonville that this was an outstanding restaurant which should be tried. Before you could say Amelia Island, Beech Street Grill was a 200 seat restaurant serving some of the most exciting food in North Florida, or for that matter, all of Florida.

With a wine cellar of over four thousand bottles, Beech Street Grill has been a winner of the Wine Spectator's Award of Excellence for four consecutive years. Their commitment to quality, consistency and creativity has earned it recognition by Florida Trend as one of Florida's top restaurants.

GRILLED YELLOWFIN TUNA
WITH KALAMATA TAPENEDE & DILL CREAM SAUCE

Simple and wonderful. The tapenade and dill cream balance one another.
Serves 2

2 7-oz. tuna filets   *1 tsp. olive oil*

Lightly rub tuna with olive oil and grill or broil to desired doneness. Pipe alternating sauces onto fish, corn row pattern. Garnish with a sprig of dill.

KALAMATA TAPENADE

³/₄ cup kalamata (Greek) olives, rinsed & pitted   *2 Tbsp. capers*
2 cloves garlic, lightly roasted   *2 Tbsp. rum*
3 anchovies, rinsed   *olive oil*

Soak olives, capers and anchovies in the rum after rinsing. Purée all in the food processor. Drizzle in olive oil to desired consistency. Keep thick in order to pipe onto fish.

DILL CREAM SAUCE

2 Tbsp. shallots   *¹/₂ tsp. white pepper*
3 Tbsp. fresh dill, chopped   *¹/₂ cup crème fraiche or sour cream*
2 Tbsp. white wine   *1 Tbsp. white wine vinegar*

In a saucepan, reduce white wine and vinegar with shallots, dill and pepper. Reduce until almost dry. Remove from fire, let cool, fold in the crème fraiche and chill.

CURRIED SWORDFISH
with GRILLED VEGETABLE COMPÔTE

A great dish - surprisingly, the curry sauce accents the fish rather than overpowering it.
Serves 2

2 7-oz. swordfish steaks (or one 14-oz. steak)

Broil or grill swordfish until just barely done. Top with curry baste and return to broiler until the curry starts to brown. Top with Grilled Vegetable Compote and serve.

CURRY BASTE

1 cup mayonnaise
1/2 bunch scallions
1 tsp. chili paste
2 Tbsp. curry powder

1 tsp. garlic
1 Tbsp. balsamic vinegar
salt, white pepper

Chop scallions in food processor. Add garlic, remaining ingredients. Cover and chill mixture until ready to use.

GRILLED VEGETABLE COMPÔTE

1/3 cup red wine vinegar
2 cups olive oil
1/2 cup balsamic vinegar
2 tsp. garlic, chopped

4 Tbsp. shallots, chopped
1 bunch fresh basil
1 bunch fresh tarragon

Mix all together to make marinade.

8 oz. cremini mushrooms
1 onion, sliced
1 bulb fennel, sliced

1 yellow squash, sliced
3 red bell peppers, roasted, peeled

Marinate vegetables, except roasted red bell peppers, for one hour. Drain marinade and grill both sides of vegetables. Remove from fire and chop all vegetables into 1/4-inch pieces. Keep warm. To serve, ladle warm vegetable compote over curried swordfish.

Herb Crusted Grouper
with Wild Mushroom & Crab Meat Ragôut

As good as it sounds . . .
Serves 2

2 8-oz. grouper filets
1/2 cup dry white wine
lemon, juice only

Bake the grouper filets on a platter with the wine and lemon juice until nearly done. Remove from oven and pack on the herb crust. Return to oven until the crust is golden brown and the fish is cooked. Top with mushroom ragout.

Herb Crust

1 bunch tarragon
1 bunch basil
1 bunch chive
1/2 bunch parsley

1/2 bunch dill
2 cups fresh ground bread crumbs
1/2 red onion, chopped very fine
4 oz. melted whole butter

Chop all herbs, mix in finely chopped bread crumbs and onion. Drizzle in melted butter. Place on grouper filets.

Mushroom Crabmeat Ragôut

4 oz. chanterelles, oyster, shiitake and/or
*   wood ear mushrooms*
3 oz. lump crabmeat
1 Tbsp. butter
1/4 cup white wine

3 oz. demi-glace
1/4 cup heavy cream
1/2 bunch chives
salt, pepper
2 Tbsp. chopped shallots

Quarter mushrooms, sauté lightly in butter. Add shallots, season with salt and pepper. Moisten with wine. Add heavy cream. Bring to a boil, simmer 1-2 minutes. Add demi-glace, bring to a quick boil and remove from heat. Fold in crab meat and chopped chives. Keep warm. To serve, ladle mushroom crab ragout over baked grouper.

BROILED SNAPPER

WITH MANGO-MELON & SOUR CHERRY SAUCE & GRILLED PINEAPPLE SALSA

If you want a special seafood presentation, this is perfect.
Serves 2

2 8-oz. snapper filets
³/₄ cup dry white wine
1 lemon, juice only

Broil the snapper filets on a platter in the white wine and lemon juice. Place the cooked filets on warm plates. Ladle the mango sauce over the fish and carefully "pipe" lines of sour cherry sauce over the mango sauce. Spoon a small amount of grilled pineapple salsa next to the filets and serve immediately.

MANGO MELON SAUCE

1 ripe cantaloupe
2 ripe mangoes
1 ancho chili
¹/₂ red onion, chopped
2 Tbsp. brown sugar

2 Tbsp. butter
2 Tbsp. orange juice concentrate
¹/₂ cup heavy cream

Sweat onion in butter. Add chopped chili, mangoes and cantaloupe, cook briefly. Add brown sugar, orange juice and cook for 3-5 minutes. Remove from heat, add the cream and purée in blender or food processor.

SOUR CHERRY SAUCE

2 tsp. oil
¹/₂ red onion, chopped
2 Tbsp. brown sugar

1 cup sour cherries (purée)
2 Tbsp. honey (apple blossom)
2 Tbsp. plum wine

Sweat onion in oil. Add brown sugar, sour cherries, moisten with plum wine, cook till thick. Remove from fire, purée. Stir in honey. Strain through fine sieve into a ketchup squirt bottle. Hold in hot water bath until ready to serve.

GRILLED PINEAPPLE SALSA

1 Tbsp. oil
1 pineapple, sliced ¼-inch lengthwise
½ red onion, chopped
2 Tbsp. brown sugar
1 red bell pepper, chopped

2 Tbsp. chopped cilantro
juice of 1 lime
2 Tbsp. red wine vinegar
½ bunch scallions, chopped

Peal pineapple, cut into ¼-inch slices lengthwise. Avoid the tough center core. Grill the pineapple slices for 1 minute on each side over medium-high heat, then cut into a small dice.

Sweat onion in oil. Add brown sugar, cook briefly with red bell pepper. Mix all ingredients together. Refrigerate until 1 hour before serving.

If brown sugar has hardened, place it in a jar with half an apple, seal and let it stand for a day. The moisture of the apple will soften the sugar.

CAFÉ CARMON

1986 San Marco Blvd., Jacksonville, Florida 32207 • (904) 399-4488

Café Carmon is the crown jewel of T. Wayne and Kitty Davis' small group of restaurants in Jacksonville. Located in the neighborhood village of San Marco, this New York-style dining spot has been one of Jacksonville's finest for over 11 years and is still the place to "see and be seen."

Their regular menu is augmented by daily specials featuring seasonal ingredients. Café Carmon has a virtual lock on the Best Desserts category by FOLIO Magazine. However, we were especially fond of their delightful seafood and pasta creations.

HERB GRILLED SHRIMP WITH RASPBERRY VINAIGRETTE

The vinaigrette works perfectly with the shrimp.
Serves 4

24 large shrimp, peeled and deveined - tails on
2 oz. rubbed sage
2 oz. thyme
mesclun salad

2 cups raspberry sauce (puréed raspberries)
2 oz. rice wine vinegar
1½ cups extra virgin olive oil

To make vinaigrette, combine raspberry sauce and vinegar in a blender on low speed. Slowly add oil until it emulsifies.

Sprinkle shrimp with herb mixture and grill for 6-8 minutes. Place on top of mesclun salad (or other fresh greens) and drizzle vinaigrette over the top.

LOBSTER & SHRIMP PASTA

A wonderful marriage of seafood and pasta!
Serves 4

16 medium shrimp, peeled and deveined
16 oz. lobster meat
2 cups diced tomatoes, seeded
2 cups chopped scallion

1 cup garlic butter
½ cup heavy cream
1 lb. fettuccine pasta
2 Tbsp. olive oil

Cook pasta according to directions and cool. Set aside.

In a skillet, add a small amount of olive oil, the lobster and shrimp, sauté for 3-5 minutes. Add tomatoes, scallions, cream and garlic butter, and cook for 5-8 minutes. Serve over pasta cooked al dente and add salt and pepper to your taste.

CHICKEN SAN MARCO

We loved this with pasta.
Serves 4

4 8-oz. chicken breasts
2 cups bread crumbs
2 cups Parmesan cheese, freshly grated
1 cup chopped fresh basil
1 qt. heavy cream

10 cloves garlic, chopped
2 cups flour
6 eggs, beaten
salt and pepper to taste

Mix together basil, Parmesan and bread crumbs, set aside.

Pound out chicken breast, coat with flour, dip in egg wash and then coat with Parmesan.

In a skillet on medium heat, add a little oil and sauté chicken until golden brown on both sides.

To make sauce, reduce heavy cream until it thickens, add garlic, salt, pepper.

"Wine is the flower in the buttonhole of society."

Werumeus Buning

THE GRILL ROOM

The Ritz-Carlton, Amelia Island
4750 Amelia Island Parkway • Amelia Island , Florida 32034 • (904) 277-1100

The Grill Room at The Ritz-Carlton on Amelia Island has been one of the finest restaurants in Florida for some time. Perhaps the word didn't get out because of its location in Northern Florida, far away from the activity of South Florida. Well, the Sunshine State and the rest of the country are standing up and taking notice of the fine dining that exists in this luxurious resort. Not only did The Grill Room recently receive a Golden Spoon Award as one of Florida's top twenty restaurants, they also received the prestigious AAA Five-Diamond Award for two consecutive years. The merit of the AAA honor is especially notable since only two restaurants in Florida received this award in 1996, and only four in the Southeast United States.

The cuisine of The Grill Room reflects the passion of Chef Matthew Medure. His desire to create beautiful food with simplicity results in new menus daily, using the freshest available ingredients and his imagination. Seafood, beef, poultry and pasta are all wonderful. Whether you prefer New World Cuisine or Southern favorites, The Grill Room's cuisine is outstanding. Additionally, the delicious creations of Pastry Chef Kevin Boxx should not be passed over, including White Chocolate Chambord Soufflé and Southern Peach Soup with Mango Citrus Gratinee.

CARAMELIZED ONION SOUP WITH THYME CROSTINI
Serves 6

10 Vidalia onions
1 qt. chicken stock
1 cup white wine
1 cup water
2 Tbsp. olive oil
Salt & ground pepper to taste
$^1/_2$ bunch fresh thyme

2 bay leaves
5 peppercorns
1 small baguette
2 Tbsp. butter
2 Tbsp. fresh thyme
2 Tbsp. Parmesan cheese

Peel and julienne the onions. Caramelize the onions in the olive oil with salt and pepper over low heat for about 30 minutes, or until the onions are golden brown in color. Deglaze with the white wine. Add the chicken stock and water. Make a sachet with the $^1/_2$ bunch thyme, bay leaves and peppercorns. Simmer for 45 minutes over low heat.

For the crostini, thinly slice 1 small French baguette. Make a mixture of $^1/_3$ Parmesan cheese, $^1/_3$ fresh thyme and $^1/_3$ butter. Spread on one side of the sliced bread and toast. Serve the crostini on top of the soup.

SOUTHERN FRIED GREEN TOMATOES
with Shrimp & Tomato Relish

If you grew up in the South you certainly enjoyed fried green tomatoes, but you never tasted fried green tomatoes this good!

Serves 2

4 ¼-inch slices of green tomato
1 cup flour, seasoned with salt & pepper
2 cups vegetable oil
8 large shrimp, peeled and deveined
1 clove garlic, minced
1 ripe red tomato, diced

1 Tbsp. butter
½ red onion, diced
1 Tbsp. sliced basil leaves
2 Tbsp. olive oil
salt & freshly ground pepper
4 ¼-inch slices of mozzarella cheese

It is best to make the relish first, so the flavors have a chance to marry. For the tomato relish, combine the diced red tomato, onion, basil leaves, 2 Tbsp. olive oil, salt and freshly ground pepper to taste.

Dredge the green tomato slices in flour seasoned with salt and freshly ground pepper. Heat the oil in a heavy pan to about 350°F. Fry the tomato slices for approximately 2 minutes, turn and cook for an additional minute. Remove and drain on paper towels.

Season the shrimp with salt and freshly ground pepper. Sauté in a hot non-stick pan for 2 minutes. Lower the heat to medium and add the garlic and 1Tbsp. of butter. Stir for 1 minute and remove from heat.

Place the tomato slices on plates, top with the mozzarella slices, sautéed shrimp and the tomato relish. Drizzle some juice from the relish around the plate.

SHRIMP WITH TOMATOES & ANGEL HAIR PASTA

Break out a good bottle of wine and Italian bread to complement this delicious recipe.

Serves 6

2 lb. large shrimp, peeled, deveined
12 Roma tomatoes, quartered
1½ lb. angel hair pasta, cooked al dente'
1 bunch fresh basil leaves, chopped
1 cup Parmesan cheese
2 cups fish stock (substitute clam juice)
1 cup white wine

2 Tbsp. shallots, chopped
2 Tbsp. garlic, minced
1 Tbsp. fresh Italian parsley, chopped
1 Tbsp. fresh basil leaves, sliced
1 cup olive oil
salt & freshly ground pepper to taste

Marinate the cleaned shrimp in a mixture of the shallots, garlic, 1/2 cup olive oil, the parsley and 1 Tbsp. basil for 30 minutes.

Heat a large sauté pan to medium-high and add the shrimp and marinade. Sauté for 3 minutes or until the shrimp are not quite done. Remove the shrimp from the pan.

Cut each quarter section of Roma tomatoes in half and add to the pan along with the remaining olive oil. Cook until the liquid starts to be released from the tomatoes, about 4 to 5 minutes. Add the white wine, bring to a simmer and add the fish stock. Bring to a boil and simmer for 1 minute. Add the cooked pasta and the shrimp. Add the Parmesan cheese and chopped basil leaves. Season with salt and freshly ground pepper to taste, toss and serve.

Shrimp & Salmon Cakes
with Fruit Salsa & Balsamic Syrup
Serves 6

12 oz. salmon filet, diced	1 1/2 Tbsp. Old Bay Seasoning
3/4 lb. cleaned shrimp, diced	2 Tbsp. mayonnaise
1 red bell pepper, diced small	1 cup bread crumbs
1 yellow bell pepper, diced small	salt & freshly ground pepper to taste
1 medium red onion, diced small	1 Tbsp. Tobasco Sauce
1 Tbsp. fresh parsley, chopped	1/2 Tbsp. Worcestershire Sauce
1 Tbsp. fresh basil, sliced	vegetable oil

Preheat oven to 350°F. Combine all of the ingredients and form into 4 oz. cakes. Sauté in a non-stick pan over medium-high heat in a small amount of vegetable oil for approximately 3 minutes per side. (You can also use a mixture of half vegetable oil and half butter.) Remove from pan, drain a moment on paper towels, and place in the oven for approximately 2 minutes. Mirror half of each plate with the Balsamic Syrup, place the Shrimp and Salmon Cakes on top and mound with Fruit Salsa.

Fruit Salsa

1 mango, diced small	1 Tbsp. honey
1 papaya, diced small	juice of 1 lemon
2 Tbsp. rice vinegar	cracked pepper to taste

Combine all ingredients and serve at room temperature with Shrimp and Salmon Cakes.

Balsamic Syrup

Combine 1 cup Balsamic vinegar and 1 cup veal or beef stock in a sauce pan and reduce to a syrup consistency over medium-high heat.

24 MIRAMAR

4446 Hendricks Avenue • Jacksonville, Florida 32210 • (904) 448-2424

24 Miramar's preeminent reputation for fine dining continues to delight epicureans in the Jacksonville area with precisely prepared and elegantly served gourmet meals. The menu changes on a seasonal basis, with new items being previewed by guest tasters. Owner Michael Thomas recently introduced new menu items, with the greatest reviews going to Thai Crab Cakes, Shrimp and Goat Cheese Capellini and of particular success was the Bouillabaise 24. As in the past, Miramar presents five or six nightly features and a special selection of tantalizing desserts which should not be passed over.

In addition to their already numerous awards, Jacksonville Magazine has again named 24 Miramar as Jacksonville's Best Restaurant.

CARIBBEAN CANNELONI

Whether you use the Kalamata pasta or regular pasta, this is a special seafood dish.
Serves 2

8 extra large shrimp, peeled and deveined
6 oz. spiny Florida lobster tail, cut into $1/4$-inch medallions
2 ears silver queen corn, roasted and cut off the cob
2 oz. yucca - fresh, peeled and medium dice
$1/4$ cup black turtle beans, cooked
4 plum tomatoes, medium dice

2 cloves garlic, minced
1 Tbsp. Cuban spice
2 cups spinach, fresh
2 sheets kalamata olive pasta (6 x 8 inch - cooked al dente)
4 Tbsp. butter, clarified
$1/4$ cup jalapeño crème fraiche
$1/4$ cup salsa
salt and pepper to taste

Heat butter over medium high heat. Sauté shrimp and lobster until no longer translucent. Add corn, yucca and beans, sauté lightly. Add tomatoes, garlic, Cuban spices and salt/pepper. Sauté lightly (trying not to break tomatoes). Add spinach and wilt in the pan. Divide mixture onto pasta sheets and roll. Garnish with crème fraiche and salsa.

VEAL MIRAMAR

Serve this delightful veal dish with your favorite pasta.

Serves 2

4 3-oz. medallions of veal loin, pounded
  very lightly
³/₄ cup oyster mushrooms, quartered
³/₄ cup crimini mushrooms, quartered
³/₄ cup shiitake mushrooms

¹/₂ cup whipping cream
¹/₄ cup Port wine
¹/₄ cup veal stock
¹/₂ cup butter, clarified
flour seasoned with salt and pepper

Dredge veal in seasoned flour. Shake off excess. Heat butter over medium high heat and brown veal lightly on both sides, reserve and keep warm. Add mushrooms, sauté until tender. Deglaze pan with wine. Add heavy cream and veal stock and reduce until sauce lightly coats the back of a spoon.

WILD MUSHROOM GRATIN

Serves 2

¹/₂ cup gruyere cheese, grated
³/₄ cup crimini mushrooms, quartered
³/₄ cup. oyster mushrooms, quartered
³/₄ cup shiitake mushrooms, quartered
2 Tbsp. shallots, finely chopped

³/₈ cup butter, clarified
¹/₄ cup Madeira wine
¹/₂ cup heavy cream
seasoned bread crumbs
salt and pepper, to taste

Heat clarified butter over medium high heat. Add shallots and sauté briefly. Add mushrooms and sauté until tender. Deglaze pan with Madeira and reduce slightly. Add cream and reduce until sauce lightly coats spoon. Place mixture into 2 rarebit dishes. Divide cheese on top. Sprinkle with bread crumbs and brown under broiler.

SHRIMP AND GOAT CHEESE CAPPELLINI

Serves 2

8 large shrimp, peeled and deveined
8 oz. angel hair, cooked al dente
4 fresh plum tomatoes, chopped
1 bunch basil, chiffonade
4 garlic gloves, minced

1 cup olive oil
salt and pepper to taste
1 cup chevre (goat cheese)
1 bunch parsley, finely chopped

Heat oil over medium high heat. Add shrimp, sauté quickly until no longer translucent. Add garlic, sauté quickly, being careful not to burn garlic. Add basil, tomato, salt and pepper. Place over angel hair. Crumble chevre over the top and garnish with parsley.

GYPSY CAB COMPANY

828 Anastasia Blvd. • St. Augustine, Florida 32084 • (904) 824-8244

In its 13 years of operation, the Gypsy Cab Company has evolved from a small house to a 100 seat restaurant with a special, laid back decor and an enjoyable atmosphere all its own. Original owner Ned Pollack refers to their culinary selections as "urban cuisine," which means the Gypsy Cab Company has been and continues to be influenced by many types of cooking. This is reflected by a menu which changes daily to continually provide new recipes for their guests to enjoy.

SWISS ONION SOUP

A lighter onion soup than the conventional beef foundation. Great with Swiss cheese melted on top.

12 sliced onions (or enough for 8 cups)
$^1/_2$ stick butter
2 qt. chicken stock
$^1/_8$ cup roux

$^1/_2$ cup heavy cream
cayenne pepper, nutmeg, salt and pepper, to taste

In soup kettle, melt butter till brown. Add onion, salt and pepper to taste. Cook till well caramelized, approximately 40 minutes. Add roux. Add chicken stock very slowly, mixing well. Add cayenne pepper and nutmeg. Bring to a boil. Simmer 45 minutes, stirring frequently. Add cream and adjust seasoning to taste.

SMOKEY SWEET POTATO SOUP

This is great with Andouille sausage.

1 large chopped onion
1 cup chopped bacon
1 cup cubed, smoked sausage
6-8 sweet potatoes, chopped
3 qt. chicken stock

1 cup heavy cream
liquid smoke to taste
1 pint sour cream
oregano, bay leaves, salt and pepper to taste

Heat sauté pan. Add bacon, sausage and onion. Sauté till onion is translucent; drain. In soup kettle, add chicken stock, sauté mixture, sweet potatoes, liquid smoke to taste and spices. Boil until potatoes are tender. Remove from heat. Remove bay leaves. Add heavy cream. Purée in food processor. Serve with a spoonful of sour cream on top.

SEAFOOD FRA DI'ABLO

Serves 2

6 oz. of fish filet in pieces
8 medium shrimp
8 bay or sea scallops, cut into bite size
   pieces
6 mussels, cleaned, bearded
10 whole mushrooms, quartered
4 Tbsp. olive oil

chopped garlic to taste
crushed red pepper to taste
chopped fresh or dried basil, to taste
2 Tbsp. clam broth
2 Tbsp. white wine
1½ cups marinara sauce
½ lb. linguine

Heat sauté pan. Add olive oil, garlic and crushed red pepper, then sauté a few minutes. Add seafood and sauté another few minutes. Add clam broth and white wine. Reduce for a few minutes. Add marinara, basil and mushrooms. Sauté and simmer a few minutes. Serve over hot linguine.

SHRIMP JAMBALAYA

A good jambalaya and a premium beer is a meal made in heaven.

¼ cup ground bacon
1 tsp. fresh chopped garlic
1 tsp. chopped jalapeño
1 cup chopped onion
1 cup chopped green pepper
1 cup diced fresh tomato
1 cup smoked sausage, diced

2 lb. peeled and deveined large shrimp
1 tsp. ground cumin
2 tsp. curry powder
2 tsp. oregano
½ cup chicken stock
6 cups cooked rice
1 cup cheddar cheese

Cook bacon over moderate heat until rendered. Add garlic and jalapeño, stir, add onion and pepper and cook 2-3 minutes. Add sausage and shrimp. Cook until shrimp is pink, about 5 minutes. Add oregano, curry, cumin, stir; add chicken stock, heat through. Add tomato and rice and heat through. Place on serving plates and top with cheese. Place under broiler for 1 minute until cheese melts.

GRILLED MARINATED GROUPER MANGO BEURRE BLANC

A wonderful seafood sauce.
Serves 2

GRILLED GROUPER

2 5-6 oz. grouper filets
1 cup olive oil
1 jalapeño pepper, roughly chopped

1 tsp. thyme
$^1/_2$ tsp. salt
juice of 1 lemon

Marinate grouper filets in olive oil, jalapeño, thyme, lemon juice, salt and pepper for about 20 minutes before grilling.
Note: Marinade should be made to taste. Grill grouper until done on outdoor barbecue or indoor grill.

MANGO BEURRE BLANC

2 ripened mangoes with pit
$^1/_4$ cup Chablis
$^1/_4$ cup cream

3 shallots
white pepper to taste
2 Tbsp. butter

Heat sauté pan. Add Chablis, chopped mango with pit and shallots. Reduce by half and remove pit. Add to food processor, purée. Add to sauce pan with cream. Heat to almost boiling. Remove from heat. Whisk in butter and pepper to taste. Serve over grilled

MARINARA SAUCE

An excellent marinara recipe. Freeze in appropriately-sized containers.
Serves 8-10

$^1/_2$ cup olive oil
1 split carrot
$^1/_2$ cup minced garlic
$^1/_3$ cup finely chopped parsley
2 bunches basil, chopped fine

dash crushed red pepper
4 white onions, chopped fine
96 oz. crushed canned tomatoes
32 oz. can plum tomatoes
1 cup Chablis

Heat kettle. Add olive oil and split carrot. Caramelize carrot. Discard carrot. Add garlic, onion, crushed red pepper and parsley; sauté until onions are translucent. Add white wine and reduce by half. Add tomato products. Bring to boil. Simmer 15 minutes. Add the fresh basil. Mix well and serve.

OLD CITY HOUSE INN & RESTAURANT

115 Cordova Street • St. Augustine, Florida 32084 • (904) 826-0781

The Old City House Inn & Restaurant is nestled in the heart of the nation's oldest city in a renovated structure originally built in 1873. The Inn has five guest rooms and a full service restaurant which commands a view of some of the most beautiful historic architecture in Northeast Florida.

The outstanding restaurant features creative American cuisine which follows the French Classical style as a base to all of its recipes. Great care is put into the unique and artistic presentation of the food, which is served in a romantic, candlelit setting. The Old City House also features an excellent selection of over 75 wines to choose from. The menu at Old City house changes nightly, with at least six new specials introduced each week, creating a challenge for both the chefs as well as the waiters.

PORK BOURSIN

A great recipe for a prime cut of pork.
Serves 2

1 pork tenderloin	egg wash (2 eggs, 2 Tbsp. water)
1/2 cup melted butter	1 tsp. dried basil
1/2 cup flour	1 tsp. dried oregano
1 cup bread crumbs	1 Tbsp. grated Romano cheese

Lightly brush the pork tenderloin with melted butter and dredge in flour. Thoroughly mix the remaining ingredients together.

Dip the tenderloin into an egg wash and then roll in the breading mixture. Bake in a 400°F. oven for 5 minutes per inch of thickness for a perfect recommended medium-rare. Top with Boursin Cheese Sauce.

BOURSIN CHEESE SAUCE

2 cups heavy cream	4 oz. boursin cheese (light, herbed goat
1 cube chicken bouillon	cheese spread)
2 Tbsp. light roux	

Bring the first 2 ingredients to a boil, add roux to thicken and remove from heat. Stir in the boursin cheese. Slice the medium-rare tenderloin at an angle and fan on the plate, then ladle on a stream of sauce.

POACHED SALMON

Serves 2

2 6-oz. salmon filets
²/₃ cup raspberry vinegar
¹/₂ cup white wine
¹/₂ cup lemon juice

3 oz. melted butter
2 tsp. pure maple syrup
2 tsp. fresh dill
pinch of salt

Mix together the raspberry vinegar, white wine, lemon juice and dill. Place filets of fresh Nova Scotia salmon in small casserole dish, sprinkle with salt, and pour mixture over fish. Drizzle with maple syrup and melted butter. Cook in a 400°F. oven for 10 minutes per inch of thickness.

GROUPER WITH BACON, DIJON & HORSERADISH

Serves 2

2 6-oz. grouper filets
1 cup sour cream (non-fat sour cream can
  be used)
¹/₂ cup chopped bacon

¹/₄ cup Dijon mustard
¹/₄ cup horseradish
pinch of salt

Blend all ingredients together and spread liberally on the fish. Bake in a 400°F. oven for ten minutes per inch of thickness.

LOW COUNTRY FRIED GRITS

For grits lovers, this is low country heaven.

¹/₂ cup diced shrimp
¹/₂ cup diced scallions

¹/₂ cup diced shiitake mushrooms
2 cups quality hominy grits

Sauté shrimp and vegetables over medium-high heat until shrimp is fully cooked, remove from heat. Cook grits (following instructions on package) in an equal mixture of chicken or seafood stock and heavy cream. Blend in shrimp and vegetables and set in a greased loaf pan, refrigerate overnight. Slice into ³/₄-inch slices, lightly coat with flour and sauté over medium heat until crispy. Top with the following "Low Country Bacon Gravy."

Sauté 1 cup raw bacon on high heat until golden brown. Sprinkle 1 Tbsp. flour over frying bacon. Add 1 cup of cream and pinches of salt, pepper and cayenne. Bring to a boil while stirring constantly. Garnish with chopped scallions and 1 grilled shrimp.

THE SOVEREIGN RESTAURANT

12 S.E. 2nd Ave. • Gainesville, Florida 32601 • (904) 378-6307

Elmo Moser is a good natured gentleman who says, "the love of cooking is what gives me pleasure." It also gives us great pleasure to see a chef/owner who gets so much enjoyment out of his work. Evidently, it also gives much of Gainesville - home of the Gators - a great deal of pleasure, as the Sovereign Restaurant has been the location for fine dining there since 1976.

Chef Elmo served his apprenticeship and attended chefs school in Switzerland before moving to America. He spent 10 years in Los Angeles prior to opening The Sovereign with his lovely wife, Lupe. The Sovereign's advertisements claim their food to be the best in this beautiful Northern Florida town and we wholeheartedly agree.

SHRIMP Á LA COVE

Serves 4 as an appetizer, 2 as an entrée

24 medium shrimp, peeled and split
2 Tbsp. flour
2 bunches scallions, chopped
1/2 tsp. granulated garlic

salt and pepper to taste
1 oz. dry white wine
1 tsp. lemon juice
1/4 cup olive oil

Dust the shrimp with flour. In a very hot skillet add the olive oil and shrimp, sauté until lightly browned. Spice with salt, pepper and garlic to taste. Add the chopped scallions, wine and lemon juice. Continue cooking for 1 minute and serve immediately.

BREAST OF CHICKEN JERUSALEM

Serves 4

4 8-oz. skinless, boneless chicken breasts
4 artichoke bottoms
1 bunch scallions
4 Tbsp. flour
1 cup sour cream

1 cup chicken stock or bouillon
1/4 cup white wine
1/2 tsp. granulated garlic
salt, pepper and Tabasco Sauce® to taste

Sprinkle chicken with salt, pepper and granulated garlic, then dredge in flour and sauté in olive oil until golden on both sides. Then add 1 tablespoon flour and stir well into pan, then add the wine and chicken stock, stirring well to prevent clumps from forming. Remove chicken and reduce sauce slightly. Correct seasoning and add Tabasco to taste.

Finish by adding the sour cream and scallions to the sauce, then continue to cook for another minute. Place the chicken on a plate with the artichoke bottom next to it, and top with the finished sauce. Serve with rice.

DRUNKEN FISH CASSEROLE

This is a quick and easy bouillabaisse with wonderful flavor.

12 large scallops
4 small flounder filets
4 small snapper filets
12 large shrimp
12 steamers (clams), cleaned
12 mussels, cleaned, bearded
2 5-oz. lobster tails, cut in half with shells on

1 Tbsp. chopped shallots
4 cups clam juice
$^1/_4$ cup bourbon whiskey
3 Tbsp. butter
1 cup diced tomatoes
salt, pepper and granulated garlic to taste

In a large pot, melt the butter, add the shallots and lightly sauté until yellowish. Add the tomatoes, clam juice and the bourbon. Let simmer for 2 minutes.

Add the fish, shrimp, scallops, clams, mussels and the lobster. Taste broth and add salt, pepper and garlic to taste. Simmer a few minutes and serve in a large bowl over rice, with garlic toast on the side.

LOMO SALTADO GRIOLLA

1½ lb. filet mignon, cut in strips
1 red bell pepper, julienne
1 yellow bell pepper, julienne
1 green pepper, julienne
1 slice of onion

2 Tbsp. olive oil
2 Tbsp. dry white wine
salt, pepper, Tabasco®, Worcestershire
Sauce® to taste

In a very hot pan, sauté the peppers and onions in olive oil until they are lightly wilted. In a second hot pan, sauté the beef strips to medium rare, add the peppers and onions and toss well. Add the salt, pepper, granulated garlic, Tabasco and Worcestershire Sauce to taste. Finish with the white wine and serve over rice.

To ripen tomatoes at home, place stem end down in a paper bag with a few holes punched through. The natural ethylene gas of the tomatoes will speed up the process. Keep the tomatoes in a location away from direct sunlight.

ARTHUR'S 27

Buena Vista Palace
1900 Buena Vista Drive • Lake Buena Vista, Florida 32830 • (407) 827-2727

To describe Arthur's 27 in just a few words to someone who has never had the pleasure of dining there is actually quite easy; the view and the cuisine are both wonderful! Appropriately set on the top floor of the Buena Vista Palace - the tallest hotel in Walt Disney World Resort - Arthur's 27 is indeed a dining delight.

Classic European touches accent Arthur's exquisite international cuisine. Among the specialties are Lobster and Red Pepper Bisque with Fennel and Sherry served in a puff pastry, and Red Snapper and Oysters with Artichoke Olives and Violet Basil. To top things off, this award-winning restaurant provides sweeping views of the nightly fireworks from the theme parks.

The Buena Vista Palace ranks among the top hotels in the Orlando region that are dedicated to maintaining the highest standard of fine dining in the grand tradition. This is evident as Arthur's 27 is consistently ranked as one of the finest restaurants in Florida.

RED SNAPPER AND OYSTERS
WITH ARTICHOKE, OLIVES AND VIOLET BASIL

The flavor of the Mediterranean delicately accents the oysters and the red snapper.
Serves 2

6 2-oz. filets red snapper
10 shucked oysters
2 artichoke bottoms
10 pitted black Niçoise olives
2 Tbsp. capers
4 Tbsp. diced tomato flesh

1 cup artichoke cooking liquor
Juice of 1 lemon
2 Tbsp. butter
2 Tbsp. violet basil
pinch cayenne pepper
pinch salt

Season red snapper with cayenne pepper and salt. Grill to doneness.

Bring artichoke cooking liquor to a simmer and add oysters for one minute. Remove oysters and arrange with red snapper on a plate.

Reduce the cooking liquor while adding the artichoke, olives, capers, tomato and violet basil. When liquid is reduced to 2 Tbsp., add butter to the pan. When butter is incorporated, spoon sauce over grilled fish and oysters. Garnish with whole sprig of violet basil.

Medallions of Veal Tenderloin
with Zuchinni, Red Pepper and Paprika

Serves 2

6 2-oz. veal tenderloin medallions
6 zucchini fans
2 Tbsp. zucchini, brunoise
2 Tbsp. red pepper, brunoise
2 Tbsp. shiitake mushroom, brunoise
2 Tbsp. toasted almonds

2 Tbsp. paprika
1 Tbsp. cayenne pepper
1 cup white veal or chicken stock
3 cups red pepper purée
1 Tbsp. finely chopped shallots

Sauté veal medallions on both sides. Remove from pan and let rest. Add chopped shallots, cayenne and paprika to the pan and toast lightly. Deglaze with stock and add red pepper purée. Pass liquid through a fine mesh strainer.

Reheat veal and arrange on a plate. Cover each piece with sauce. Sauté brunoise vegetables and sprinkle over top.

Finish with toasted almonds and favorite herb. Serve with favorite pasta.

Breast of Chicken
with Glazed Apples, Sugar Snap Peas
& Black Trumpet Mushrooms

This wonderful dish is excellent with rice.
Serves 4

4 4-oz. chicken breasts, boneless
2 apples, peeled, diced
16 sugar snap peas
10 black trumpet mushrooms
1 cup apple cider

1 cup chicken stock
4 Tbsp. Apple Jack Brandy®
2 Tbsp. butter

Season chicken breast with salt and white pepper. Sauté each side until golden brown and then add apples. Flambé pan with the Apple Jack Brandy and add cider and stock. Reduce liquid gently while cooking the chicken.

Remove chicken when cooked. Continue reducing liquid to ¼ cup. Add sugar snap peas and black trumpet mushrooms. Incorporate butter and spoon over chicken breasts. Garnish with favorite herbs.

ATLANTIS

Stouffer Renaissance Orlando Resort
6677 Sea Harbor Drive • Orlando, Florida 32821 • (407) 351-5555

Atlantis is the perfect name for the signature restaurant at the Stouffer Renaissance Resort in Orlando. Though the Atlantis menu contains a full complement of meat dishes, including an outstanding Roasted Duck Breast with Thai Curry Sauce, the specialty is seafood, and the menu varies nightly with chef creations based on the freshest available ingredients. Overall, the cuisine of this outstanding AAA Four-Diamond Award-winning restaurant is eclectic in nature, emphasizing creative dishes with lighter, healthier sauces.

The impeccable reputation Atlantis enjoys in Orlando is a reflection of their outstanding food, professional service and the lovely setting. Guests at Atlantis are surrounded by an atmosphere of polished mahogany, etched glass, hand painted ceiling murals and a beautiful art collection. A pleasurable way to enjoy all of this is to indulge in a made-to-order dessert soufflé after an exquisite meal.

WARM SHRIMP SALAD WITH ASPARAGUS & MANGO

Serves 10

FOR THE SALAD

2 lbs. large shrimp, peeled & deveined
2 cups white wine
2 cups fish or chicken stock
1 Tbsp. shallots, minced
$^1/_2$ tsp. black peppercorn, cracked

10 red leaf salads
1 lemon, juice only
5 mangoes
40 asparagus, trimmed and blanched

FOR THE DRESSING

$^3/_8$ cup balsamic vinegar
$^3/_8$ cup olive oil (marinate olive oil over-
    night with chopped fresh basil, thyme,
    garlic and shallots)

salt and pepper
$^1/_8$ cup honey
$^1/_8$ cup orange juice, with zest

Combine the stock, wine, shallots, peppercorns and the juice of one lemon and bring to a boil. Add the peeled shrimp and shallow-poach until the shrimp are just cooked. Remove the shrimp and set aside.

Combine the vinegar, oil, honey, orange juice and zest and adjust the seasoning of the dressing. Arrange the lettuce, mangoes, asparagus and shrimp on the plate. Drizzle each portion with 2 tsp. of vinaigrette.

SALMON FILET

WITH MUSHROOMS BAKED IN PHYLLO SHEETS

SERVED WITH SAFFRON SAUCE

The saffron sauce is heavenly.
Serves 4

4 4-oz. salmon filets
2 Tbsp. olive oil
4 phyllo sheets
2 cups mushrooms (morels, shiitake,
    button mushrooms)
2 Tbsp. butter
1 Tbsp. shallots, minced
1 tsp. garlic, minced
salt and pepper

SAFFRON SAUCE

$^1/_4$ cup white wine
$^1/_8$ tsp. saffron threads (crushed)
2 Tbsp. shallots, chopped
1 Tbsp. chives, sliced
$^1/_4$ cup heavy cream
1 cup chicken stock
2 Tbsp. corn starch

    Season the salmon with salt and pepper. Heat the olive oil and sear the salmon 2 minutes on both sides. Set aside.

    Wash and slice the mushrooms of your choice. Heat the butter and sweat the shallots, garlic and mushrooms until all the released liquid has cooked away.

    Remove from the heat and let cool completely. Put the mushrooms on top of the salmon, wrap the salmon in the phyllo and bake in a 350°F. oven for about 8 minutes.

    To make the sauce, heat the wine and shallots and steep the saffron in it. Add the chicken stock and simmer until a deep golden color is reached. Add the cream and thicken lightly with cornstarch. Add chives just before serving.

PEPPER SEARED RARE YELLOWFIN TUNA

WITH BALSAMIC VINEGAR, LEMON GRASS & MANGOES

Serves 1

7 oz. center cut tuna
1 Tbsp. soy sauce
1 Tbsp. truffle juice
1 Tbsp. balsamic vinegar
1 tsp. sesame oil
1 Tbsp. sherry wine vinegar

$^3/_8$ cup basil oil
1 Tbsp. chopped shallots
1 Tbsp. chopped lemon grass
1 Tbsp. cracked black pepper
1 tsp. truffle, julienne
1 mango fan for garnish

    Combine above ingredients. Use half as marinade and half as sauce. Marinate for $^1/_2$ hour. Sear tuna and cook to desired temperature. Cover with warm sauce, garnish with a mango fan.

Baked Filet of Red Snapper
with Pistachio Crust

The Orange Blossom sauce is splendid with this crusted fish.
Serves 1

7 oz. red snapper
$^1/_2$ cup pistachio crust*
2 Tbsp. vinaigrette

$^1/_4$ cup orange blossom vinaigrette
1 tsp. capers
1 Tbsp. cilantro

Sear fish, then brush with vinaigrette. Spread with the pistachio crust and bake at 350°F. until done. Cover with orange blossom sauce and garnish with orange, lime & grapefruit wedges.

Pistachio crust - equal parts ground pistachios & white bread crumbs.

Orange Blossom Vinaigrette

$^3/_8$ cup marinated olive oil (marinate with garlic, thyme, basil, shallots, rosemary, cracked white pepper)
2 Tbsp. vinegar ($^1/_2$ sherry and $^1/_2$ balsamic)

2 Tbsp. reduced orange juice
1 orange rind
1 tsp. honey
pinch of salt and pepper

Combine all ingredients and bring to a simmer.

If you have forgotten to soften the butter, grate it and it will soften quickly.

DUX

The Peabody Orlando
9801 International Drive • Orlando, Florida 32819 • (407) 352-4000

Since its inception in 1987, Dux has endeavored to become the leader of innovative food preparation and presentation in the state of Florida. The Peabody Orlando culinary group creates menus that are new and exciting- on the cutting edge that will excite the senses. Dux (pronounced "ducks") has already received acclaim as one of Florida's 10 best restaurants. Though the cuisine is often referred to as "American," the style is best described as globally inspired, with the menu and special preparations being based on the availability of the finest fresh ingredients. Dux does an outstanding job of presenting numerous lighter dishes which certainly do not suffer any lack of flavor due to reduced fat or lowered calories.

This smoke-free restaurant provides a delightful setting with vivid floral arrangements and original works of art (almost exclusively ducks). The restaurant staff, like that of the hotel, is both professional and courteous. Incidentally, duck is NEVER on the menu at Dux!

KALBI SHORT RIBS
Some of the best ribs ever!

5 lbs. beef short ribs, $^1/_2$-inch cut
1 lb. ginger
1 head garlic
2 qt. soy sauce
1 cup sugar

4 cups water
1 Tbsp. dried chili flakes
$^1/_2$ cup sesame oil
$^1/_2$ cup daikon

Chop ginger, garlic and daikon and mix with soy, water, sugar, chili flakes and sesame oil to form marinade. Marinate the ribs overnight and grill...Yum! Serve with sticky rice and cold beer.

PORTOBELLO POTSTICKERS WITH GOAT CHEESE CREAM
Serves 4

POTSTICKERS

2 or 3 Portobello mushrooms
3 Tbsp. olive oil
3 Tbsp. balsamic vinegar
$^1/_2$ tsp. black pepper

3 oz. goat cheese
4 scallions
24 won ton skins
1 Tbsp. whole butter

SAUCE

1 shallot

1 teaspoon olive oil

1 cup white wine

1¹/₂ cups cream

4 oz. goat cheese

FOR THE POTSTICKERS

Remove stem and gills from mushrooms. Marinate in oil and vinegar for 5 min. and grill over coals 3-4 minutes on each side. Dice and mix with chopped scallions and goat cheese. Place 2 teaspoons of the mixture in the center of wonton square, wet edges with water and fold into triangle. Wet tips of triangle and pinch together to shape. Steam potstickers 5 minutes and sauté in butter to brown on one side.

FOR THE SAUCE

Briefly sauté chopped shallot in olive oil and wine and reduce to syrup. Add cream and reduce by a half. Add goat cheese and stir until smooth. Serve with Potstickers.

MAYAN PUMPKIN & CORN BISQUE

This soup has an incredibly exotic taste - absolutely wonderful . . . and easy!

Serves 8

1 qt. good chicken stock

2 lb. winter squash (orange)

6 ears fresh corn

1 cup coconut milk

2 habañero chiles

2 cups cream

4 Tbsp. honey

1 tsp. turmeric

1 Tbsp. salt

1 bunch scallions

1 red bell pepper

Roast pumpkin or squash in oven until tender (about 30 minutes) and remove skin and seeds. Clean corn and cut from cob. Add pumpkin and corn to simmering stock and cook 10 minutes, then add coconut milk, diced chiles, cream, honey, turmeric and salt and cook another 10 minutes. Purée mixture briefly, leaving some chunks. Garnish with chopped red peppers and scallions.

Baked Grouper with Sundried Tomato Tapenade

This results in a very moist, flavorful fish.
Serves 4

4 6-oz. grouper filets
1 cup sundried tomatoes
$^1/_2$ cup kalamata olives

2 Tbsp. roasted garlic
$^1/_4$ cup olive oil
2 tsp. black pepper

Purée sundried tomatoes, pitted Greek olives, roasted garlic, pepper and olive oil in a food processor until smooth. Spread $^1/_4$-inch layer on top of each piece of fish and bake at 400°F. untill done. (Depends on thickness of fish, 1 inch = 10 min.) Serve with pasta or rice and grilled veggies.

Almond Lace Baskets

You can be as creative as you want to be with the filling.

$^1/_2$ lb. sugar
4 oz. sliced almonds
$^1/_2$ lb. butter
$^1/_2$ cup flour

Melt butter and constantly stir while adding sugar, nuts and flour. Do not bring to a boil, heat while stirring to completely blend ingredients. Stir while cooling to prevent separation. Roll into 2 oz. balls and place 5 inches apart on a teflon baking sheet. Press to slightly flatten. Place in 350°F. oven until golden. When lace cookies are cool enough to touch but are still pliable, place over upside-down coffee cups to form basket. Allow basket to dry until hard. Lift off and fill with homemade ice cream and fresh berries.

With all BBQ sauces using sugar, baste the meat only during the last 10 minutes to avoid burning.

ENZO'S

1130 S. Hwy. 17-92 • Longwood, Florida 32750 • (407) 834-9872

Fifteen years ago, Enzo Perlini discovered a lovely, secluded lakefront home which was built in the style of an Italian villa. It was here that he built his restaurant faithful to the simple yet sophisticated cuisine of his native Rome. This is not a totally out of the ordinary ambition, since Enzo's father also owned a restaurant in Rome. Enzo is not only the owner and the manager of the restaurant, he is also the head chef, and is skilled in both traditional and modern Italian cuisines.

The freshest of ingredients are woven into a menu that emphasizes the culinary heritage and diversity of Enzo's birthplace, offering many dishes which can be found nowhere else in Central Florida. An elaborate antipasto table welcomes guests to the main dining room which overlooks the lake. A wonderful setting for outstanding Italian cuisine.

SHIITAKE AL PEPE
(PEPPERED SHIITAKE)

Appetizer serves 4

1 lb. shiitake mushrooms	salt
3 Tbsp. extra virgin olive oil	coarse black pepper

Remove stems from mushrooms, wipe cap with clean paper towel. Place steel skillet on medium high heat, add oil. When warm, add mushrooms, cap down. Sauté two minutes, pressing cap with spatula. Add salt and pepper. Turn mushrooms, sauté as before. Arrange mushrooms on a serving platter and sprinkle platter edge with pepper as decoration.

ARROASTO FARCITO CON PATATE

This turned out to be one of the finest veal dishes we tried.
Serves 4

1¹/₂ lbs. of veal loin (beef or pork may be used)	1 branch fresh rosemary
	¹/₄ cup olive oil
3 oz. truffle paté	1¹/₄ cups dry white wine
3 oz. shiitake or a mix of wild mushrooms	salt and black pepper
4 Idaho potatoes	

Pre-heat oven to 350°F. Clean and dry potatoes thoroughly, slice lengthwise into 6 to 8 wedges and place in bowl. Add 2 Tbsp. olive oil, salt and pepper to taste. Strip half of rosemary branch and sprinkle over potatoes. Toss well, then place in a large baking dish, leaving enough space to place roast in center and place in oven.

Sauté mushrooms in 1 Tbsp. olive oil until soft. Open loin, remove excess fat. Rub entire loin with olive oil, salt and pepper. Spread the length of loin with paté and mushrooms. Close loin and tie with kitchen string. After potatoes have cooked for 30 minutes, place loin in center of pan. Pour remaining olive oil over roast and place remaining rosemary sprig on loin. Cook for 30 to 35 minutes more. Add 1¼ cups dry white wine over loin for final 3 minutes of cooking time. Remove from oven. Slice and arrange on platter with rosemary potatoes.

RAVIOLI NUDI
(NAKED RAVIOLI)

(Excellent with Angel Hair Pasta)
Serves 4

1 lb. ricotta cheese
8 oz. breast of chicken (all fat and carti-
lage removed)
4 oz. frozen spinach
6 oz. Parmesan Reggiano

2 egg yolks
pinch of nutmeg
salt and white pepper to taste
1 cup flour

Purée breast of chicken and spinach in food processor. In bowl, mix ricotta, spinach/chicken mixture, 4 oz. Parmesan, 2 egg yolks, nutmeg, salt and white pepper. Form into 1 inch balls. Roll balls in flour until covered. Set aside.

In sauce pan, bring water to boil. Add 1 Tbsp. salt. Drop balls in boiling water. Remove when balls float on top and set on plate. Serve with your favorite sauce and sprinkle with Parmesan. Balls can be made smaller and served as a soup in your choice of broth.

STRAWBERRY ALLA CARDINALE

The Strega and Kirschwasser are an exotic taste combination.
Serves 4

1 lb. fresh strawberries (washed, dried and
cut in quarters)
1 pt. fresh whipped cream
4 Tbsp. Strega® liquer

2 Tbsp. Kirschwasser liquer
fresh ground black pepper
1 lemon (remove seeds)

Place strawberries in crystal bowl and cover with 5 turns of pepper grinder (medium grind) and squeeze lemon over berries and pepper. Add Strega, Kirschwasser and fresh whipped cream. Toss mixture well and serve in champagne cup. (Fresh raspberries may be substituted.).

MAISON & JARDIN

430 S. Wymore Road • Altamonte Springs, Florida 32714 • (407) 862-4410

This Mediterranean villa sits on five magnificently landscaped acres secluded by majestic oaks. Inside, you are surrounded by exquisite antiques and Austrian crystal chandeliers and served with the attention you would find in an elegantly appointed family home.

Swiss Chef Hans Spirig has commanded the kitchen here for eighteen years. Adapting his classic European training and his devotion to the freshest local ingredients has resulted in a style best described as contemporary continental cuisine. His interest in serving the freshest regional ingredients is legendary. He has grown organic herbs and vegetables on the property for years. The result of his efforts has earned national acclaim, including the AAA Four Diamond Award and the DiRoNA Distinguished Dining Award.

MACADAMIA NUT CRUSTED FILET OF RED SNAPPER
WITH PAPAYA SALSA

Very easy, very elegant. This is one of our favorite methods of preparing snapper.
Serves 6

6 6-oz. red snapper filets, American
    preferred
2 cups white bread crumbs, fresh
$^1\!/_2$ cup Macadamia nuts, chopped medium
    fine
2 tsp. melted butter

$^1\!/_3$ cup good quality mayonnaise
pinches of salt and pepper
$^1\!/_3$ cup melted butter
1 Tbsp. water

Mix together the bread crumbs, Macadamia nuts and melted butter to form the crust mixture. Spread the mayonnaise on top of the fish filets, then top with the crust mixture and season with salt and pepper.

Mix the water with the melted butter and baste the crust. Bake for approximately 20 minutes at 400°F. Serve the fish filet over papaya salsa and garnish with cilantro.

PAPAYA SALSA

Serves 6

1 fresh papaya, peeled & diced
1 lime, juice only
3 Tbsp. red onion, chopped fine

5 sprigs fresh cilantro, chopped
3 Tbsp. extra virgin olive oil

Blend all of the ingredients together and allow time for flavors to marry.

Spring Salad With Basil Vinaigrette

Serves 6

$^1/_2$ head radicchio
2 heads red oak leaf lettuce
2 heads frisse
1 head endive
2 heads red chicory

$^3/_4$ cup basil vinaigrette
$^1/_2$ cup pecans, chopped coarse
$^1/_2$ cup Montrachet cheese, broken into
    small pieces

Clean the lettuce and tear into bite size pieces and mix together. Toss with the vinaigrette dressing and assemble on plates. Sprinkle the cheese and pecans over the top.

Basil Vinaigrette Dressing

Yield: 2 cups

1 cup fresh basil, chopped
$^1/_4$ cup red wine vinegar
2 Tbsp. shallots, chopped fine

$^3/_4$ cup extra virgin olive oil
$^1/_2$ tsp. Dijon mustard
pinch of salt and pepper to taste

Combine all ingredients and emulsify in a blender or processor.

Three Mushroom Cream Soup

A delightful starter with a rich, creamy texture.
Serves 12

4 oz. butter
1 small onion, chopped medium
2 stalks celery, diced fine
1 tsp. garlic, chopped
4 oz. oyster mushrooms, sliced
4 oz. shiitake mushrooms, sliced
4 oz. cremini mushrooms, sliced

3 cups heavy cream
1 cup sherry
6 cups chicken stock
$^1/_4$ cup cornstarch, dissolved in water
1 Tbsp. fresh thyme, chopped fine
1 Tbsp. fresh rosemary, chopped fine

In a heavy pot, sauté the onion, celery and garlic in the butter over medium heat until the onions are transparent. Add the mushrooms and the heavy cream and simmer for 10 minutes. Add the sherry and reduce for a few minutes.

Add the chicken stock and boil for 10 to 15 minutes. Add the cornstarch, rosemary and thyme and simmer for another 5 to 7 minutes. Salt and pepper to taste and serve while hot.

Sautéed Shrimp & Scallop Appetizer
With Saffron Beurre Blanc

Serves 4

20 threads saffron
¹/₄ cup dry vermouth
4 fresh large scallops
8 fresh large shrimp, peeled, deveined,
    butterflied
pinch of pepper
¹/₄ cup flour
¹/₄ cup olive oil

1 tsp. shallots, chopped fine
2 Tbsp. heavy cream
¹/₄ lb. butter, at room temperature
¹/₂ lemon, juice only
2 drops of Worcestershire®
salt and pepper to taste
2 Tbsp. sundried tomatoes, soaked over-
    night

Soak the saffron in vermouth for 20 minutes. Season the scallops and shrimp with salt and pepper, dredge in flour and sauté in hot olive oil for 2 minutes on each side. Reserve, keeping warm.

In the same pan with the remaining juices, sauté the shallots a moment and add the vermouth and saffron. Reduce by half.

Add the heavy cream and reduce until thick. Incorporate the butter a small piece at a time, being careful not to boil the sauce. Season with lemon juice, Worcestershire sauce, salt and pepper. Reserve. Simmer the sundried tomatoes a few minutes and strain.

To assemble, on each plate pour some saffron beurre blanc sauce. Arrange shrimp and scallops on the plates, and top with the sundried tomatoes. Place wild rice on radicchio leaves and set on the plate next to the shrimp and scallops.

Freshly grated nutmeg is always preferable to ground nutmeg, which quickly loses its potency and flavor on market and kitchen shelves.

PALIO

Walt Disney World Swan
1200 EPCOT Resorts Blvd. • Lake Buena Vista, Florida 32830 • (407) 934-3000

Named for the horse races that have been run in tiny village squares throughout Italy since the Renaissance, this outstanding restaurant offers guests the flair of Tuscany, a taste of Italy and the elegance of Europe. Notable on Palio's menu are the zesty antipasto, imaginative pasta dishes and traditional Italian entrées, including scampi, veal and calamari, all complemented by a fine list of Italian wines.

Located in the beautiful Walt Disney World Swan Hotel, Palio has the authentic look and feel of a fine Tuscan restaurant. Replicas of the legendary patterned flags that each rider carries in the races decorate each of the tables. The open kitchen includes a wood fired pizza oven and broilers which tantalize diners with the rich aromas of Italian food while they enjoy a view of the resort's scenic waterways.

TEGLIA DI PESCE SPADA

This is typical of so many fine dishes at Palio. The Mediterranean flavor is just wonderful.
Serves 6

6 7-oz. swordfish steaks
salt and freshly ground pepper
1 cup dry white wine
1 sprig fresh rosemary, whole
4 cloves garlic, finely chopped

$^1/_4$ cup extra virgin olive oil
2 Tbsp. bread crumbs
3 Tbsp. capers, drained and chopped
1 lemon, juice only

Place the swordfish steaks in a bowl and season with salt & pepper, pour in wine and add rosemary and garlic. Marinate one hour. Drain and reserve marinade. Brush skillet with a little oil and heat. Sprinkle fish with bread crumbs and capers. Add to skillet and brown to golden color on both sides, basting with reserved marinade. Whisk the rest of the oil with the lemon juice. Pour over fish, bring to boil, and serve.

MOZZARELLA IN CARROZA

Serves 6

2 eggs
salt
12 slices firm, coarse-textured bread
 without crust, $^3/_8$-inch thick
6 mozzarella slices (same size as bread)

1 cup milk
1 cup flour
oil for frying
cilantro for garnish
1 cup marinara sauce

Beat eggs with salt in wide dish. Line up the slices of bread on work surface and place a slice of mozzarella on six of them. Top with the other six bread slices. Dip the sandwich quickly in milk and then flour, then soak them for a few seconds in beaten egg. Heat oil in skillet until smoking. Add sandwiches and fry on both sides until golden. Drain on paper towels and serve immediately.

SPAGHETTINI AL CARTOCCIO

Serves 1

3 large shrimp
3 large scallops
2 clams
2 oz. calamari, cut in rings

³/₄ cup marinara sauce
4 oz. fresh spaghettini
julienne of basil

Sauté seafood in casserole, just to brown (30 seconds). In a piece of parchment paper that has been rubbed with olive oil, put the pasta and sauce, and arrange the seafood on top. Sprinkle with herbs. Fold the paper around and seal. Bake in oven at 375°F. for 10 minutes and serve.

CALAMARI ALLA GRIGLIA

The beauty of this is its simplicity . . . wonderful with garlic bread and wine.
Serves 1

5 oz. calamari steak, marinated in olive oil and garlic
pinch cilantro
1 Tbsp. lemon juice
salt & pepper to taste

Season and marinate. Broil quickly. Top with sautéed cilantro. Deglaze with lemon juice. Pour over top of calamari steak. Serve with gnocchi and fennel.

SCAMPI VENEZIANA

When you taste this, you will feel you are in Venice . . . very authentic.
Serves 1

6 oz. med. shrimp, peeled and deveined
1 Tbsp. olive oil
1 Tbsp. garlic, chopped
1 Tbsp. shallots, chopped
1 cup tomato concasse

pinch fresh oregano
¹/₄ cup white wine
2 Tbsp. butter
salt and pepper to taste

Sauté the shrimp in olive oil. Add garlic and shallots. Deglaze with white wine and add oregano, tomato. Remove shrimp onto shirred egg dish. Reduce sauce and finish with butter. Adjust seasoning and serve.

PARK PLAZA GARDENS

319 Park Avenue South • Winter Park, Florida 32789 • (407) 645-2475

Located on charming Park Avenue in historic Winter Park, this quaint restaurant has been delighting local patrons since 1979.

Park Plaza Gardens was recently rated by the Zagat Survey as Central Florida's most popular restaurant. The live trees below a glass roof adds to the candlelight atmosphere. The extensive menu of Chef Luis Colon features unique presentations of fresh Florida seafood as well as lamb, venison and poultry. A leisurely Sunday champagne brunch is enhanced by a tuxedoed trio playing mellow jazz. The staff is professional and the wine list is extensive.

WEST INDIAN SALMON

The most popular seafood dish at Park Plaza Gardens.
Serves 4

1 lb. salmon filet	*1 egg for bread crumb mixture*
1 cup bread crumbs	*1 egg for egg wash*
¹/₂ cup grated horseradish root	*flour*
¹/₄ cup pickled horseradish	*salt and white pepper*
¹/₂ tsp. thyme	*peanut oil*
¹/₂ tsp. parsley	

Season salmon with salt and pepper. Combine horseradish root, pickled horseradish, egg, thyme, parsley and bread crumbs. Dust salmon in flour, dip in egg wash, then bread crumb mix top side only. Heat oil in sauté pan until smoking hot, add salmon, bread crumbed side down, skin side up, and sauté for 30 seconds. Finish cooking in a 350°F. oven for 8 minutes.

CHICKEN AMARILLO

Serves 4
The blend of flavors and temperatures is heavenly.

2 boneless chicken breasts, skin on	*3 cups olive oil*
3 green bell peppers	*¹/₄ cup onions*
cilantro - 1 bunch of leaves, no stems	*¹/₂ tsp. cumin*
1 tsp. garlic	*1 tsp. lemon juice*

Season chicken with salt, pepper and cumin, grill skin side down. Lightly burn the skin then turn over and grill, turning occasionally until fully cooked.

For sauce: purée bell peppers, onions, garlic and cilantro in food processor - slowly add olive oil and season with lemon juice. Remove from processor and chill. Pour chilled sauce over hot chicken and enjoy!

WALNUT BREAD PUDDING

This one you will have to hide from the kids and the neighbors. News about good bread pudding travels fast!

Serves 8

1 loaf of bread (unsliced)
1 quart of heavy cream
6 egg yolks
$^1/_2$ cup sugar
1 tsp. cinnamon

$^1/_2$ cup walnut oil
1 tsp. vanilla extract
1 cup chopped walnuts
1 cup raisins

Slice bread about $^1/_2$-inch thick, lengthwise, trimming off top crust, place in a pan. This should make 2 layers of bread. In a mixing bowl add egg yolks, sugar, cinnamon, and vanilla - whip on high until fluffy (about 2 minutes). Change speed to slow and add cream, whip until evenly incorporated. Sprinkle walnuts and raisins over each layer of bread, then drizzle walnut oil and $^3/_4$ of the cream mixture over each layer. All left-over cream mixture should be set aside until pudding is baked. Cover pan with aluminum foil and bake for 15 minutes in a 350°F. oven. Pour remaining mixture over cooked pudding and serve.

SEAFOOD PALM BEACH

Very simple, very elegant.

Serves 4

6 oz. large shrimp
6 oz. large scallops
6 oz. lobster meat
$^1/_4$ cup shallots
1 tsp. garlic
$^1/_2$ cup peanut oil
$^1/_2$ tsp. paprika

$^1/_2$ tsp. thyme
1 lemon, juice only
$^3/_4$ cup unsalted butter
1 cup Chardonnay
$^3/_4$ cup flour
salt and pepper

Cut lobster into the same size as the shrimp and scallops so the seafood will all cook evenly. Heat the peanut oil in a sauté pan until very hot. Flour seafood and sauté for 30 seconds. Add shallots and garlic, then add Chardonnay and thyme, cook until the wine is almost gone. Add butter and stir with spoon until the wine and the butter develop a creamy sauce. Add paprika and season with lemon juice, salt and pepper. Serve over pasta or rice.

SUM CHOWS

Walt Disney World Dolphin
1500 EPCOT Resorts Blvd. • Lake Buena Vista, Florida 32830 • (407) 939-3463

Executive Chef Chris Salansky describes Sum Chows' menu as exciting and eclectic, featuring items from the Pacific rim and highlighting such far away places as Japan, Thailand, China and Vietnam. The elegance and beauty of the cuisine are showcased in a style of the modern classics. Favorites include Spring Lamb Canton with Sesame Crust and Delicate Lemon Sauce, as well as Wok-Seared Lobster with Truffles and Sweet Peppers.

The signature restaurant of the beautiful Walt Disney World Dolphin Resort at EPCOT, Sum Chows has been honored by numerous food writers and food critics, including The American Automobile Association, Southern Living Magazine, Orlando Magazine, New York's WCBS radio and Florida Trend Magazine as one of the finest restaurants in the state. Chef Chris has had the privilege of serving guests as diverse as former President George Bush, Axel Rose, Vanna White and Shaquille O'Neal. For special occasions and celebrations, we suggest the Chef's Table.

SNOWY MOUNTAIN BEEF

This is just one of the many tasteful dishes that makes Sum Chows a must when visiting Walt Disney World.
Serves 2

DIPPING SAUCE

8 oz. sirloin of beef
1/2 cup daikon radish, fresh (ground in food processor)
1 lemon, thinly sliced
2 scallions, thinly sliced

(mix together)
2 Tbsp. Japanese soy sauce
2 Tbsp. water
2 1/2 Tbsp. fresh lemon juice
1/2 tsp. Shishimi to garnish (Japanese 7-spice pepper or cayenne pepper, to taste) optional

Completely remove all fat and silver skin from beef and season lightly with salt. Sear beef in a non-stick pan over high heat for 30 seconds on each side. The beef should be very rare on the inside. Allow to cool in refrigerator.

Slice beef thinly (as London Broil), arrange on cold plates. Top with ground daikon, lemon slices and scallions. Serve with small bowls of dipping sauce on the side.

Suggested accompaniments are sliced cucumber, pickled ginger, pickled daikon and sesame seeds.

FIRECRACKER SNAPPER

The heat of this magical sauce may be adjusted by the amount of hot oil added.
Serves 2

SAUCE

1 lb. red snapper filets
1 small Italian eggplant
2 stalks broccoli
2 sprigs fresh herbs for garnish
2 edible flowers for garnish

$^3/_4$ cup water
$^1/_2$ cup sugar
$^1/_2$ cup white vinegar
$^1/_2$ cup ketchup
$^3/_4$ tsp. garlic (minced)
$^1/_2$ tsp. fresh ginger (minced)
2 Tbsp. soy sauce
1 Tbsp. hot oil
2 Tbsp. finely sliced scallion for garnish
cornstarch to thicken

BATTER

2 whole eggs
1$^1/_2$ cups flour
water

Rinse and dry snapper filets, eggplant and broccoli. Score cross-hatch pattern on skin side surface of snapper. Trim ends off eggplant and cut in half. Cut broccoli into spears.

Place sauce ingredients into sauce pan, heat. Mix together batter ingredients with enough water to make slightly more loose than a pancake batter.

As sauce boils, thicken with cornstarch mixed with cold water; it should coat a spoon. Remove from high heat, keep warm. Dust snapper, eggplant and broccoli with flour, dip in batter and deep fry until done. Arrange on a hot plate and add scallions to the sauce. Then ladle the sauce on the plates and garnish with herb sprig and flower.

Note: For hot oil, crush two hot, dry red peppers and combine with $^1/_2$ cup vegetable oil. Allow to sit for 6 hours.

KABUKI SCALLOPS

This is simply out of this world!
Serves 6

2 lb. large sea scallops
18 fresh shiitake mushrooms
6 wonton skins
3 red bell peppers
3 green bell peppers
3 yellow bell peppers
6 shiso leaves* (fresh)
2 cups Chinese salsa (recipe included)
$^1/_4$ cup Kikkoman® soy sauce

$^1/_4$ cup water
$^1/_4$ cup rice vinegar, unseasoned
$^1/_8$ cup sugar
1 ruby red grapefruit
6 edible flowers
oil to fry
cornstarch
sake

Remove stems and seeds from all peppers. Separately purée the peppers in a food processor, adding water as needed to create a liquid. Place each puréed color pepper separately in sauce pans over medium heat. Bring to a boil. Thicken with cornstarch diluted in cold water, just enough so sauce coats a spoon. Season with salt. Strain through fine sieve. Reserve.

Heat about four cups canola oil to 350°F. Place wonton skin on oil's surface and depress center with back of a metal spoon to create a cup. Fry until crispy. Remove to paper towels to drain. Peel grapefruit and cut into uniform segments. Remove stems from shiitake mushrooms and cut decoratively.

Mix soy sauce, water, rice vinegar and sugar. Heat and thicken with cornstarch and reserve. In a cold sauté pan, lay out scallops and shiitake mushrooms in one layer. Splash with Japanese sake (enough to cover bottom quarter of scallops).

Preheat burner and place pan on high heat. Scallops should be prepared to medium rare. When the sake boils, flip the scallops and shiitake mushrooms and immediately remove from heat. Using the three pepper purées and sauce, decorate the serving plate.

Place scallops and shiitake in circle, add shiso leaves and wonton cup. Place spoonful of Chinese Salsa in the cup and top with a grapefruit segment and edible flowers.

* Shiso is a Japanese herb similar to basil but with a minty flavor. If unavailable, substitute with fresh basil and mint.

CHINESE SALSA

3 large vine ripe tomatoes, seeded and
    peeled
1 green bell pepper, seeded
2 Tbsp. minced fresh garlic
$^1/_4$ cup Kikkoman® soy sauce

$^1/_4$ cup rice vinegar
2 Tbsp. sugar
2 tsp. Vietnamese chili paste
4 shiso leaves, fresh and shredded

Finely dice tomatoes and peppers into small pieces. Mix all ingredients together. Keep refrigerated. This is best if flavors are allowed to marry overnight. Will keep one week.

✤

VICTORIA & ALBERT'S

Disney's Grand Floridian Beach Resort
Walt Disney World, Florida 32830 • (407) 939-3463

Located in the exquisite Grand Floridian Beach Resort, Victoria & Albert's offers a very special dining experience in a setting described as a nostalgic trip back in time when the ritual of dining out was civilized, stylized and lavish. Chef Scott Hunnel and his culinary staff prepare modern American cuisine that features products gathered from the international marketplace. Seven course table d'hotel menus change every day, offering the Resort's most innovative and elaborate creations.

For small, intimate dinner parties, the restaurant features an elegant private dining room that seats up to twelve persons. Royal Dalton china, Sambonet silver, Schott-Zweisel crystal and an elegant fireplace make this private room a very special place to entertain. Victoria & Alberts has won many awards, including the prestigious Four Diamond Award from the American Automobile Association.

MAINE LOBSTER TAIL
WRAPPED IN PHYLLO AND FILLED WITH A DUXELLE OF HAZELNUTS, TOMALLEY AND RAMPS WITH LEMON-THYME BUTTER SAUCE

Serves 6

DUXELLE

2 cups hazelnuts, toasted and peeled
1/4 cup lobster tomalley
1 tsp. chopped, fresh lemon-thyme

1 tbsp. hazelnut oil
fresh bread crumbs to bind
2 bulbs ramps

Roast hazelnuts in 350°F. oven for 10 minutes, let cool. Rub in between coarse cloth to remove hazelnut skin. Separate stems from lemon-thyme, chop leaves. Purée hazelnuts, tomalley, and lemon-thyme, drizzle in hazelnut oil. Add bread crumbs to tighten. Double blanch 2 bulbs ramps, chop fine, blend into duxelle.

LEMON-THYME BUTTER SAUCE

4 bulbs shallots
2 cloves garlic
1/2 cup Champagne vinegar
1 tsp. lemon-thyme

2 cups heavy cream
1/2 lb. butter chips
2 cups Chardonnay
1 tsp. clarified butter

Sweat shallots and garlic in clarified butter. Add Champagne vinegar and Chardonnay, reduce by one-half. Add lemon-thyme and heavy cream, reduce by one-half. Whisk in butter chips over low heat.

ASSEMBLY

6 8-oz. Maine lobster tail
6 sheets phyllo dough
1 cup clarified butter

Poach Maine lobsters (2½ lb. size) for 7-8 minutes; plunge into ice bath, let cool. Separate tail from body, remove tomalley from body. Reserve for duxelle. Remove all shell from tail except lower portion. Remove claw meat from shell.

Split tail, insert hazelnut duxelle. Cut each phyllo sheet in quarters; paint with clarified butter as you wrap the lobster tail. Bake in 400°F. oven until golden brown. Carve with an electric knife and place on lemon-thyme butter sauce.

FILET OF GULF COAST YELLOWTAIL SNAPPER
WITH TAMARIND AND TROPICAL SCOTCH BONNET SAUCE

The flavor of the Scotch bonnet pepper is wonderful with snapper.
Serves 6

6 6-oz. portions yellowtail snapper	*3 oz. butter*
2 oz. tamarind concentrate	*salt and pepper*
1 large size boniato, peeled, shredded	*3 Tbsp. Scotch bonnet oil*

Place yellowtail snapper skin side down on a sizzle platter that has a slight film of Scotch bonnet oil. Season snapper and paint with tamarind concentrate. Shred peeled boniato and apply to top of snapper; season lightly and drizzle with butter. Place under medium heat of broiler until boniato is golden brown.

To serve, make a bed of tropical Scotch bonnet sauce, place snapper on top, garnish with strawberry blossoms.

TROPICAL SCOTCH BONNET SAUCE

3 Tbsp. infused Scotch bonnet oil	*1 papaya, peeled and sliced*
2 cloves garlic, chopped	*2 Tbsp. passion fruit*
4 shallots, chopped	*½ cup dark rum*
½ cup Coco Lopez®	*1 oz. key lime juice*
1 mango, peeled and sliced	*½ cup heavy cream*

Sweat chopped garlic and shallots in Scotch bonnet oil, add fruit and cook slightly, deglaze with dark rum and key lime juice. Add Coco Lopez, heavy cream and reduce.

SCOTCH BONNET INFUSED OIL

4 cups canola oil
10 Scotch bonnet peppers

Wear rubber gloves while splitting Scotch bonnet peppers. Heat oil with peppers and let cool. The longer the oil sits, the hotter it will become.

VICTORIA & ALBERT'S
CARAMELIZED PINEAPPLE SOUFFLÉ

We made this with the coconut and loved it.

Prepare 8-10, 6-oz. ramekins or a 2¹/₂ qt. soufflé dish by rubbing with butter and dusting with sugar, chill until ready to fill.

1 cup flour
¹/₂ cup butter
1 cup sugar
2¹/₂ cups milk
4 Tbsp. dark rum
1 vanilla bean, split
1¹/₂ cups pineapple (preferably fresh, cut
into half inch pieces)
10 eggs, separated

** Other optional ingredients:
¹/₂ cup melted milk or dark chocolate
¹/₂ cup toasted coconut
¹/₂ cup chopped, toasted Macadamia nuts
1 tsp. allspice

Bring the milk, ¹/₂ cup sugar and vanilla to a boil. Remove from heat. In a separate pan make a roux by melting the butter over medium heat and stirring in the flour; cook for 4 minutes, stirring constantly.

Remove vanilla bean from milk. Slowly add some of the milk to the roux, stirring to make a smooth paste, then add the remaining milk. Remove from heat.

Beat in 6 eggs yolks, two at a time, until incorporated and batter is smooth and glossy. In a sauce pan on high heat, caramelize the pineapple pieces which have been drained and sprinkled with the remaining ¹/₂ cup of sugar, allowing the pieces to brown without burning, for several minutes on each side. Put in a large bowl with any resulting juices and the rum to cool. Mix in the base mixture adding any optional ingredients at this time.

In a standing mixer, whip the 10 egg whites until stiff but not dry. Beat ¹/₃ of the whites into the base until fully incorporated. Carefully fold in the remaining whites.

Fill the chilled ramekins and bake at 350°F. in a water bath for 35 - 40 minutes or until soufflé is pulled and set. A larger soufflé may require more time and should have a paper or foil collar attached around the dish, which is carefully removed before serving.

CHALET SUZANNE

Chalet Suzanne Restaurant and Country Inn
3800 Chalet Suzanne Drive • Lake Wales, Florida 33853 • (813) 676-6011

Nestled in the rolling citrus hills in the heart of Florida lies the legendary Chalet Suzanne Restaurant and Country Inn. The restaurant is the Crown Jewel of this precious 30-room Inn, and the foundation of Chalet Suzanne's reputation is its food. Chef-owner Carl Hinshaw insists, "quality and consistency are the keys to holding the standards we have set for over 60 years. The appreciation of returning guests is our reward."

The one of a kind assemblage of five dining rooms on different levels, as well as the entire resort, is the very epitome of originality and charm. The Prix Fixe menu features classic dishes with regional touches. A Golden Spoon Award winner for an incredible 25 years, plus the Mobil Guide Four-Star Award attest to the dedication of Mr. and Mrs. Hinshaw and their staff.

TANGY TROPICAL SALAD

large ripe avocado, peeled and sliced
4 oranges, sectioned and seeded
2 medium onions, sliced thinly

Marinate oranges and onions in a dressing of:

$^3/_4$ cup oil to $^1/_4$ cup red wine vinegar
salt & pepper to taste
1 Tbsp. sugar
$^1/_3$ cup ketchup
$^1/_4$ cup snipped parsley

Arrange avocados in a bowl on bed of lettuce. Put oranges and onions on a tray and drizzle dressing over all.

Do not put on too much dressing.

SHRIMP CURRY SUZANNE

$^1/_3$ cup butter or margarine
3 Tbsp. flour
1 to 2 tsp. curry powder
$^1/_2$ tsp. salt
$^1/_4$ tsp. paprika
dash nutmeg
2 cups light cream or half-and-half

3 cups shrimp, cleaned, cooked
1 Tbsp. candied ginger, finely chopped
1 Tbsp. lemon juice
1 tsp. cooking sherry
1 tsp. onion juice
dash Worcestershire Sauce®
salt to taste

Melt butter; blend in flour, curry powder, salt, paprika, and nutmeg. Gradually stir in cream; cook until mixture thickens, stirring constantly. Add remaining ingredients; heat through. Pour into casserole dish and bake in 400°F. oven about 10 minutes, or until top is lightly browned. Serve with curry condiments: currant chutney, finely shredded orange peel, flaked coconut, chopped roasted peanuts and watermelon pickles.

GATEAU CHRISTINA

MERINGUE

2 egg whites
³/₄ cup sugar
¹/₄ cup blanched ground almonds

Preheat oven to 250°F. Cut four rounds of aluminum foil about 4-in. diameter. Lightly grease foil rounds. Whip egg whites until stiff, gradually adding sugar and ground almonds as eggs begin to hold their shape. Spread meringue on foil rounds with rubber spatula. Transfer rounds to a baking sheet and bake 15 minutes, or until meringue is dry. Carefully turn meringues over and bake 5 additional minutes. Baking time will vary depending on atmospheric humidity and individual oven.

CHOCOLATE FILLING

1 egg white
¹/₄ cup sugar
1 Tbsp. sweetened cocoa
¹/₂ cup butter, softened
2 oz. semisweet chocolate, melted

In the top of a double boiler, over hot - not boiling - water, beat egg white until foamy. Gradually add and whisk: sugar, cocoa, softened butter and melted chocolate. Beat until thick and creamy, then remove from heat. Allow to cool.

To assemble the gateau: Reserve some chocolate filling for icing. Place the best meringue layer on bottom, spread with chocolate. Top with another meringue circle, pressing down lightly to make layers fit together well. Spread with chocolate. Repeat procedure until all meringue circles are used. Carefully top with reserved filling. Refrigerate the gateau at least 24 hours. Gateau keeps well under refrigeration. It may be made and stored in tin boxes for Christmas gifts.

Yield: One 4-layered 4-inch gateau.

THE MANGO TREE

118 N. Atlantic Ave. • Cocoa Beach, Florida 32931 • (407) 799-0513

In India, the mango tree is sacred. In Cocoa Beach, the Mango Tree Restaurant is magical. Owner Betty Price and her son, Bob, have transformed this original settler's bungalow into an excellent restaurant which features a profusion of lavish, fresh floral creations, all from their flower shop next door. The waterfall, the baby grand piano, the lily pond filled with Japanese Koi, the original works of art, Persian rugs and cushioned wicker chairs are all a feast for the senses.

The Mango Tree's menu is a straightforward list of traditional beef, veal and seafood which are all prepared to perfection. As a writer for Long Island's Newsday wrote, "There are absolutely no clunkers on the menu."

APPLE PEANUT BREAD

¹/₂ cup firmly packed dark brown sugar
¹/₂ cup granulated sugar
¹/₂ cup peanut oil
2 cups grated apple (from about 2 large apples)
2 Tbsp. fresh orange juice
2 tsp. cinnamon

2 cups all-purpose flour
1 tsp. salt
2 large eggs
1 cup coarsely chopped, unsalted, roasted peanuts
¹/₂ tsp. baking soda
¹/₂ cup peanut butter

In a large bowl, with an electric mixer, beat together the sugars and the oil, beat in the peanut butter until it is well mixed. In a small bowl, stir together the apple, the juice and the cinnamon. In a bowl whisk together the flour, the baking soda, and the salt.

To the sugar mixture add the eggs, 1 at a time, beating well after each addition, and beat in the flour mixture, beating until the mixture is just combined. Stir in the apple mixture and the peanuts, stirring until the batter is just combined. Turn the batter into a well-buttered 9 x 5-inch loaf pan, and bake the bread in the middle of a preheated 350° F. oven for 45 to 55 minutes, or until a tester comes out clean. Let the bread cool in the pan on a rack for 30 minutes, turn it out onto the rack, and let it cool completely.

KIR ROYALE SORBET

Yield: 1 qt.

²/₃ cup sugar
²/₃ cup water
2¹/₂ cups raspberries

1 cup champagne
¹/₄ cup creme de cassis
1¹/₂ Tbsp. fresh lemon juice

In a small heavy saucepan, combine sugar and water and bring to a boil, stirring until sugar is dissolved. Remove pan from heat. In a blender or food processor, purée raspberries with champagne, creme de cassis, and sugar syrup until smooth. Force purée through a fine sieve set over a bowl, pressing hard on solids and stir in lemon juice. Chill mixture until cold and freeze in an ice-cream maker.

Marinated Lamb Chops

These are also great on the grill!
Serves 4

$1/4$ cup olive oil
1 Tbsp. balsamic vinegar
4 garlic cloves, minced

8 Frenched 1-inch-thick rib lamb chops
(about 1 lb. total)

In a small bowl, whisk together oil, vinegar, garlic, and salt and pepper to taste. On a plate or in a shallow dish, coat lamb chops on both sides with the marinade and let stand at room temperature - turning once - for 30 minutes. Preheat broiler. Broil chops on rack of a broiler pan 2 inches from heat for 7 minutes, turning after 5 minutes for medium-rare meat.

Lemon Pepper Chicken

We first tried this on a grill, basting the marinade with excellent results.
Serves 2

$1/4$ cup fresh lemon juice
2 garlic cloves, minced
2 shallots, minced
4 fresh thyme sprigs
1 bay leaf

$1/2$ cup olive oil
1 $2^{1}/_{2}$-lb. chicken, halved
1 Tbsp. freshly grated lemon zest
2 tsp. coarsely ground fresh black pepper

In a large shallow bowl, whisk together the lemon juice, the garlic, the shallots, the thyme, the bay leaf, and the oil. Add the chicken, turning to coat it with the marinade, and let it marinate - skin side up, covered and chilled - for 2 hours.

Arrange the chicken, skin side up, on a rack in a roasting pan. Sprinkle it with the zest, the pepper, and salt to taste, and roast it in the middle of a preheated 450°F. oven for 35 to 45 minutes, or until a meat thermometer inserted into the fleshy part of a thigh registers 180°F. and the juices run clear when the thigh is pierced with a skewer. Serve immediately.

TOPAZ CAFÉ & PORCH

1224 Oceanshore Blvd. • Flagler Beach, Florida 32136 • (904) 439-3275

In 1984, the Hampton sisters took the largest risk of their lives and opened the Topaz Café, located in the then badly neglected Topaz Hotel. The hotel was inhabited by seagulls and a host of nasty creatures. Through hard work and creativity the Topaz Café has evolved into a fine dining experience combining great food and a unique atmosphere. Thanks to Paul Lee, who purchased the complex in 1989, the cobwebs and other unwelcome creatures have been replaced by Victorian furnishings and a vast collection of antiques.

The seaside location has been further enhanced by the addition of a wrap around Victorian porch with outdoor dining.

The menu is eclectic and changes every 3 weeks, featuring fresh seafood, meat, pasta and vegetarian dishes. As a bonus, jazz recording artist Bobby Branca and his swing band play in the cozy bar room four nights a week.

Japanese Noodle & Spinach Salad
with Soy-Ginger Vinaigrette

A favorite at the Topaz Café for many years - the soy ginger vinaigrette is delightful!
Serves 4

1 package Udon noodles	1½ cups soy sauce
1 package of pre-washed spinach	¾ cup Dijon mustard
2 Tbsp. chopped fresh ginger	4½ cups vegetable oil
1¼ Tbsp. chopped fresh shallot	dash of hot pepper sauce
1 Tbsp. chopped garlic	2 Tbsp. toasted sesame oil

Insert metal blade in food processor and individually chop the ginger, garlic and shallots; measure and set aside. Replace blade and add soy, Dijon, ginger, garlic and shallots. With machine running, slowly pour oil through the feed tube, add hot pepper sauce and chill.

Udon noodles are available at most natural or oriental food stores. Cook and drain according to package directions. Toss with toasted sesame oil and chill.

Purchase pre-washed spinach. Remove stems and toss leaves with soy-ginger vinaigrette. Serve in a large bowl surrounded by the udon noodles. Optional toppings: grilled scallops wrapped in bacon, snow or sugar peas, red onion, grilled sliced chicken or beef. Pass additional vinaigrette over toppings or serve on the side.

Banana Vanilla Muffins

These are just plain great.

$^1/_4$ cup vegetable oil
1 egg
2 mashed bananas
$^1/_3$ cup sugar

$^1/_2$ cup Breyer's® light vanilla ice cream
$^1/_4$ cup no-fat sour cream
2 Tbsp. pure vanilla

Mix the above ingredients together with a wire whip.

2 cups flour
$^1/_2$ cup graham cracker crumbs
1 Tbsp. baking powder

Sift together the flour and baking powder, add graham cracker crumbs and add the flour mixture to the banana mixture, stirring until completely mixed. Spoon into greased muffin tin, filling slightly more than half full. Bake in pre-heated 375° F. oven for about 20 minutes.

Chilled Asparagus Salad
with Raspberry Cream

Serves 4

1 bunch pencil-thin asparagus spears
Boston lettuce and radicchio

$^1/_4$ cup toasted pine nuts
raspberry cream

In a shallow wide pot bring to boil enough water to cover asparagus spears lying lengthwise. Place spears in boiling water and cook 3-4 minutes. Do not cover pan or overcook! Remove spears with tongs and place in cold water. Drain, pat dry and chill. In 350°F. oven, toast pine nuts until brown.

Raspberry Cream

16 oz. plain, no-fat yogurt
3 Tbsp. no-fat mayonnaise
3 Tbsp. whipped heavy cream

$^1/_4$ cup frozen raspberry concentrate,
    unthawed- available at natural food
    stores

Blend all ingredients well and chill. Decoratively arrange Boston lettuce leaves and radicchio leaves at the top of the plate. Fan asparagus spears under lettuce leaves and sprinkle with toasted pine nuts. Put dollop of raspberry cream on lettuce leaves.

Grilled Japanese Eggplant & Coconut Pesto
with Black Beans, Rice and Papaya Salsa

It seems there is no end to the exciting creations at the Topaz Café
Serves 4

4 Japanese eggplants, cut lengthwise
1 cup black beans, cooked according to
  package directions

1 cup white rice, cooked according to
  package directions

Papaya Salsa

2 ripe papayas, peeled, seeded and cut in
  small dice
1/2 bunch cilantro, chopped
1 red bell pepper, finely chopped
1 jalapeño pepper, finely chopped

3 Tbsp. each of lime, lemon and pineapple
  juice
1/4 cup rice wine vinegar
1 small red onion, finely chopped

Gently blend all ingredients and chill.

Coconut Pesto

3 cloves chopped garlic
2 cups fresh coconut, shredded or unsweetened coconut- available at natural
  food store

1 bunch fresh basil, chopped
1/2 cup coconut cream or milk- available at
  oriental food store

Blend all ingredients together in a bowl with a spoon and refrigerate. Grill eggplant slices on each side about 3 minutes or until tender. Top with coconut pesto. Mix black beans and rice together. Top with papaya salsa.

THE OCEAN GRILL

Sexton Plaza • Vero Beach, Florida 32964 • (305) 231-5409

In the original restaurant built by Waldo Sexton in 1941, The Ocean Grill's famous seafood is as good as ever. For those who appreciate a good, no nonsense seafood restaurant with a great view of where the fish live, The Ocean Grill is pretty close to perfect. The Replogle family from Milwaukee (land of Walleyed Pike and Yellow Perch) purchased the venerable Vero Beach restaurant 30 years ago and have not missed a beat in serving the residents and guests of this oceanside community. One addition they have made to the menu is the duck, which they naturally import from Wisconsin.

The sauces served with the broiled fish are outstanding. Our favorite is the apricot butter which often accompanies the pompano.

CONCH FRITTERS

These are excellent with cocktail sauce and a cold beer.

2¹/₂ lbs. whole conch
¹/₂ cup chopped onion
¹/₂ cup chopped celery
¹/₂ cup chopped tomato
³/₈ cup chopped parsley
¹/₂ Tbsp. chopped garlic
¹/₂ Tbsp. Worcestershire® sauce

1¹/₂ Tbsp. Old Bay Seasoning®
¹/₂ Tbsp. baking powder
¹/₂ Tbsp. Tabasco®
¹/₈ tsp. black pepper
2 cups cracker meal
4 large eggs, separated

Grind conch in food processor. Mix with onions, celery, tomato, parsley, garlic, salt, and Old Bay Seasoning. Then process this mixture together. Add Worcestershire, baking powder, Tabasco, pepper and cracker meal. Mix well. Whip egg yolks and blend into mixture. Whip egg whites and fold in thoroughly. Refrigerate until ready to use. Deep fry in canola or peanut oil at 350-360°F.

APRICOT BUTTER

1 cup sherry
¹/₂ cup water
¹/₂ bag dried apricots, chopped
2 lbs. butter

1 jar apricot jelly
1 tsp. Tabasco®
1 tsp. Worcestershire®

Simmer sherry, water and apricots together. Add jelly and melt. Add Tabasco and Worcestershire sauce. Add butter a little at a time, whisking until it melts. Serve on broiled fish. (1 cup of pineapple and ¹/₂ cup pineapple juice can be substituted for apricots and water to make pineapple butter.)

This is used on their fresh broiled fish, most often pompano.

Jake's Red Peppercorn Citrus Butter

for Fresh Seafood and Fish

¹/₂ lb. lightly salted butter
¹/₂ Tbsp. orange juice concentrate
¹/₂ tsp. lime zest, finely chopped
3 oranges peeled, cut into segments and chopped (save peel)
1¹/₂ Tbsp. fresh lemon juice

2 tsp. finely chopped orange zest (from peel)
¹/₂ tsp. white pepper
¹/₄ tsp. salt
¹/₂ cup whole red peppercorns

Whip butter in mixer until double in volume. Mix remaining ingredients, except peppercorns, into butter with mixer on low speed. Mix in peppercorns. Spoon mixture onto parchment paper and roll into cylinder. Chill in freezer or refrigerator. To use, cut into coins and place on fish or scallops after cooking.

Place fish under broiler just until butter begins to bubble.

Serve immediately. Wrap extra butter tightly in clear wrap, mark and store in freezer for later use.

Ultra-pasteurized cream has a longer storage life but poorer whipping quality than regular cream.

ARMANI'S

Hyatt Regency Westshore
6200 Courtney Campbell Causeway • Tampa, Florida 33607 • (813) 874-1234

Armani's is located high atop the Hyatt Regency Westshore, with panoramic views of Tampa Bay and the city skyline. The focal point is the incredible Antipasto Bar, where each guest may create their own selection from an extensive array of cold appetizers. Northern Italian cuisine is the theme, with veal and seafood given special treatment.

The credentials and cuisine of Armani's are both outstanding, earning it the prestigious Golden Spoon Award as one of Florida's top twenty restaurants for the fifth time. However, we feel Armani's Lounge and Bar should also receive a special award as the best spot for an after dinner drink while overlooking old Tampa Bay and enjoying soothing piano music.

ARMANI'S SHRIMP SCAMPI

Serve with crispy Italian bread for the wonderful juices.
Serves 4

20 med. shrimp, peeled and deveined
1/2 cup extra virgin olive oil
3 cloves fresh garlic, chopped fine
4 whole plum tomatoes, peeled and diced
   fine

1 1/2 cups fresh basil, chopped
salt and pepper to taste
3/8 cup dry white wine

In a sauté pan over medium heat add olive oil, the garlic and shrimp.

Cook shrimp on each side for one minute. Add remaining ingredients and bring to a slow boil for 5-6 minutes. Garnish with fresh basil.

GRILLED SWORDFISH WITH LEMON BUTTER & CAPERS

Serves 4

4 8-oz. swordfish steaks
1 stick butter
2 lemons, juice only

1/4 cup capers
1/2 cup extra virgin olive oil
salt and pepper to taste

Brush steaks lightly on both sides with olive oil and place on grill for five minutes on each side. Remove and place on a serving plate. In sauté pan over low heat, add butter, lemon juice and capers. Reduce for 5-6 minutes and then pour directly over swordfish. Garnish with lemon wheel and fresh rosemary.

Tomato and Red Onion Salad

A perfect lunch when served with iced tea and a crispy baguette.
Serves 4

4 beefsteak tomatoes, sliced
4 sundried tomatoes packed in oil, drained
   and chopped
1 red onion, finely chopped
salt and freshly ground pepper
2 Tbsp. red wine vinegar

pinch of sugar
3 Tbsp. extra virgin olive oil
4 Tbsp. chopped mixed fresh herbs, such
   as basil, oregano, parsley, chives, dill
   and cilantro
herb sprigs to garnish

Layer tomatoes, sundried tomatoes and onion in a shallow serving dish. Season with salt and freshly ground pepper.

Mix together remaining ingredients except herb sprigs in a small bowl, then pour over salad. Garnish with herb sprigs.

Chicken Rollatini

Serves 4

4 6-oz. skinless chicken breasts
4 full fresh spinach leaves
8 slices thin mozzarella cheese
1 bunch basil

1 cup extra virgin olive oil
2 cups flour
2 cups Italian bread crumbs
3 eggs, beaten

Pound chicken to ¼ inch thickness. Place spinach, basil and mozzarella on each chicken breast then roll and insert two toothpicks to hold together.

Pre-heat oven to 400°F., dip each chicken roll in flour, then dip in egg and roll in bread crumbs.

Place in pre-heated sauté pan with olive oil until golden brown. Remove from sauté pan and drain excess oil, then place on a baking sheet and place in the oven for 5 minutes. Garnish with fresh basil.

Adding a little water to eggs and beating only until the whites and yolks are just combined will result in a more moist, tender omelet.

THE BLUE HERON

3285 Tampa Road • Palm Harbor, Florida 34684 • (813) 789-5176

Chefs Robert Stea and Larry Lloyd call their style "fusion cuisine," a creative mix of Caribbean, Southwestern, Far Eastern and Pacific Rim elements. The result is an inspiring dining experience full of visual and gastronomic delight. The Blue Heron specializes in fresh Florida seafood, as well as duck and game. The ambience at the Blue Heron is elegant yet casual — their motto is "everyone from tennis to tuxedo." Located 10 minutes north of Clearwater in Palm Harbor, The Blue Heron is another example of outstanding cuisine that's well worth the drive.

SALMON & RED PEPPER BISQUE

Serves 4

6 oz. jumbo lump crab (for garnish)
2 lg. red bell peppers, seeded and rough chopped
1 med. onion, rough chopped
2 cloves garlic, crushed

6 oz. salmon filet, rough chopped
1 stalk celery, rough chopped
1 qt. heavy cream
2 cups white wine
parsley for garnish

On high heat sauté peppers, onion, celery, salmon and garlic until limp and salmon is cooked, then add white wine. When mix comes to a boil, turn to medium heat for three minutes. Remove from heat and let cool for ten to fifteen minutes. Put the mixture through a blender.

In a soup pot, reduce the heavy cream to desired consistency and combine with blended pepper mixture. Add salt and white pepper to taste.

Put entire mixture through a fine sieve; heat and serve, garnished with parsley and jumbo lump crab meat.

LUMP CRAB, ARTICHOKE & HEARTS OF PALM

TOSSED IN LEMON BASIL OIL

Serves 4

$^1/_2$ lb. lump or jumbo lump crab
12 large artichoke hearts (canned), quartered
12 large hearts of palm (canned), rinsed and cut in $^1/_2$-inch lengths

1 small head red cabbage (cored and cut chiffonade)
1 each red and yellow bell pepper, seeded and julienne

Toss all ingredients in a large mixing bowl. Cover and refrigerate.

Basil Oil

1 to 1½ bunches fresh basil
1 shallot, minced
2 cloves garlic, minced
1 tsp. black pepper

juice of 1 lemon
2 cups olive oil
salt to taste

Place all ingredients in a blender and process.
Toss basil oil into salad. Arrange on plate. Garnish with basil and chopped chives.

Marinated Grilled Swordfish
with Florida Citrus Sauce

Blue Heron's citrus sauce is perfect with grilled swordfish.
Serves 4

4 6-oz. swordfish steaks
2 Tbsp. olive oil
juice of 2 limes
2 Tbsp. white pepper

Marinate swordfish steaks in olive oil and lime juice for 3 minutes. Season and grill steaks 3 to 4 minutes per side. Keep warm until ready to serve.

Florida Citrus Sauce

2 lg. pink grapefruit
1 lg. orange
2 key limes (or regular limes)
1 tsp. Dijon mustard
1 tsp. tomato paste
1 Tbsp. extra virgin olive oil
6 leaves fresh basil, finely chopped

1 Tbsp. cornstarch, diluted in ¼ cup cold
water (if you desire thicker sauce)
scallions, chopped, for garnish
3 cups cooked brown rice (or grain of your
choice)

Squeeze the first three ingredients and reserve the juice. Place juice, Dijon mustard and tomato paste in a sauce pan and reduce by half, stirring occasionally. If desired add cornstarch in cold water for thicker consistency. When reduced, whisk in olive oil. Simmer and reduce slightly while whisking. Turn off heat, add fresh basil and stir. Immediately serve over grilled swordfish, garnished with chopped scallions. Serve with cooked rice.

THE COLUMBIA RESTAURANT

2117 East 7th Avenue • Tampa, Florida 33505 • (813) 248-4961

Freshly baked Cuban bread, fresh roasted coffees and fresh seafood from the Gulf of Mexico have been a tradition at the world famous Columbia Restaurant since 1905. With its original location in Ybor City, the Columbia Restaurant is both Florida's oldest restaurant and the world's largest Spanish restaurant.

The Columbia Restaurant emphasizes authentic Spanish and Cuban cuisine. Consistently winning recognition for its high standards of food and service, the Columbia Restaurant has been voted the number one Spanish restaurant by readers of the St. Petersburg Times, Tampa Bay Tribune and Sarasota Herald. (NOTE: Enjoy an authentic Flamenco dance show in the original Ybor City restaurant 6 nights a week.)

BLACK BEAN SOUP

Some people add chorizo, but this basic recipe is so good we like it just as it is.
Serves 4

1 lb. black beans
2 qts. water
3 medium size onions, chopped fine
2 green peppers, cut in strips
4 cloves garlic, minced

1 bay leaf
1 tsp. oregano
$^1/_4$ tsp. ground cumin
$^1/_2$ tsp. black pepper

Before washing beans, spread on flat surface and pick broken beans out. Look for foreign particles such as tiny little stones. Wash beans well and soak overnight in 2 quarts of water.

Next day, pour beans into 4 quart soup kettle and boil in the same soaking water. Cover and cook on medium heat.

Meanwhile, in a skillet, sauté onions and green peppers in olive oil until light golden, then add crushed oregano, bay leaf, cumin and minced garlic. Add to the beans, stirring well. Add salt and pepper and cook slowly until beans are tender. Serve over white rice and top with chopped onions.

CHICKEN AND YELLOW RICE

The Columbia recipe for this traditional dish is perfection.
Serves 4

1 3-lb. fryer, cut in quarters
2 onions, chopped
1 green pepper, chopped
2 medium size tomatoes, peeled, seeded
   and chopped
2 cloves garlic, minced
¼ cup olive oil
1 bay leaf

2 cups long grain rice
4 cups chicken broth
½ tsp. saffron
1 Tbsp. salt
½ cup small green peas (frozen)
2 pimentos, cut in half
4 asparagus tips
¼ cup white wine

Cut fryer in quarters. In a skillet, sauté chicken in heated oil until skin is golden. Remove chicken and place in casserole. In the same olive oil sauté onion, green pepper, tomatoes and garlic for 5 minutes. Pour over chicken and add chicken broth, saffron and rice. Bring to boil, cover casserole and bake in oven at 350°F. for 20 minutes. Take out of oven, sprinkle with wine and garnish with peas, pimentos and asparagus tips. (*NOTE: Use a casserole dish which can be used on a burner.*)

SPANISH CUSTARD

Serves 6

3 cups of sugar
6 eggs
1 tsp. vanilla
1 pinch of salt
1 pint of boiling milk

Boil a cup of sugar and half cup of water until brown, then pour the caramel into six molds. Beat 6 eggs, add two cups of sugar, a teaspoon of vanilla, a pinch of salt and beat again. Add 1 pint of boiling milk little by little, then strain through cloth or china colander. Pour mixture into molds, put molds in water filled pan and bake for 30 minutes at 350°F. in oven — don't let water boil, or custard will be filled with holes. Cool in refrigerator.

When ready to serve, press edges of custard with spoon to break away from mold, then turn upside down. The caramel then tops the custard.

DONATELLO

232 North Dale Mabry Hwy. • Tampa, Florida 33609 • (813) 875-6660

When it comes to top quality Northern Italian cuisine in the Tampa area, Donatello is the restaurant which gets the nod. The cuisine and the wine list are both classic, authentic Italian, reflecting the background of the owner, manager and the chefs.

Both veal and pasta dishes are outstanding, but the desserts which are all made on site should not be passed over. In addition to outstanding cuisine, the entire staff at Donatello is both friendly and professional. Every city should have an Italian restaurant like Donatello.

LINGUINE FANTASIA

This is what Italian seafood is all about.
Serves 2

4 Tbsp. olive oil
2 cloves of fresh garlic, finely chopped
2 Tbsp. of chopped Italian parsley
$^1/_2$ cup dry white wine
4 jumbo shrimp
$^1/_2$ lb. sliced calamari
$^3/_4$ cup scallops

6 oz. chicken stock
tomato, sliced
small head of broccoli, florets only
salt & pepper to taste
$^1/_2$ lb. linguine, cooked al dente

In a sauté pan heat oil and garlic until golden. Add parsley, seafood and white wine and sauté until wine is reduced by half. Add chicken stock and cover for 2 minutes. Add sliced tomato and broccoli florets and cover for 1 minute. Toss with linguine which has been cooked al dente. Serve immediately.

LINGUINE WITH CRAB MEAT

Quick, easy and great.
Serves 4

4 Tbsp. olive oil
3 cloves fresh garlic, chopped
2 Tbsp. Italian parsley, chopped
$^1/_2$ tsp. crushed red pepper
1 lb. fresh or canned jumbo crab meat

$^1/_2$ cup dry white wine
1 cup clam juice
salt and pepper to taste
1 lb. linguine
1 Tbsp. butter

In a sauté pan heat oil, add garlic and sauté until golden. Add parsley, red pepper, crab meat and wine. Sauté until wine is reduced by $^1/_2$. Add clam juice and salt and pepper and simmer for 2 minutes. Toss sauce with cooked pasta over high heat with the butter for 2 minutes. Serve immediately.

PASTA & BEAN SOUP

Great with garlic bread and white wine.
Serves 4

2 tablespoons olive oil
¹/₂ cup chopped onion
2 stalks chopped celery
1 stem fresh rosemary, finely chopped
2 slices of bacon

2 8-oz. cans of cannelini beans, drained
1¹/₄ cup chicken stock
2 Tbsp. tomato sauce
salt and pepper to taste

In a large pot using the olive oil, sauté the vegetables, rosemary and the bacon until slightly golden. Add the beans, chicken stock and the tomato sauce for color.

Bring the soup to a boil, reduce heat and allow to simmer uncovered for 10 minutes. Salt and pepper to taste. Add the cooked pasta of your choice and serve.

The vitamin A content of a fresh apricot is one hundred times greater than the average in other fruits.

THE HERITAGE GRILLE

234 Third Avenue North • St. Petersburg, Florida 33701 • (813) 823-6382

The Heritage Grille in St. Petersburg has been a leader in New American cuisine since 1990. The casual, yet elegant Grille is like an art gallery within a restaurant, with cocktails being served from a bar that once graced the home of Jefferson Davis.

The Grille's exciting food is noted for its creative blending of contemporary cuisines. The selections may include the bold flavors of the Caribbean to the influences of classical French, mixed according to freshness and a respect for Florida's culinary resources. Under the direction of Executive Chef Henri Chaperont, The Heritage Grille has earned the coveted Golden Spoon Award for four consecutive years.

SHRIMP AND SCALLOP POT PIE

You will love this seafood variation.
Serves 4

1 lb. medium shrimp
3/4 lb. medium scallops
1 each green and red pepper
1 red onion
6 plum tomatoes
4 Tbsp. garlic, chopped
1/2 cup ancho chili oil

1/4 tsp. cayenne pepper
1 Tbsp. shallots, chopped
1/4 tsp. chili powder
salt, white pepper to taste
1/4 cup sherry wine
puff pastry dough
3/4 cup cheddar cheese

Dice all your vegetables to 3/4-inch pieces, peel and devein the shrimp. Sauté shrimp and scallops in hot ancho chili oil, deglaze with sherry wine and add all your vegetables and seasonings. Serve in a soup plate or soup terrine topped with puff pastry dough and shredded cheddar cheese. Bake in a 350°F. oven until golden brown.

YUCCA AU GRATIN

Serves 4

2 lbs. fresh yucca
1/2 tsp. salt
1/4 tsp. white pepper

1 pt. heavy cream
1/4 tsp. nutmeg
1/4 stick of unsalted butter

Peel and core yucca. Cook in boiling water until tender. Combine yucca, salt and pepper, heavy cream, nutmeg in a bowl with an electric mixer. Grease baking pan with butter. Add yucca and top with your choice of cheese, bake at 325°F. until cheese is melted and becomes brown.

Blackened Salmon with Papaya & Mango Salsa

Serves 4

Seasonings:

1 tsp. sweet paprika
2½ tsp. seasoned salt
1 tsp. onion powder
1 tsp. garlic powder
1 pt. cayenne pepper

1 tsp. white pepper
1 tsp. black pepper
½ tsp. dried thyme leaves
1½ tsp. dried oregano leaves

4 6-oz. salmon filets
1 stick butter, melted

Combine all seasonings in a bowl and set aside. Dip each filet into melted butter and sprinkle the seasoning mix on the filets. Heat a cast iron skillet until extremely hot. Place the filets in the hot skillet and cook until the seasoning on the fish looks charred. Turn filets over and repeat the process. Pour a small amount of butter over the filets and continue cooking until filets are firm.

Papaya and Mango Salsa

Can be served over Blackened Fish.
Serves 4

1 fresh mango
1 fresh papaya
½ fresh pineapple
1 medium tomato

1 bunch cilantro
½ lime - juiced
½ lemon - juiced

Peel mango, papaya, pineapple, tomato and dice very fine. Wash cilantro, pick leaves and chop into fine pieces. Combine all ingredients in a bowl with the lime and lemon juice and stir.

White Chocolate Mango Tart

Serves 8-12

Sweet Pastry Dough

2 Tbsp. sugar
3 cups flour
½ tsp. salt

3 sticks cold unsalted butter
3 Tbsp. ice cold water

Combine dry ingredients in a bowl with electric mixer. Using a paddle, work in the butter until it becomes the size of small peas. Slowly pour in water until dough just comes together, then refrigerate for 30 minutes. Roll out ¼-inch thick in a tart shell and prebake at 325°F. for about 15 minutes.

White Chocolate Filling

12 oz. white chocolate, chopped
¹/₂ cup heavy cream
4 Tbsp. butter, softened

Melt chocolate with heavy cream over a double boiler. Stir in butter. Pour into pre-baked pie shell. Refrigerate until firm. Arrange mango slices and/or any fruit of your choice on top of tart.

Resist lifting the lid when crockery cooking. The lost steam and heat may take up to 30 minutes to replace.

MARCHAND'S BAR & GRILL

Renaissance Vinoy Resort
501 Fifth Avenue N.E. • St. Petersburg, Florida 33701 • (813) 894-1000

Marchand's Bar & Grill is one of four excellent restaurants at the Renaissance Vinoy Resort. The cuisine at Marchand's is a delightful combination that highlights Florida's fresh seafood and a variety of dishes with a light handed Mediterranean influence. Master Chef Thomas Chin also injects a Pan Asian flavor to a number of seafood specialties that are determined according to freshness and availability. Florida Trend Magazine honored Marchand's Bar & Grill as one of Florida's outstanding new restaurants a year after its opening, and now rates it as one of Florida's finest.

The showplace of St. Petersburg's scenic waterfront, the Renaissance Vinoy Resort is a full service resort that recalls the style and glamour of another era. Situated on sparkling Tampa Bay and surrounded by lush grounds and park lands, this opulent resort surrounds guests with grand furnishings and vintage architectural detail. In addition to a host of amenities, the Renaissance Vinoy features a private marina with 74 slips.

GRILLED SNAPPER
WITH FRESH TOMATO, CAPER & BLACK OLIVE SALSA
Serves 2

2 6-oz. snapper filets	1 cup Tomato, Caper & Black Olive Salsa
1 Tbsp. olive oil	salt & freshly ground pepper to taste

Brush olive oil lightly on both sides of fish and season with salt and pepper. Place the filets on a hot grill and cook for approximately 1 minute, turn over and cook until fish is done. Place the fish on two plates and serve the Tomato, Caper & Black Olive Salsa over the fish.

TOMATO, CAPER & BLACK OLIVE SALSA

1 Tbsp. olive oil	1/2 Tbsp. Kalamata olives, pitted, chopped
1 Tbsp. shallots, chopped fine	1/2 tsp. fresh thyme, chopped
1/4 tsp. garlic, chopped fine	2 cups tomatoes, peeled, seeded, diced into
1 Tbsp. balsamic vinegar	1/2-inch pieces
1 Tbsp. capers, rinsed	salt & freshly ground pepper to taste

Heat a non-stick sauté pan, add olive oil, chopped shallots, garlic and cook for approximately 30 seconds. Add Balsamic vinegar, tomatoes, capers, olives and fresh thyme. Simmer for about 3 minutes. Adjust seasoning with salt and freshly ground black pepper to taste.

PENNE PASTA
with Roasted Fennel, Artichokes and Tomatoes
Serves 2

8 oz. penne pasta
1 roasted fennel bulb, 1/4-inch julienne
1 Tbsp. garlic, chopped fine
1 Tbsp. shallots, chopped fine
6 fresh baby artichokes, blanched, trimmed
  and halved
1/2 cup tomatoes, peeled, seeded,
  diced into 1/2-inch pieces

3 Tbsp. olive oil
1/4 cup fresh Romano cheese, grated
1/8 cup tightly packed fresh basil,
  chopped
1 whole fennel bulb, all stems removed
1 Tbsp. olive oil
salt & freshly ground black pepper

Cook pasta until just done. Heat a non-stick sauté pan and add olive oil, shallots, garlic, fennel, artichoke hearts and sauté for 1 minute. Add drained pasta and the chopped basil, mix thoroughly and continue heating for another minute. Adjust seasoning with salt and pepper.

Divide into two pasta bowls, arranging half of the artichokes on each plate. Sprinkle with Romano cheese and garnish with chopped tomatoes.

For the Roasted Fennel, preheat oven to 400°F. Cut fennel bulb in half lengthwise and lightly brush with olive oil. Place in oven and roast for 15-20 minutes. Remove and cool to room temperature.

MACADAMIA CRUSTED GROUPER
with Citrus Papaya Salsa
Serves 2

2 6-oz. Grouper filets, skinned
Egg wash (1 egg mixed with 2 Tbsp. water)
1/2 cup flour, seasoned with salt & pepper
1 cup bread crumbs

1 cup macadamia nuts, finely
  chopped
1/2 cup canola oil
1 cup citrus papaya salsa

Dredge grouper filets through seasoned flour, shake off any excess flour. Dip the filets into the egg wash. Mix together the bread crumbs and chopped macadamia nuts in a bowl, and press the filets into this mixture until evenly coated

Heat a large non-stick sauté pan with canola oil. Add the filets and cook for until for 1 minute, turn over and continue cooking until done. (If filets are thick, you may want to finish cooking in 350°F. oven to avoid burning macadamia crust in sauté pan.) Remove and place on absorbant paper.

CITRUS PAPAYA SALSA

1 papaya, peeled, seeded,
  diced into ¹/₂-inch pieces
¹/₈ cup tomatoes, peeled, seeded,
  diced into ¹/₂-inch pieces
¹/₄ cup diced red onions
1 Tbsp. fresh cilantro, chopped

¹/₈ cup red wine vinegar
¹/₄ cup fresh orange juice
¹/₈ cup olive oil
salt & freshly ground pepper to taste

Place all ingredients into a stainless steel or glass bowl and mix thoroughly. Place 1/4 of this mixture into a blender and puree. Stir the puree into the salsa mixture. Adjust seasoning with salt and freshly ground pepper to taste.

GRILLED SWORDFISH
WITH WHITE BEANS, BACON AND SHERRY CHIVE VINAIGRETTE
Serves 2

2 Tbsp. olive oil
2 6-oz. Swordfish steaks, skin & bone removed
2 cups white beans, cooked
3 slices uncooked smoked bacon, diced
1 cup tightly packed fresh spinach, chopped
1 Tbsp. shallots, chopped fine

1 tsp. garlic, chopped fine
¹/₂ cup tomatoes, peeled, seeded,
  diced into ¹/₂-inch pieces
¹/₂ cup Sherry-Chive Vinaigrette
salt & freshly ground white pepper

Lightly oil fish and season with salt and pepper. Place fish on hot grill and cook for approximately 30 seconds, make a quarter turn and continue to grill for antoher 30 seconds. Turn over and repeat process until fish is done. Remove and hold on warm plate.

Heat a non-stick sauté pan , add diced bacon and cook until rendered. Add shallots, garlic and spinach and sauté for 1 minute. Add diced tomatoes, white beans and cook until beans are hot. Adjust seasoning with salt and pepper. Divide beans onto two plates, top with cooked swordfish, and drizzle Sherry-Chive Vinaigrette around beans.

SHERRY CHIVE VINAIGRETTE

1 cup sherry vinegar
2 cups olive oil
3 cloves garlic

4 peeled shallots
1 cup fresh chives, chopped

Place vinegar, garlic, shallots and chives in blender. Puree until smooth. Turn blender to low speed and slowly drizzle olive oil into the mixture until emulsified. Season with salt and freshly ground black pepper. This vinaigrette will hold for 5-7 days under refrigeration.

THE MARITANA GRILLE

The Don Cesar Beach Resort
3400 Gulf Blvd. • St. Petersburg Beach, Florida 33706 • (813) 360-1881

The Maritana Grille is seemingly submerged in more than 1,500 gallons of salt water, as exotic fish swim through massive tanks lining an entire wall of the restaurant. The Maritana Grille, which replaces the long popular King Charles restaurant, brings unique "Floribbean" specialties to Florida's legendary "Pink Palace."

Signature dishes include Fire-Roasted Gulf Fish with Flaming Herbs, Cous-Cous Filled Eggplant with Bitter Greens and Atlantic Salmon with Horseradish Crust. Many of the selections are carefully prepared over a pecan and cherry wood burning grill. The Maritana Grille was recently selected as one of the Florida's outstanding new restaurants by Florida Trend Magazine.

The Mediterranean flair exhibited by The Maritana Grille combines Florida cuisine and attentive, professional service to make a very special dining experience - a great new restaurant in a venerable institution with a perfect Gulf front location.

PROSCIUTTO WRAPPED PRAWNS
WITH CAPELLINI, GRILLED VIDALIA ONIONS AND PARSLEY

The prosciutto and shrimp make a great combination.
Serves 4

20 extra large tiger prawns
$^1/_2$ lb. capellini
1 sm. Vidalia onion, julienne
1 tsp. garlic, minced
1 tsp. shallots, minced
$^1/_2$ cup Italian parsley, chopped
2 yellow plum tomatoes, seeded and diced

2 red plum tomatoes, seeded and diced
Parmesan cheese to taste
10 slices prosciutto, sliced thin
$^1/_2$ cup Chardonnay wine
$1^1/_2$ cups fish stock
$^1/_2$ cup chives, chopped

Cut prosciutto in half the lengthwise, then wrap around prawn. Season with chopped herbs and pepper, grill till medium rare. Set aside. Cook pasta and rinse, then set aside. Sauté onions, garlic and shallots till soft. Add white wine and reduce by half. Then add fish stock, tomatoes, parsley and pasta. Add prawns until lightly cooked and serve at once. Garnish with Parmesan cheese and chives.

SEARED YELLOW FIN TUNA
WITH JICAMA SALAD AND WASABI DRESSING

Fun, interesting and tasty - the Wasabi dressing is wonderful.
Serves 4

TUNA

1 lb. yellow fin tuna, center cut
1/2 tsp. black pepper
1/4 cup cilantro, chopped

1 tsp. BBQ spice
2 Tbsp. sesame oil
2 Tbsp. red shallots, chopped

Mix all ingredients for tuna in a bowl. Take tuna loin and marinate for one hour. When tuna is ready, pack all herbs and spices around tuna and sear in hot skillet until golden brown. Set aside in colander. Tuna should be rare inside.

JICAMA SALAD

1 jicama, grated
segments from 1 orange
juice from 1 lime
1/2 each red and yellow pepper, diced

salt and pepper, diced
2 Tbsp. cilantro
2 Tbsp. sesame seed oil

Skin and shred jicama in a bowl, add all ingredients mix well and chill.

WASABI DRESSING

3 cups olive oil
2 Tbsp. sesame oil
1 Tbsp. wasabi paste
1 Tbsp. sugar

1 Tbsp. shallots, chopped
2 Tbsp. tarragon
2 Tbsp. mint

Whisk together all ingredients expect olive oil. Add the olive oil slowly while whisking continuously. Chill for serving.

Arrange the Jicama salad in the center of each plate. Fan the tuna next to the salad and drizzle the Wasabi dressing over the tuna.

FALLEN CHOCOLATE SOUFFLÉ

This sounded so interesting, and it was - the tiramisu paste adds a subtle flavor.
Great with ice cream!
Serves 12

7 oz. butter
13 oz. bittersweet chocolate
2 oz. tiramisu paste
15 egg yolks

15 egg whites
1/2 cup cake flour
1 1/4 cups plus 2 Tbsp. sugar

Melt chocolate with butter and tiramiso paste. Whip yolks and sugar till sabyonne texture. Then fold into chocolate mixture and sift in flour. Whip egg whites until soft peaks form, then fold into chocolate mixture.

Bake at 350°F. for 25-30 minutes. Garnish with fresh berries and vanilla balsamic ice cream.

Twenty minutes in the freezer is roughly the equivalent of the cooling effect
of 1 hour in the refrigerator.

TIO PEPE RESTAURANTE

2930 Gulf to Bay • Clearwater, Florida 34619 • (813)799-3082

Since 1976, Tio Pepe has offered the Bay area authentic "Old Country" Mediterranean continental cuisine with a distinctive Spanish Flair. One would naturally expect an excellent selection of tapas, but Jesus Exposito and Joseph Rodriguez also feature Iowa and Nebraska corn fed beef, as well as lamb, pork and veal. Fresh seafood includes pompano, snapper, lobster and salmon (flown in daily). Desserts and breads are made in their in-house bakery.

Located in a landmark Spanish-style house with rare antiques and mementos, Tio Pepe recently earned a 1994 Golden Spoon Award as one of Florida's finest restaurants, and has received the Award of Excellence from the Wine Spectator for eight consecutive years.

SPANISH SAFFRON RICE

Like all dishes at Tio Pepe, this is perfectly authentic.
Serves 6

3 cups long grain enriched white rice
5 cups chicken broth
1 Tbsp. ground garlic
1 small green pepper, finely chopped
1 small onion, finely chopped

1 tsp. salt
5 Tbsp. olive oil
pinch of toasted saffron
splash of Tio Pepe sherry

In a casserole dish over medium heat, add 4 Tbsp. olive oil; add garlic, green pepper and onion. Sauté until transparent. Stir in rice to coat with oil. Add boiling chicken broth, add salt and a pinch of saffron. Stir to dissolve, and bring to a full boil. Cover and move to a pre-heated oven at 350°F. for 30 minutes. Then uncover and let stand for 5 minutes. Add 1 Tbsp. olive oil and a splash of sherry. Stir and serve.

STRAWBERRY ROYAL

The Amaretto Cream is heavenly.

1 quart strawberries

AMARETTO® CREAM

1 cup whipping cream
5 Tbsp. sugar
3 oz. Amaretto Di Saronno®

sliced toasted almonds (optional)
juice of 1 lemon

Pour sugar and the Amaretto into a bowl. Add the cream and whip at high speed for approximately 3 to 3¹⁄₂ minutes, or until cream is a nice consistency but not real heavy.

Rinse strawberries well and remove stems. Sprinkle with sugar and a little lemon juice. Cover and let them rest in refrigerator. When dessert time comes, spoon strawberries into a glass or dish of your preference. Pour the Amaretto cream mixture on top and serve.

TENDERLOIN TIPS SALTEADO

you should have a bottle of good red wine to do justice to this excellent dish.
Serves 6

24 oz. of prime filet (tenderloin) cubed,
  one inch thick
1¹⁄₂ large potatoes (peeled and cubed in ¹⁄₂-
  inch pieces) salt to taste
²⁄₃ cup olive oil
2¹⁄₂ Tbsp. pure ground garlic
1 tsp. ground white pepper
1 tsp. crushed oregano
¹⁄₂ tsp. salt
pinch of nutmeg

1 medium green pepper, finely chopped
1 medium onion, finely chopped
2 bay leaves
3 chorizos (Spanish sausage) sliced thin
4 oz. ham, cubed ¹⁄₂-inch
4 large fresh mushrooms, sliced thin
¹⁄₄ cup red wine
¹⁄₂ cup green peas
1 red pimento cut in 6 pieces

Season cubed tenderloin with 2 Tbsp. of garlic (reserve remaining ¹⁄₂ Tbsp.), ²⁄₃ tsp. white pepper, ¹⁄₂ tsp. oregano and salt to taste, set aside. In a skillet, heat oil over medium heat, add remaining ¹⁄₂ Tbsp. garlic and cook potatoes until light golden. Remove potatoes.

In second skillet: 6 Tbsp. of oil and at medium heat, sauté the green peppers until almost transparent and then add onions, ¹⁄₂ tsp. oregano, ¹⁄₃ tsp. white pepper, pinch of nutmeg and salt. Add chorizo, ham, mushrooms and continue to cook until vegetables are soft and transparent. Mix in potatoes.

In the first skillet, heat remaining oil at high heat. When oil is sizzling hot, add the cubed tenderloins and sear quickly. When they start sticking to the skillet, add the red wine and mix with the sauté ingredients. Cook for about one minute; stir and reduce heat. Cook according to your taste (rare, medium rare). For presentation, sprinkle green peas all over and strips of red pimentos. Serve with saffron rice.

MISE EN PLACE

442 W. Kennedy Blvd. • Tampa, Florida 33606 • (813) 254-5373

If the entrées were any more unusual they'd be fictitious, or so says one reviewer of Chef Marty Blitz's cuisine at Mise en Place. The urban setting with a clean and romantic design sets the stage for this hands on operation which daily changes its mix of 17 appetizers, 3 soups, 6 salads and 15 to 18 entrées. Some would call Chef Blitz crazy, most call him a genius, and all call him crazy about food.

Marty started his career in a local deli at the age of 12. He and his wife, Maryann, now own and operate a perennial Golden Spoon Award-winning restaurant which is praised by critics and patrons alike as one of Florida's finest restaurants.

What gets the kitchen most fired up is to explore an ethnic cuisine in depth and to bring those ideas to a Modern American interpretation. Specialty of the house? It depends on who you talk to, but the things they will all mention are the commitment to an unparalleled dining experience....and fun.

RED AND GREEN SALAD
WITH FRIED FETA AND SUNDRIED TOMATO VINAIGRETTE

8 sundried tomatoes, julienne	$^1/_4$ cup red wine vinegar
$^1/_4$ cup Madeira	1 cup olive oil
4 cloves garlic, finely chopped	salt to taste
2 Tbsp. basil, chopped	cracked black pepper to taste

In a small dish, add the tomatoes and the Madeira allow to sit for 1/2 hour. Combine all ingredients in a stainless steel bowl (including the Madeira the tomatoes were soaking in). Whisk until ingredients are combined well. Set aside.

FRIED FETA CHEESE

4 slices feta cheese	eggwash (1 egg, $^1/_4$ cup milk)
olive oil - for sauté	$^1/_4$ cup sesame seeds, a 50/50 mix of black
$^1/_2$ cup flour (for dusting)	and white

Heat sauté pan. When hot, add olive oil. Dredge feta in flour, eggwash and sesame seeds. Sauté till golden brown.

THE SALAD

1 head radicchio lettuce
1 head bibb lettuce
1 head red oak lettuce
1 head green oak lettuce

1 vine ripened fresh tomato, cut into 4
thick slices
fried feta cheese
sundried tomato vinaigrette

Wash and dry bibb, radicchio and oak lettuces. To assemble the salad, arrange the bibb, radicchio, oak and tomato on the plate. Place the fried feta on top and drizzle the vinaigrette over the entire salad. Serve immediately.

Note: As with all recipes, the quality of the raw ingredients determines the success of your final product. Look for fresh, local greens, a high quality feta and sundried tomatoes from a local gourmet store.

SHRIMP, MANCHEGO CHEESE & CHORIZO GRITS
WITH PUERTO RICAN RED BEAN SALSA

It may sound unusual, but trust Chef Blitz - it is superb!
Serves 4

FOR GRITS

3 cups shrimp stock (substitute clam juice)
3/4 cup grits
4 Tbsp. butter
1/4 lb. manchego cheese, grated

1/4 lb. cooked shrimp, diced
1/8 lb. chorizo, cooked and diced
salt, black pepper to taste

Heat stock, slowly add grits while stirring constantly. Cook approximately 20 minutes. Add butter, cooked shrimp, chorizo and cheese. Season with salt and pepper. Grits are ready to serve.

FOR RED BEAN SALSA

2 cups cooked red beans
2 cloves garlic, chopped
1 red onion, chopped
2 sour oranges - juice only
2 serrano chilis, seeded and chopped

2 Tbsp. fresh Puerto Rican cilantro,
chopped
1 Tbsp. sherry vinegar
2 Tbsp. olive oil

Mix all ingredients together. Let sit minimum of 2 hours to develop and meld flavors. Place hot grits in serving bowl. Top with salsa and garnish with fried plantains and Puerto Rican cilantro.

Veal Stack of Polenta, Portobello Mushrooms, Oven Roasted Tomatoes & Toma Cheese
With Madeira Sage Sauce

The title of this dish is a mouthful, visually this impressive dish is an eyeful.
The taste is simply wonderful and the sage sauce is perfect.
Serves 2

8 oz. veal scallopine, pounded thin
flour for dredging
salt & pepper to season
2 Tbsp. olive oil

Heat sauté pan, add oil, lightly dust veal in flour, shake off excess, season with salt and pepper, and sauté until golden brown. Remove from pan and set aside.

2 Portobello mushrooms
2 plum tomatoes
6 oz. instant polenta
¹/₄ cup toma cheese, grated

Lightly rub mushroom and tomatoes with olive oil, salt and pepper. Roast in 400°F. oven for 30 minutes until tender. Set aside.

Make polenta according to instructions on package. Pour into flat cookie pan ¹/₂-inch thick and chill.

To assemble stack, place in heating pan in the following order: Polenta cut in rectangles, top with sautéed veal, then oven roasted sliced Portabello and tomatoes, and finally, toma cheese. Bake at 400°F. for 5 minutes. Serve with Madeira Sage Sauce.

Madeira Sage Sauce

1 tsp. chopped shallots
1 clove of garlic, chopped
¹/₂ cup Madeira
1 tsp. fresh sage
1 cup beef or veal stock

Sauté shallots, sage and garlic in some olive oil for one minute. Deglaze with Madeira and reduce by ³/₄. Add stock and bring to boil. Cook for 5 minutes and strain.

NEXT CITY GRILLE

2902 W. Kennedy Blvd. • Tampa, Florida 33609 • (813) 879-1990

Situated in a quaint 1908 Florida bungalow, the Next City Grille opened its doors in 1993. Since then, the restaurant has earned high accolades locally, regionally and nationally. The diners are indeed treated as "house guests," with quiet professionalism.

Next City Grill changes its menu frequently, emphasizing "fusion cuisine" with a delicate marriage of Florida resources and Pan-Asian inspiration. Flavors and presentations involve a balance of heights, colors and textures. Owners Dwight and Lauren believe that dining is an experience of all of the senses, and approach each one individually.

Next City Grill was the proud recipient of the Florida Trend "Best Newcomer Award" in 1993, as well as continued recognition as one of the top 200 restaurants in Florida.

TAHITIAN VANILLA BEAN CRÈME BRULÉE

This créme brulée is certainly more basic than its counterparts, but the clean simplicity of the vanilla bean flavor is a winner.
Serves 4

1 cup whole milk
1 cup heavy cream
1 vanilla bean (cut lengthwise, scrape beans from pod)

¹/₂ cup sugar
3 egg yolks
1 whole egg

Scald the first 4 ingredients in a heavy sauce pan. In a separate bowl, whisk the 3 egg yolks and 1 whole egg. Add the scalded cream mixture to the whisked eggs.

Pour the mixture into 4 oven-proof cups and place the cups in a cold water bath, at least halfway up the sides of the cups.

Bake in a preheated 350°F. oven for approximately 45 minutes. Remove from the oven and let cool. Once cool, sprinkle the tops with granulated sugar and caramelize the tops under direct heat and serve immediately.

Soy Roasted Chicken Breasts
with Ponzu Glaze

Ponzu is a seasoned citrus sauce available at Asian markets. This is truly a wonderful and exotic dish with a taste we loved.

Serves 4

(Served with Cucumber and Habañero Cole Slaw)

4 boneless chicken breasts
$^1/_2$ cup soy sauce
$^1/_4$ cup sesame oil
2 Tbsp. unseasoned rice wine vinegar
$^1/_2$ cup ponzu (available at Asian markets)

1 lemon, juice only
1 orange, juice only
1 Tbsp. ginger root, minced
$^1/_4$ cup fresh chives, finely chopped

Mix the soy sauce, sesame oil and rice vinegar in a bowl and add the 4 chicken breasts to $^3/_4$ of the marinade.

Turn occasionally, allowing to stand for 30 minutes.

Heat a sauté pan over high heat. Add 1 tsp. olive oil. Allow the olive oil to briefly smoke and place the chicken breasts skin side down in the pan. Lower the heat by half immediately.

To make the ponzu glaze, combine the last 5 ingredients. When the chicken is done, quickly spoon the ponzu glaze over the chicken and serve immediately.

Cucumber & Habañero Cole Slaw

2 cucumbers, seeds removed, julienne
$^1/_2$ habañero pepper, seeds and ribs removed, julienne

1 medium red onion, julienne
1 bunch fresh mint, julienne

Toss with the $^1/_4$ of the marinade mix which was reserved from the soy roasted chicken above. Chill until ready to serve. Serve with the soy roasted chicken with ponzu glaze.

MARINATED GULF SHRIMP SPRING ROLLS
WITH TOMATILLO & MANGO SALSA

This exciting dish is a good example of the Pan-Asian cuisine at Next City Grille.
Serves 4

$^1/_4$ lb. medium shrimp, peeled, deveined,
   diced
$^1/_4$ cup virgin olive oil
3 Tbsp. annato seeds
1 lime, zest and juice only
salt and pepper to taste
1 small red onion, diced

2 cups Napa cabbage, diced
1 red bell pepper, seeds & ribs removed,
   diced
6 tomatillos, diced
1 mango, peeled, diced
$^1/_4$ cup fresh cilantro, finely chopped
1 pkg. spring roll wrappers

Heat the olive oil in a sauce pan until wisps of smoke are seen. Turn off the heat and add the annato seeds. Let set until cool, then strain off the oil and discard the seeds. Add the lime juice and zest. Place the shrimp in this olive oil mixture 30 minutes.

Combine $^1/_2$ of the diced onion, all of the cabbage and red pepper, and toss lightly in 2 Tbsp. of the olive oil mixture. In a large sauté pan, add the onion, cabbage and red pepper, and toss quickly. Add the shrimp and remove from heat and let cool.

Soak the spring roll wraps in cold water. Work no more than 4 wraps at a time to prevent drying. Place approximately 3 to 4 oz. of the cooled filling in the bottom center of each wrap. Fold from the bottom once, fold from the sides once, and then roll up.

Heat $^1/_4$-inch of olive oil in a large sauté pan. Place the rolls in the pan seam side down. Cook evenly on all sides. Remove from pan and drain on paper towels. Serve with tomatillo and mango salsa.

For the mango and tomatillo salsa, combine the tomatillos, mango, remainder of onion and the cilantro in a bowl. Salt and pepper to taste. Chill until ready to serve.

*"Wine nourishes, refreshes and cheers…Wherever wine is lacking,
medicines become necessary."*
The Talmud

BEACH BISTRO

6600 Gulf Drive • Holmes Beach, Florida 34217 • (941) 778-6444

Sean Murphy was an illegal alien searching for a site to start a sailboat rental business when he discovered the breathtaking Gulf front location for the Beach Bistro. Ultimately, Sean found himself in charge of this bustling beach front restaurant which has become respected as one of the best on Florida's Gulf Coast.

The Bistro blends classics like Bouillabaisse and Rack of Lamb with new world ingredients and imaginative techniques to create truly memorable meals. The Beach Bistro recently added a beach bar, the perfect spot to have an after dinner drink or one of the exceptional Bistro desserts. This is also a wonderful location to take in a Gulf sunset or a walk on the beach after dinner.

SMOKED SALMON PIZZA

The crème fraiche "sauce" is the perfect accompaniment to the salmon.
Serves 1

6-inch pizza shell
2 Tbsp. crème fraiche with fresh dill (see
     page 250)
5 slices of smoked salmon
1 Tbsp. capers
1 Tbsp. small diced red onion

Preheat oven to 400°F. Top pizza shell with crème fraiche, salmon, capers and onions. Bake 5 minutes or until hot.

TOMATO MOZZARELLA SALAD

Serves 2

3 large, ripe tomatoes, sliced
4 Tbsp. pesto
1 cup mozzarella cheese, sliced

2 Tbsp. capers
8 calamata olives
mixed greens

Placed torn mixed greens on plate. Top with sliced tomato. Spread pesto on tomato and top with fresh mozzarella, capers and olives. Serve with an herb vinaigrette and crusty French bread.

GRILLED TUNA WITH PAPAYA MANGO SALSA

The Beach Bistro has a way with seafood. Their dishes are straight forward and delightful.

Serves 2

2 6-oz. tuna filets
1 papaya
1 mango
¹/₂ red pepper

¹/₄ cup scallions
¹/₄ cup red onion
1 lime, juice only
salt and pepper to taste

Lightly brush tuna with olive oil and set aside. Finely dice the remaining ingredients, allow to marry for at least ¹/₂ hour and refrigerate until chilled. Grill tuna to medium rare and serve with salsa.

SALMON BENJAMIN

Serves 2

2 6-oz. salmon filets
2 large Idaho potatoes
2 lemons, juice only

1 Tbsp. salt
¹/₂ cup vegetable oil

Place 2 cups of water in a bowl with juice of 1 lemon and salt. Thinly slice potatoes and soak in the lemon water for 1 hour. Remove and then soak in 2 cups of water with juice of 1 lemon until ready to use. Wrap salmon filets with potato slices and sauté until golden brown in vegetable oil. Remove from pan and finish for 8 minutes in hot oven. Serve on a bed of sautéed leeks and brush with lime-dill butter.

GROUPER PICASSO

Serves 2

2 6-oz. grouper filets
1 cup dry white wine
4 Tbsp. butter
banana

strawberries
raspberries
fresh pineapple
kiwi fruit

Lightly flour and pan sauté grouper on both sides in vegetable oil, remove fish from pan and keep warm. Discard any fat from the pan and deglaze with white wine. Reduce and add fruit(s) of your choice. Finish with cold butter and serve over fish.

CARMICHAEL'S

1213 Palm Ave. • Sarasota, Florida 34236 • (941) 951-1771

When Carmen Gillett was looking for a site to open her restaurant in 1987, she came across an old Spanish style home that was built in 1923. The home, which is located in Sarasota's Theater District, was perfect for the intimate restaurant she had envisioned, however, its status as a national and state historical landmark involved a fair amount of red tape. Ultimately, the restaurant she envisioned was completed with a total seating capacity of 62 guests.

The cuisine of Carmichael's reflects the New American style with continental overtones. Chef Peter Kim, a graduate of the prestigious Culinary Institute of America at Hyde Park, performs wonders with beef and seafood entrées, while the outstanding desserts are all created in the kitchen daily. Carmichael's has received accolades from numerous writers and publications, included recognition by Florida Trend Magazine as one of the top 100 restaurants in Florida.

MARYLAND STYLE CRAB CAKES
WITH LEMON & GREEN PEPPERCORN REMOULADE

Chef Kim works wonders with this remoulade.
Serves 4

1 lb. Pepperidge Farm® white bread, crust
   removed
1 lb. jumbo lump crab meat
1 cup mayonnaise
2 eggs, beaten
1 Tbsp. Dijon mustard
1 Tbsp. fresh parsley, chopped

1 Tbsp. fresh chives, chopped
1 tsp. Old Bay Seasoning®
1 tsp. hot sauce
1 tsp. Worcestershire Sauce®
1 tsp. baking powder
olive oil for sautéeing crab cakes

Cut the bread into cubes. Carefully pick over the crab meat, removing any shell. Gently mix in the bread, trying not to break up the crabmeat. Combine the rest of the ingredients together, then gently blend with the crabmeat to form thick patties. Heat oil in a heavy skillet and add the crab cakes and sauté until golden brown on both sides. Serve with Lemon & Green Peppercorn Remoulade.

LEMON & GREEN PEPPERCORN REMOULADE

1 cup mayonnaise
1 Tbsp. Dijon mustard
2 Tbsp. fresh parsley, chopped
1 Tbsp. fresh chives, chopped
1 Tbsp. capers, chopped

2 tsp. green peppercorns
1 tsp. minced anchovy filets
1 Tbsp. chopped dill pickle (Claussen®)
1 tsp. fresh lemon juice
pepper to taste

THE SPECIAL TASTE OF FLORIDA

In a bowl, mix the mayonnaise and mustard until thoroughly blended. Stir in the rest of the ingredients and serve.

Tomato, Jicama, Red Onion & Feta Cheese Salad
with Key Lime Cilantro Vinaigrette

Serves 2

2 large, ripe tomatoes, cored and cut into wedges
4 Tbsp. crumbled feta cheese

4 oz. jicama, peeled and cut into match sticks
1/2 small red onion, sliced

Combine all ingredients with the Key Lime-Cilantro Vinaigrette and toss.

Key Lime-Cilantro Vinaigrette

1/2 cup olive oil
1/3 cup fresh key lime juice (approx. 4 small limes)
1/4 cup fresh cilantro, minced

1 small garlic clove, chopped
1 Tbsp. sugar
1/4 tsp. ground cumin
salt and pepper to taste

Whisk together oil and lime juice. Stir in the rest of the ingredients and chill for 1 hour before serving.

Horseradish Crusted Grouper
with Braised Fennel & Capers

Serves 4

4 7-oz. grouper filets
3/4 cup prepared horseradish
1/2 cup corn flakes
1 Tbsp. fresh parsley, chopped
1 Tbsp. fresh chives, chopped

1 Tbsp. fresh thyme, chopped
salt and pepper to taste
1 cup olive oil
egg wash (2 eggs, 1 Tbsp. water)

Combine horseradish, crushed cornflakes and fresh herbs. Season filets with salt and pepper. Brush egg wash on the top side of the filets, and then coat with the horseradish mixture and refrigerate until cooking time.

Heat the olive oil to medium high in a heavy, non-stick pan. Place the filets crust side down, cook slowly until golden brown, turn and cook on the other side. Serve on warm plates with braised fennel and capers.

Braised Fennel and Capers

1 small fennel, sliced
1 tsp. shallot, chopped
salt and pepper to taste

3 Tbsp. olive oil
3 Tbsp. capers

Heat olive oil over medium low heat in a frying pan, add chopped shallot and sliced fennel and cook slowly. Do not brown. Add capers and season with salt and pepper.

Low-Fat Chocolate Angel Cake

16 slices at 90 calories per serving

1¹/₄ cups cake flour
¹/₃ cup cocoa powder
1 tsp. baking powder
12 large eggs, whites only

1³/₄ cups powdered sugar
1 tsp. cream of tartar
2 Tbsp. butter, melted then cooled
2 tsp. vanilla extract

Sift the flour, cocoa and baking powder together twice and reserve.

Beat the egg whites until they are thick and foamy. Gradually beat in the sugar and cream of tartar and continue to beat to a medium peak.

Fold the sifted dry ingredients into the beaten egg whites gently, to retain as much volume as possible. Add the butter and vanilla, and fold them into the batter.

Pour the batter into a tube pan or a springform pan that has been sprayed with vegetable oil (Pam®) and lined with parchment. Bake the cake in a preheated 325°F. oven until the cake pulls away from the side of the pan. Allow to cool completely before removing the cake from the pan.

A variety of sauces and toppings may be served with this cake.

To keep pancakes warm until serving, keep them on an oven-proof plate in a 300°F. oven.

CHEF CALDWELL'S

20 South Adams Drive • Sarasota, Florida 34236 • (941) 388-5400

Frank Caldwell, a very popular Southwest Florida chef, together with his lovely wife Jean, opened their own restaurant on St. Armand's Circle in the summer of 1993. The success of Chef Caldwell's has exceeded their expectations, as recipient of Sarasota Magazine's Best New Restaurant Award and Florida Trend's Best Newcomer Award. It comes as no surprise that Chef Caldwell has added to a long list of awards for his culinary talents.

The restaurant's offerings at lunch are served on oak pub tables with fresh flowers, which are transformed into a sophisticated setting of white linens and candlelight for dinner. Chef Caldwell's menu features many contemporary and decidedly creative dishes, including their popular "heart healthy" entrées and dessert items.

HEART HEALTHY EGGPLANT PARMESAN

For those of us who love eggplant parmesan, but hate the oil absorbed by the eggplant.
Serves 6

white from 1 large egg
2 Tbsp. water
$1/2$ cup seasoned dried bread crumbs
1 large eggplant, sliced in $1/3$-inch thick rounds

vegetable cooking spray
2 cups low-fat marinara sauce
$1 1/2$ cups shredded non-fat mozzarella cheese
$1/4$ cup grated Parmesan cheese

Heat oven to 425°F. Have ready a wire rack on a cookie sheet and a lightly greased shallow oval baking dish. Put egg white and water into a shallow dish and beat with a fork until egg is well broken up. Spread bread crumbs on waxed paper. Dip eggplant in egg mixture, then bread crumbs to coat. Put slices on rack. Spray lightly with vegetable cooking spray. Bake about 30 minutes until tops are golden brown. Turn slices over and spray again. Bake 10 to 15 minutes until tops are golden brown and crisp and centers are soft.

Turn oven to 375°F. Spread $1/2$ cup marinara sauce in baking dish. Arrange $1/2$ of the eggplant slices over sauce. Top with $1/2$ cup marinara, $3/4$ cup of mozzarella and 2 Tbsp. Parmesan cheese. Repeat layers using remaining ingredients. Bake 20 to 25 minutes until cheese is melted and sauce bubbly.

HEART HEALTHY MARINARA SAUCE

A heart healthy recipe which is also an absolute winner.
Makes 6 - ¹/₂ cup servings

1 cup chopped onion
1 Tbsp. minced garlic
¹/₂ cup chicken stock
1 tsp. fresh fine chopped oregano
³/₄ tsp. fresh fine chopped basil

1 bay leaf
¹/₂ tsp. ground black pepper
2 cups sliced fresh mushrooms (optional)
3 cups canned tomato sauce
2 cups canned tomato purée

In a large saucepan, sauté onion and garlic in stock with crushed herbs, bay leaf and black pepper until onions are tender.

Add mushrooms and cook 5 minutes. Add tomato products. Cover and simmer over low heat for 1 hour. Remove bay leaf before serving over pasta.

GRILLED MEDALLIONS OF PORK LOIN
WITH RASPBERRY BARBECUE GLAZE

A real attention-getter on the grill.
Serves 4

1¹/₂ lb. pork tenderloin (6 1-oz. medallions
per serving - slice after grilling)

RASPBERRY BARBECUE GLAZE

1 8-oz. can no-salt tomato sauce
³/₄ cup chopped red onion
¹/₂ cup plus 2 Tbsp. no salt chili sauce
¹/₂ cup raspberry vinegar
1 Tbsp. honey
1 tsp. low sodium Worcestershire®

1 clove garlic, minced
¹/₂ tsp. mustard
¹/₂ tsp. cinnamon
¹/₄ tsp. ground cloves
¹/₈ tsp. ginger

Combine first six ingredients in a saucepan. Add garlic, mustard, cinnamon, ginger and cloves. Bring to a boil; reduce heat and simmer 10 minutes.

While glaze is simmering, place pork loin on hot grill. Grill 3 minutes, turn, brush on glaze, grill 3 more minutes. Chicken can be substituted for pork loin.

Escargot Florentine

Serves 4

1 can escargot
2 Tbsp. chopped garlic
1 cup sliced mushrooms
2 cups fresh chopped spinach

3 cups heavy cream
3 Tbsp. butter
$^1/_2$ cup Parmesan cheese
salt and pepper to taste

Sauté escargot, garlic, butter and mushrooms. Simmer 3 minutes. Add cream, Parmesan cheese and spinach. Simmer until mixture thickens. Garnish with fresh Parmesan cheese. Serve immediately.

When threading poultry, fish or meats on skewers, leave at least $^1/_4$" of space between each piece to ensure even cooking and eliminate raw areas between pieces.

THE COLONY DINING ROOM

The Colony Beach & Tennis Resort
1620 Gulf of Mexico Drive • Longboat Key, Florida 34228 • (941) 383-5558

The Colony Dining Room is located at The Colony Beach & Tennis Resort on the sugar sand beaches of Longboat Key, where both the resort and restaurant guests are treated to a relaxed friendliness which seems just about perfect for this island resort. The restaurant has been family owned and operated for over 26 years, making it the longest standing fine dining restaurant tradition in the Sarasota area.

The innovative American cuisine and fresh seafood are both outstanding in this exquisite restaurant that overlooks the Gulf of Mexico. A special tip of the hat to The Colony Dining Room for their Annual Stone Crab & Seafood Festival, which takes place at the end of October each year. In a true culinary spirit, the Klauber and Moulton families host seven of the finest chefs in the United States, as well as selected vintners, all working in concert to provide 3 days of seafood splendor in this elegant, intimate festival.

GROUPER PAILLIARD

Seafood at The Colony Dining Room is as good as it gets on the West Coast of Florida.
Serves 2

2 6-oz. grouper filets	¹/₄ cup flour
4 oz. chopped pecans	eggwash (1 egg, 1 tsp. water)

Chop pecans in food processor and mix in ¹/₄ cup flour.

Set up breading station with some flour, the eggwash and the pecan mixture. Dredge filets in the flour, then eggwash, then pecan mixture.

Sauté in clarified butter until slightly browned and finish in 350°F. oven. Serve over beurre blanc and garnish with pecan halves and tomato concasse.

BEURRE BLANC

1 lb. butter	¹/₄ cup lemon juice
³/₄ cup heavy cream	¹/₄ tsp. cayenne pepper
1 shallot, diced	salt
3¹/₂ oz. white wine	

Place white wine, lemon juice and shallots in a heavy saucepan. Reduce wine by half, add heavy cream and reduce by half (or when cream reaches desired consistency).

Slowly whip in whole butter. When butter has been incorporated, season to taste with salt and cayenne pepper.

THE COLONY'S ULTIMATE COOKIES

Unbelievably wonderful!
Yield: 144 cookies.

2 lb. butter
3 cups sugar
1 lb. light brown sugar
4 tsp. salt
4 tsp. vanilla

6 eggs
4 tsp. baking soda
9 cups bread flour
2 lb. pecans
5 lb. semi-sweet chocolate chunks

Cream butter, salt, vanilla and both sugars. Dissolve soda in a small amount of hot water and add to mixture with the eggs, mix. Add flour, mix well, fold in pecans, then fold in chocolate. Do not over mix chocolate! Make tablespoon size balls and bake at 325°F. on a sheet pan with parchment paper (recipe may be halved or quartered).

BAKED AMERICAN RED SNAPPER

Serves 2

2 6-oz. red snapper filets (preferably
    American)
4 oz. lump crabmeat
2 oz. sundried tomatoes
¹/₂ cup clarified butter

¹/₂ bunch chopped basil
¹/₂ cup beurre blanc
¹/₂ cup white wine
paprika

Place snapper in a baking pan, coat with clarified butter and white wine and dust with a small amount of paprika. Bake to desired temperature. In a sauté pan, heat crab and basil, add beurre blanc and sundried tomatoes. Serve snapper with sauce on top.

> *To freeze whipped cream, spoon it into mounds on a baking sheet lined with waxed paper. Freeze until firm and place the mounds into a freezer container. The mounds will last for 2 to 3 days. They will thaw in 5 to 10 minutes.*

EUPHEMIA HAYE

5540 Gulf of Mexico Drive • Longboat Key, Florida 34228 • (941) 383-3633

Euphemia Haye's menu is as inspired and eclectic as the art and antiques that adorn the award winning restaurant. Chef Ray Arpke integrates classical training, experience and innovative flair in an extraordinary selection of international, American classic and contemporary cuisine.

In 1980, Chef Ray and his wife, D'Arcy Arpke, bought Euphemia Haye from Les Buntin, who had named the restaurant in honor of his grandmother. Euphemia Haye has now won two consecutive Golden Spoon Awards from *Florida Trend* magazine as one of the top twenty restaurants in the state.

Well-considered expansions have culminated in four intimate dining rooms and the Haye Loft, all while maintaining the casual elegance that is Euphemia Haye's charm. The Haye Loft comprises a dessert room and a comfortable lounge which serves premium spirits, fine wines and imported beers in a relaxing atmosphere of live music. The dessert room also features exotic coffees and, according to Robert Tolf of *Florida Trend*, "outrageous desserts."

QUENELLES OF SALMON AND SCALLOPS WITH DILL
Serves 4

*2 cups cubed salmon meat - free of all
   bones and skin*
1 cup scallops
1 egg white
*2 tsp. fish base (may substitute chicken
   cube)*

½ cup half-and-half
1 dash white pepper
1 Tbsp. fresh dill

Blend the salmon, scallops, egg white, fish base, dill and pepper in a food processor until smooth. Add the half-and-half through the fill tube while mixture is still processing. Process for a minute or two until you have a very smooth consistency. You may have to scrape the bowl a few times.

In a large fry pan, place water about 2 inches deep and bring to a slow boil. Salt the water to your taste. Take a tablespoon and scoop salmon mixture in a rolling fashion, so as to make little eggs about 1" x 2" and carefully place them in the water.

After they are cooked through (about 4 to 5 minutes) you may serve the quenelles on top of the sour cream dill sauce.

SOUR CREAM DILL SAUCE

1 Tbsp. chopped shallots
1/8 cup clarified butter
1/8 cup flour
2 cups heavy cream
1 Tbsp. fish base

1 dash cayenne pepper
2 Tbsp. chopped fresh dill
1/2 cup white wine
1/2 cup sour cream

Sauté shallots in butter for one minute. Add flour and cook 2 minutes longer. Add white wine, and cook 2 minutes longer. Add cream, fish base and pepper and cook 2 minutes longer. Turn mixture off and whisk in sour cream and dill. Serve at once or retain for later use. Important: Do not let mixture boil when reheating.

STRAWBERRY SHORTCAKE

Hooray for this outstanding traditional dessert.
Serves 6

2 cups all purpose flour
1 Tbsp. baking powder (heaping)
2 Tbsp. sugar

1/3 cup shortening
2/3 cup buttermilk
6 Tbsp. melted butter

Preheat oven to 450°F. Mix dry ingredients together. Add shortening and mix with fingers until crumbled and mealy. Stir in buttermilk to make a semi-stiff dough. Divide in half. Place half in a buttered and floured 8-inch cake pan. Press dough into bottom of pan. Butter the top of the dough and place the other half of the dough on top. Press dough flat again. Bake for 15 minutes and lower heat to 325°F. Bake 20-25 minutes longer. Remove from pan and cool on a rack for one hour. Split layers in 2.

STRAWBERRY SAUCE FOR SHORTCAKE

1 qt. fresh strawberries or one 12 oz. bag
   frozen strawberries
1/4 cup sugar

1/3 cup water
1 Tbsp. corn starch mixed with 1 Tbsp.
   water

Bring the berries, sugar and water to a boil. Stir in carefully the cornstarch mixture and boil until thick. Remove and chill in refrigerator until cold.

SWEETENED WHIPPED CREAM

1 1/3 cups whipping cream
1/2 cup powdered sugar
1 tsp. vanilla extract

Whisk ingredients together until soft peaks are formed.

To Assemble Cake

Place bottom layer on a decorative cake plate. Pour ¹/₃ the sauce on top of the bottom layer. Spread ¹/₃ whipped cream over sauce. Place 2nd layer on top. Add ¹/₃ sauce on top of 2nd layer. Pipe whipped cream on top in a decorative fashion. Top with remaining sauce and garnish with fresh strawberries.

Grouper Jamaican

The taste of the Caribbean is also performed to perfection at Euphemia Haye.
Serves 4

1 lb. grouper filets, in four pieces
¹/₄ cup Meyers's® Rum
5 oz. bottle Pickapeppa® sauce
¹/₂ cup unsalted butter, softened to room
    temperature
2 - 4 large onions
¹/₂ - 1 cup white wine

¹/₂ - 1 cup water
1 - 2 chicken bouillon cubes
1 large banana, sliced into 12 diagonal
    slices
salt and pepper to taste
strawberries, orange zest or other fruit for
    garnish, if desired

In a heavy, non-aluminum saucepan, heat the rum and set it alight. Remove from heat and add Pickapeppa sauce. When the flames have died down, return the pan to the heat and simmer for one minute; if it flames up again, remove from heat briefly. Turn heat to low, move the pan to one side, and whisk in the butter. Return pan to low heat just to warm - do not allow it to simmer or the sauce will separate. Remove the pan from heat and keep warm on the back of the stove while you poach the fish.

Slice the onions into rings and use them to cover the bottom of one or two large frying pans, depending on the size of your filets. (You will need one to two onions for each pan.) Add a bouillon cube to each pan and just enough water and wine, in equal proportions, (about ¹/₂ cup each for each pan) to barely reach the top of the onions. Bring to a boil and cook just until the onions are transparent, about 60 seconds. Add more liquid only if absolutely necessary.

Place grouper filets gently on top of the onions. (They should not sink into the stock.) Season with salt and pepper, cover the pan, and poach the fish gently for three to four minutes, just until the centers are no longer transparent. Top each filet with sliced banana, cover and simmer just long enough to warm, not cook the fruit.

To serve, spoon sauce onto individual plates. Remove filets, along with onions, with a slotted spatula, allowing them to drain briefly over pan. Place filets in center of sauce and garnish with additional sliced fruit and a small amount of orange zest, if desired.

Liver Paté

1 lb. duck, goose, pheasant or chicken
    livers
¹/₄ lb. ground veal
1 medium onion
2 eggs
1 cup mushrooms
¹/₂ lb. butter

¹/₂ lb. cream cheese
1 tsp. each of allspice, thyme, pepper,
    clove, bay leaf, nutmeg, mustard,
    ginger
salt to taste
4 cloves garlic
1 Tbsp. chicken base

Cut onions into tiny dice and sauté with the mushrooms. Add the remaining ingredients, except eggs, and cook until well done. Fold in eggs and cook 1 minute longer. Place in food processor with ¹/₂ lb. butter and ¹/₂ lb. cream cheese. Process for 5 minutes, scraping bowl occasionally. Place in loaf pan and chill for a minimum of 4 hours.

Zaboglione or Sabayon

Serves 12

6 egg yolks
1 cup sugar (heaping)
1 cup white wine
1 Tbsp. liqueur

Serves 2

1 egg yolk
3 Tbsp. sugar
3 Tbsp. white wine
1 dash liqueur

Whisk all ingredients over hot water bath or direct flame, until thick. Serve hot over fresh berries or fruit. Use the liqueur of your choice.

The Red Delicious apple was discovered in Peru, Iowa in 1872. Then called the "Hawkeye," the name was changed by the nursery that bought the propagation rights.

MICHAEL'S ON EAST

1212 East Avenue South • Sarasota, Florida 34239 • (941) 366-0007

Michael's on East has won Florida Trend's coveted Golden Spoon Award for four consecutive years, as well as consistently voted Sarasota's "best all around restaurant." The reason is simple - fresh, inspiring menus, an outstanding wine list, impeccable service and an inviting, casually sophisticated ambiance.

Proprietors Michael Klauber and Philip Mancini keep their Florida cuisine on the cutting edge with dishes that are artful to the eye as well as pleasing to the palate. Michael's also responds to the whims of their customers, providing weekend jazz, pre-theater menus, heart healthy menus and a catering service. Additionally, Michael's new wine shop is a natural outlet for these owners who share an appreciation of fine wines and gourmet foods with their customers.

CHILLED JUMBO SHRIMP
WITH GAZPACHO DIPPING SAUCE

Actually three recipes used for one dish. Michael's on East adds an interesting twist by using filo pastry to easily create an attractive bowl for presentation of this appetizer.
Serves 4

12 jumbo shrimp, peeled, deveined
2 cups fish stock or clam juice
4 pieces of 4" X 4" filo pastry
2 Tbsp. melted butter
1 cucumber, julienne

1 carrot, julienne
¼ bunch fresh cilantro, chopped
¾ cup Citrus Vinaigrette
¾ cup Gazpacho Sauce

Heat stock to a boil and add shrimp for 2 minutes or until just cooked. Shock with ice water.

Cut filo pastry to size and lightly brush both sides with melted butter. Press each filo sheet into an ovenproof cup or cupcake pan to act as a mold, and bake in a 350°F. oven until lightly golden, about 5 minutes. Allow to cool. Remove the filo "bowls" from their molds.

Combine the cucumber, carrot and cilantro and toss with Citrus Vinaigrette. Use remaining vinaigrette to toss with shrimp. Fill the filo pastry "bowls" with tossed julienne vegetables. Arrange shrimp on the vegetables and garnish each with 4-inch cut chives, placed vertically into the vegetables. Serve with a ramekin of Gazpacho Dipping Sauce.

CITRUS VINAIGRETTE

1 fresh orange
1 fresh lemon
1 fresh lime

1 1/2 oz. vinegar
1/3 cup olive oil
1/3 cup canola oil

Zest and juice each of the fruits. Bring some water to a boil and blanch the zest three times, placing the zest in ice water between blanchings. This will remove any bitterness from zest. A metal strainer works best for this. Mix together all of the ingredients, including the juices from the fresh fruits.

GAZPACHO DIPPING SAUCE

1 cucumber, peeled and seeded
$^1/_2$ green bell pepper, seeded, chopped
$^1/_4$ small onion
$^1/_2$ cup crushed tomatoes

$^1/_4$ cup tomato juice
1 dash Tobasco sauce
salt & pepper to taste

Grind the cucumber, bell pepper and onion in a processor, or finely dice. Add the tomato products and season with Tobasco, salt and freshly ground black pepper to taste.

LONG ISLAND DUCKLING CONFIT
WITH RED CURRANT SAUCE
Serves 4

2 ducks, quartered, ribs removed
8 baby carrots, peeled blanched
8 snow peas, blanched
8 asparagus, blanched
1 green bell pepper, julienne

1 yellow pepper, julienne
1 red pepper, julienne
1 bunch scallions, sliced on bias
1 Tbsp. black sesame seeds for garnish
salt & pepper to taste

If uncertain about quartering or removing the ribs from your duck, have your butcher handle the job. They are normally more than happy to do this for you. Cook the duck for 1 $^1/_2$ hours at 350°F. in either duck fat, chicken fat or salad oil, or a combination of these. Cook until the meat shrinks away from the bone and the color turns brown.

Sauté the peppers and scallions in vegetable oil until they are just cooked. Salt and pepper to taste. Sauté the snow peas and carrots in butter for just a couple of minutes. Salt and pepper to taste.

Arrange the Rice Pilaf in the center of plates. Surround this with the Currant Sauce. Arrange the snow peas, asparagus and baby carrots on top of the rice. Place the duck quarters on top of the rice, first the leg, then the breast. Place the peppers and scallions on top of the duck and sprinkle with black sesame seed.

Red Currant Sauce

1 cup red currants
1 cup veal or beef stock

1 tablespoon sugar
1 Tbsp. arrowroot

Puree the first 3 ingredients together and bring to a boil. Slow to a simmer and add the arrowroot until thickened to a sauce consistency.

Wild Rice Pilaf

1/2 medium onion, diced
2 ribs of celery
1 carrot, diced
1 Tbsp. butter
1 lb. wild rice
1 qt. chicken stock

1 qt. chicken stock
1 sprig rosemary, chopped
1 sprig thyme, chopped
1/2 bunch sage, chopped
salt and pepper to taste

Sauté the onions, celery and carrots in the butter for just a few minutes. Add the wild rice to this and sauté over high heat for two minutes while stirring. Add the chicken stock and bring to a boil. Reduce to a simmer. Add the rosemary, thyme and sage, cover and cook until the rice is tender. Salt and pepper to taste.

Poached Pears in Frangelico Syrup

Serves 6

4 cups sugar
4 cups water
4 cups white wine
4 cinnamon sticks
1 cup hazelnuts

1 Tbsp. anise seeds
2 oranges, zest only
2 lemons, zest only
6 pears
1 cup Frangelico®, or to taste

Retain some of the fruit zest for garnish. Bring all of the ingredients to a boil in a large pot.

Peel the pears, core from the bottom and remove seeds. Place the pears in the liquid and simmer until tender when pierced. Remove pears and place in an ice bath.

Take 2 cups of the poaching liquid and flavor to taste with Frangelico. Strain and divide into martini glasses or small bowls.

Toast the hazelnuts, being careful not to burn them, peel the skins off and roughly chop. Stuff the pears with the nuts and place the pears into the serving bowls. Drizzle with additional Frangelico. Garnish with zest.

OPHELIA'S ON THE BAY

9105 Midnight Pass Road • Siesta Key, Florida 34242 • (941) 349-2212

Wonderfully situated on the banks of Little Sarasota Bay, this enchanting waterfront restaurant is renowned for its colorfully presented selections rich with the flavors and produce unique to Florida and the Caribbean. Ophellia's On The Bay captures the essence of Southwest Florida with a New World Cuisine.

Fresh, locally grown organic produce and fish from the bountiful Gulf of Mexico become delicacies in the hands of this culinary master. Guests may dine inside overlooking the bay, or outside among the tropical foliage of the dockside patio. Ophelia's has been selected as one of Florida Trend's Top 100 restaurants for 6 consecutive years and has earned the Mobil three-star rating.

BAKED VIDALIA ONION STUFFED WITH GULF SHRIMP
& WILD MUSHROOMS WITH A CHIVE CREAM SAUCE

Serves 6 as an appetizer

6 Vidalia onions, the size of baseballs
4 oz. shiitake mushrooms, chopped
$1/2$ lb. large Gulf shrimp, peeled, deveined and chopped
2 Tbsp. roasted garlic, pureed
$1^1/2$ Tbsp. fresh basil, chopped

$1^1/2$ oz. Parmesan cheese, very good quality
1 cup bread crumbs
1 large egg, whole
$1/2$ cup melted butter, unsalted
salt and fresh ground black pepper, to taste

Preheat oven to 350°F. With a knife, carefully trim off the top eighth of each onion and peel off the very outer skin, leaving the root end of the onion attached. When the outer skin is removed, trim only enough of the root end off so that the onion will stand on its own. Carefully hollow the onion out and reserve the onion that is scooped out. Chop the reserved onion and sauté with the mushrooms and shrimp with $1/4$ cup butter until the onions are translucent and the shrimp are cooked. Remove to a mixing bowl and add remaining ingredients except remaining butter and $1/2$ oz. Parmesan cheese. Mix well and season to taste.

Divide stuffing amongst the onions and fill them until they are overflowing. Make sure the onions are firmly packed. Place in baking dish making sure they do not touch. Sprinkle the remaining Parmesan cheese and butter over the tops. Fill the baking dish with approximately $1/2$-inch water and cover loosely with foil and bake for 1 hour or until tender.

CHIVE CREAM SAUCE

1 tsp. garlic, chopped fine
1 tsp. shallots, chopped fine
2 cups heavy cream

2 Tbsp. fresh chives, finely snipped
3 Tbsp. olive oil
salt and white pepper

Sauté garlic and shallots in the olive oil until the garlic is translucent. Add the heavy cream and reduce by 1/4. Thicken with diluted cornstarch, if necessary. Season to taste with the salt and white pepper and strain. Add chives just before serving so they do not turn black.

To Serve, divide sauce among six plates and place onion in the middle of the plate. Garnish with whole sprigs of chives.

OVEN ROASTED GULF SNAPPER, WITH JAMAICAN JERK SPICES
TROPICAL FRUIT COULIS & SPICY GAZPACHO SALSA

Serves 4

4 8-oz. filets of fresh snapper
Jamaican jerk spices
salt to taste

Lay fish on a plate and generously coat the fish with the spices and refrigerate until ready to cook. Preheat oven to 350°F.

TROPICAL FRUIT COULIS

1 ripe mango, peeled and diced
1 ripe papaya, peeled and diced
1 small pineapple, peeled and diced
1 small jalapeño, seeded and chopped fine
1 Tbsp. fresh cilantro, chopped fine

1 cup shrimp stock or chicken stock
salt and white pepper

Place all ingredients, except cilantro, in a non-corrosive pan and simmer until all the fruit is tender. Remove from heat and purée until smooth. Add cilantro and season to taste with the salt and white pepper.

Spicy Gazpacho Salsa

3 large tomatoes, seeded and diced small
1 cucumber, peeled, seeded and diced small
$^1/_2$ small red bell pepper, diced small
$^1/_2$ small yellow bell pepper, diced small
1 small jalapeño pepper, seeded and
    chopped fine
4 green onions, finely sliced on the bias

1 Tbsp. fresh cilantro, chopped fine
$^1/_2$ cup tomato juice
2 Tbsp. rice wine vinegar
2 Tbsp. olive oil
salt and black pepper

Mix all ingredients together and adjust seasonings to taste.

Place snapper filets on an oven-proof baking dish and bake for approximately 10-12 minutes.

To assemble, divide the tropical fruit coulis on each serving plate and swirl the plate so that the sauce evenly coats the bottom of each plate. Place one filet of each plate directly in the center. Top each filet with a generous amount of the salsa. Garnish with sprigs of fresh cilantro.

Grilled Orange & Basil Cured Cobia
with Arugula Pasta and Citrus Basil Broth

Serves 4 as an entrée or can serve 8 as an appetizer.

8 4-oz. cobia filets
2 Florida oranges, zested; finely chop the
    zest, reserve the oranges for the broth

2 Tbsp. fresh basil, chopped
3 Tbsp. olive oil
salt and white pepper to taste

Coat each snapper filet with the above ingredients and refrigerate until ready to grill.

For Broth

8 lb. white fish bones, chopped
1 large carrot, diced
4 celery stalks, diced
1 large onion, diced
1 Tbsp. chopped garlic
$^1/_2$ cup butter
2 large bay leaves
$^1/_4$ tsp. chili flakes

1 tsp. black peppercorns
1 cup white wine
1 bunch parsley
2 bunches basil
2 lemons, zested
3 oranges, zested and juiced
water to cover bones

Sauté the bones, carrot, celery, onion and garlic in the butter until the meat on the bones begins to look cooked. Add the remaining ingredients and cover with just enough water to cover the bones. Simmer for 2 hours, adjusting the heat so that the broth has a slight bubble and does not boil. After 2 hours, strain through a fine mesh strainer lined with cheesecloth and adjust the seasoning to your taste.

For Pasta

1 cup blanched arugula leaves
2 large eggs, beaten
3¹/₂ cups high-gluten flour (bread flour)

NOTE: The use of high-gluten flour allows for more water absorption, allowing for a greener pasta.

Combine the arugula leaves and eggs in a food processor and purée until smooth. On a table, pour the flour onto the table and form a well in the middle. Pour the arugula mixture into the well and slowly incorporate the mixture and flour together. When it is well blended, begin kneading the dough until it is smooth. Wrap in plastic and refrigerate until ready to use. When ready to use, roll the dough through a pasta machine and cut to the desired thickness and shape; linguine would be best.

For assembly:

Heat a grill to medium high heat and add some wood chips that have been soaked in water.

Bring a large pot of water to a boil and add a touch of salt. When at a boil, cook pasta until al dente. Return the broth to the stove and heat until hot; do not bring to a boil. Grill the cobia for approximately 3 minutes on each side. In a large pasta bowl, place the pasta in the middle and two filets of cobia, one on each side of the pasta. Pour approximately 8 oz. of broth into the bowl. Garnish with a chiffonnade of fresh arugula and orange zest sprinkled around the dish.

SAUTÉED PLANTAIN CRUSTED GROUPER
WITH BAHAMIAN SLAW & TROPICAL FRUIT SALSA

This entrée is absolutely wonderful!
Serves 4

4 8-oz. filets of grouper   salt and white pepper

Lay the grouper filets on a plate and season with salt and white pepper. Place in refrigerator until ready to cook.

FOR BAHAMIAN SLAW

1 head celery cabbage, finely shredded
1/2 red bell pepper, fine julienne
1/2 yellow bell pepper, fine julienne
1 ripe papaya, peeled and diced small
1 ripe mango, peeled and diced small
3 green onions, thinly sliced
2 Tbsp. cilantro, finely chopped

1/2 vanilla bean, split in half, seeds scraped
    out
1 Tbsp. Jamaican jerk seasonings
1/4 cup Consorzio five pepper oil
1/4 cup rice wine vinegar
salt and pepper to taste

Mix above ingredients together and reserve until ready to serve.

FOR PLANTAIN CRUST

3 cups plantain chips
1/2 cup bread crumbs
1/4 cup shredded coconut

pinch ground allspice, coriander, cinnamon and nutmeg
salt and white pepper to taste

Combine in food processor. Process until smooth. Reserve.

FOR TROPICAL FRUIT SALSA

3/4 cup ripe mango, small dice
3/4 cup ripe papaya, small dice
3/4 cup ripe pineapple, small dice
2 Tbsp. shredded coconut
3 Tbsp. red bell pepper, small dice

2 green onions, thin slice
1 Tbsp. cilantro, finely chopped
1 lime, juiced
1/2 tsp. habañero, finely chopped
salt and pepper to taste

Combine and reserve.

Preheat oven to 350°F. Coat grouper with plantain crust mixture by pressing the mix into each side. In a sauté pan over medium heat, add olive oil and sauté grouper until golden brown on both sides and then place in the oven for 10-15 minutes.

To assemble the plates:

Divide the slaw evenly on four plates. Place one grouper filet on top of the slaw on each plate. Top with the tropical salsa. Garnish with fresh cilantro sprigs.

GREENHOUSE GRILL

2407 Periwinkle Way • Sanibel Island, Florida 33957 • (941) 472-6882

It is worth noting that the finest chefs in Florida have a high regard for each other. Competitive by nature, they still share a common bond and a healthy respect for each other's work. They often meet at special exhibitions or culinary festivals, with each one having a reputation that precedes him or her. One of the most popular and respected chefs in this group is Danny Mellman, who owns and operates the Greenhouse Grill on Sanibel Island with his wife, Ariel.

The Greenhouse Grill has grown substantially since its early days on Captiva Island, and is now a popular gathering spot for breakfast and lunch. When the sun goes down, this relaxed bistro continues its tradition of dining excellence with creative dishes and flawless presentations that are well known to those who live and vacation on this barrier island. The Greenhouse Grill's specialty is fresh Florida seafood, but the prime meats, farm-raised game, creative pasta and vegetarian fare are all excellent.

JACKETED SCALLOPS WITH SHRIMP & GINGER

This delicate appetizer is delicious! An elegant presentation and a breeze to prepare.
Serves 4

4 jumbo sea scallops
4 medium shrimp, chopped fine
2 scallions, chopped fine
1 Tbsp. pickled ginger (Oriental stores)
2 sheets nori (Oriental stores)

$^{1}/_{2}$ tsp. light soy sauce
$^{1}/_{2}$ tsp. sesame oil
Pinch of ground cumin
1 Tbsp. sesame oil (to cook scallops)
$^{1}/_{2}$ tsp. sesame oil (to cook shrimp)

Butterfly the scallops horizontally and flatten slightly.

Add $^{1}/_{2}$ tsp. sesame oil, scallions and shrimp to a hot, non-stick pan. Cook for one minute. Add to the pickled ginger in a small bowl, toss to mix and set aside.

To cook the scallops, add 1 Tbsp. sesame oil to a hot, non-stick pan. Sear the butterflied scallops for one minute on one side, turn, and another 30 seconds on the other side. Remove from heat and allow to cool.

"Stuff" the butterflied shrimp with the shrimp mixture. Combine $^{1}/_{2}$ tsp. sesame oil, the soy sauce and cumin in a small cup. Brush the outside of the scallops with this mixture. Cut the nori in long strips. These should be as wide as the scallops are tall. Wrap the nori around the sides of the scallops. Cover and place in the refrigerator to chill until service.

Pepper Seared Breast of Duck
with Caribbean Potato Salad & Fruit Ketchup

The Greenhouse Grill is known for their creative dishes. You will love the Caribbean Potato Salad, and the Fruit Ketchup makes this dish a delight.

Serves 4

4 3-oz. boneless, skinless duck breasts
2 Tbsp. fresh orange juice

2 Tbsp. fresh lemon juice
2 Tbsp. freshly ground black pepper to taste

When you remove the skin from the breasts, leave the thin fat layer just below the skin. Marinate the breasts in the fruit juices and pepper for 2 hours.

Remove the breasts from the marinade. Sear the duck on the side the skin was removed in a non-stick pan until crisp. Turn and brown the other side for 2 minutes. Remove from pan and slice on the diagonal. Mirror each dish with the fruit ketchup. Mound one fourth of the Caribbean Potato Salad on each plate, then fan the sliced duck adjacent to the potato salad.

Caribbean Potato Salad

10 oz. potatoes, purple, red bliss or other firm potatoes suitable for salad
1 small fennel bulb
1/2 red bell pepper, roasted, skinned, julienne
1 Tbsp. orange zest
1 Tbsp. lemon zest
1 Tbsp. rice vinegar

1 Tbsp. fresh parsley, chopped
1 Tbsp. extra virgin olive oil
1 Tbsp. orange juice
1/2 small red onion, julienne
Salt and pepper to taste
1 orange, peeled, in segments

Boil the potatoes until just tender, being careful not to over cook. Cut the potatoes into desired size pieces. Grill the fennel just a few minutes on each side, then slice into a fine julienne. Gently toss all of the ingredients together to mix well.

Fruit Ketchup

1 cup blueberries, fresh or frozen
1/2 small onion, outside peel removed
1/2 green apple, peeled, cored
1/2 cup sugar

1/2 cup raspberry vinegar
1/2 tsp. alspice
1 Tbsp. salt
1 cup water

Bring all ingredients to a boil and simmer for 20 minutes. Puree in a food processor or blender.

GREENHOUSE GRILL KEY LIME PIE

This is not your basic Key Lime Pie. A layer of chocolate over the graham cracker crust, then a white chocolate mousse topping over the key lime filling, all topped off with chopped macadamia nuts. (Yes, you may cheat and start out with a store-bought pie crust.)

One 9-inch Pie
2 cups graham cracker crumbs

1 stick very cold butter, in 8 pieces
1 egg

In the bowl of a mixer, place the graham cracker crumbs on slow speed. Add the egg, then slowly add the butter, one piece at a time. Mix to the consistency of gravel. Do not overmix.

Press into a 9-inch high sided pie tin. Bake at 350°F for 12 to 15 minutes, until hard, not crisp.

8 oz. bittersweet chocolate

1/2 cup heavy cream

Bring cream to a boil, remove from heat and add to chocolate in a bowl. Slowly stir with a wooden spoon until uniformly mixed, with no cream showing. Pour the crust into the warm crust, tilting from side to side to uniformly distribute chocolate all over the crust.

$^1/_2$ cup key lime juice
$^1/_4$ to $^1/_2$ cup sugar, depending on
   desired tartness
2 eggs

3 egg yolks
1 Tbsp. heavy cream
4 Tbsp. butter, sliced

In a stainless or heat proof bowl, place all the filling ingredients except the butter. Briskly wish over simmering water until the mixture is smooth and doubled in volume. Filling is finished when it leaves a ribbon-like trail when the whisk is removes, approximately 8 minutes. Place the sliced butter on the filling, allow to melt, then gently stir into the filling. Allow to cool and then add the filling to the chocolate covered pie shell.

6 oz. white chocolate
4 Tbsp. melted butter

2 cups heavy cream
$^1/_2$ cup macadamia nuts, toasted &
   chopped

In a double boiler or microwave on medium, melt the white chocolate. Incorporate the melted butter using a wooden spoon and allow to cool. In a chilled bowl, whisk the heavy cream until stiff. Slowly fold the cooled chocolate mixture into the whipped cream

Spoon the mousse into the center of the filled pie shell. Slowly spread towards the sides, leaving the mousse mounded higher in the center. Sprinkle with the macadamia nuts and chill for two hours befor serving. Cut with a warm, sharp knife.

KING'S CROWN

South Seas Plantation Resort & Yacht Harbour
Captiva Island, Florida 33924 • (941) 472-5111

The King's Crown dining room and South Seas Plantation both have an interesting history. The restaurant, which overlooks Pine Island Sound, is housed within the historical commissary of the original key lime and coconut plantation of the property. Prior to its inhabitation by farmers, Captiva Island was home to the captured women held by plundering pirates, hence the name of the Island.

South Seas Plantation was established in the late 1920's by Clarence Chadwick, who chose the name because of its tropical similarity to the south seas islands. Though initially a working plantation, this 330-acre property with 2½ miles of private beach has evolved into a world-class resort.

King's Crown features more than just an outstanding setting, with creative pasta, seafood, poultry and beef dishes. The wine list offers more than 250 selections, earning an Award of Excellence from The Wine Spectator for five consecutive years.

SEARED GROUPER MEDALLIONS
WITH APPLE MANGO RELISH AND CURRIED BASIL SAUCE

The apple mango relish and the curried basil are perfect together.
Serves 4

8 3-oz. grouper medallions
½ cup white rice
2 Tbsp. coconut milk
¾ cup milk
10 basil leaves, julienne
1 Granny Smith apple, peeled and diced
1 mango, peeled and diced
1 red bell pepper, diced

2 Tbsp. peanut oil
1 clove garlic, minced
2 Tbsp. curry powder
¼ tsp. cumin
4 cups clam juice
1 plum tomato, diced
1 bunch parsley, chopped

FOR THE SAUCE

Heat peanut oil in a sauté pan over medium heat, add garlic, toss quickly and add clam juice. Add curry powder, cumin, salt and pepper; simmer and reduce by ½. Add ¾ of the basil, mango, apple and tomato; simmer one additional minute. Remove from heat and keep warm.

For the Rice

Cook rice over medium heat with coconut milk, regular milk and salt and pepper. Cook till rice is tender. Fold in remaining basil. Keep warm.

For the Grouper

Season medallions with salt and pepper; in a skillet on medium heat, sear medallions two minutes per side and finish for five minutes in a 350°F. oven.

For the Plate

Place rice in the center of the plate with two medallions. Drizzle with sauce around plate. Sprinkle mango, tomato and apple around the rice on the edge of the plate.

Fresh Shrimp & Crayfish
with Angel Hair Pasta

Serves 4

8 jumbo shrimp, peeled & deveined
8 2-oz. crayfish tails, peeled
8 oz. angel hair pasta, cooked
$^1/_4$ cup corn, shucked off the cob
4 cloves garlic, minced

2 scallions, chopped
$^1/_2$ oz. Cajun spiced ham
1 tsp. fresh rosemary, chopped fine
salt & white pepper to taste
1 Tbsp. tomato infused olive oil

For the tomato infused olive oil, rough chop two tomatoes and add in a container with 1 cup of extra virgin olive oil. Let stand for two days. Strain and season with salt and pepper.

For the Pasta

At medium-high heat in a sauté pan, add in $^1/_2$ Tbsp. of olive oil and sauté corn, garlic, scallions, the spiced ham for one minute. Add in shrimp and crayfish; continue to cook for four minutes. Add angel hair, fresh rosemary, salt and pepper.

Arrange seafood on plate; swirl cooked angel hair pasta in the center, drizzle with remaining tomato olive oil and garnish with rosemary sprigs.

GRILLED TRUFFLE DUSTED POMPANO
WITH ROASTED TOMATOES, ARTICHOKES AND SHIITAKE FRICASSE

A wonderful and delicate taste combination.
Serves 6

6 6-oz. pompano filets, skinned and boned
4 plum tomatoes, quartered and roasted
4 globe artichokes, cleaned and julienne
4 shiitake mushroom caps, julienne
2 shallots, julienne
1 cup white wine

$^1/_4$ cup cream
salt & pepper to taste
$^1/_8$ tsp. truffle dust, available at specialty
  stores
1 Tbsp. olive oil

In a sauté pan over medium high heat, add the olive oil, shallots, garlic and sauté quickly for two minutes. Add shiitakes, artichokes and roasted tomatoes; toss gently and deglaze with white wine and cream. Season and simmer for seven minutes. Keep warm.

For the pompano, season with salt and pepper, lightly dust with truffle powder and grill on open face grill for five to seven minutes until cooked medium well.

Serve fricasse in the center of the plate with the pompano placed on top; garnish with chopped parsley.

Note: For roasted tomatoes, quarter and bake for 1$^1/_2$ hours in a 250°F. oven on a rack. Season before roasting with garlic, salt and coarse ground black pepper.

"Let us have wine and women, mirth and laughter, sermons
and soda water the day after."

Lord Byron

THE MUCKY DUCK

Andy Rosse Lane • Captiva Island, Florida 33924 • (941) 472-3434

How The Mucky Duck came to be is an interesting story. In 1975, two families - the Mayerons and the Webbs - purchased the old "Gulf View Inn," thinking maybe rental property would be a success on Captiva Island.

While doing some research at the courthouse in Ft. Myers they were informed of a beer and wine license that had expired, which they could activate for $100.00.

Everyone was excited about opening a restaurant, and Webb, being a bobby in London for 20 years, had the idea of an English pub. The Webbs remembered a pub in Stratford-on-Avon they used to frequent called the Black Swan, but referred to by the locals as "The Mucky Duck."

When the new Mucky Duck opened in January 1976, there was a dart board, player piano and a limited menu of nice English dishes and fresh seafood. From its first day, The Mucky Duck was special - a local spot to savor cold beers, play darts, enjoy sunsets from its Gulf front location, sing and talk to the wee hours of the morning.

Not much has changed about The Mucky Duck in the past 19 years except for its reputation. It is a very special place to visit, run with the spirit and enjoyment that was experienced back in 1976. When on Sanibel or Captiva Island, stop by The Mucky Duck for lunch or dinner and say hello. It's like going back to Captiva, 1976.

SMOKED AMBERJACK SPREAD

This has been one of the most requested menu items at The Mucky Duck for many years. Make it once and it will be in your family for generations to come.

2 lb. smoked amberjack, skinned and boned	²/₃ cup mayonnaise
¹/₄ cup red onion, chopped	3 Tbsp. capers
¹/₄ cup celery, chopped	2 Tbsp. horseradish
¹/₂ cup red pepper, chopped	black pepper to taste

Break the smoked Amberjack up in a bowl into small pieces. Combine all the ingredients, mix well and chill for 1 hour or until needed. Serve scooped on a plate garnished with fresh lemon slices and crackers or toast points.

GRILLED TUNA
WITH LEMON BUTTER

We tried this interesting recipe with both tuna and wahoo. The "lemon butter" was one of our favorites on grilled fish.

Serves 4

4 8-oz. tuna steaks, skinned
seasoned salt
2 sticks butter
$^1/_4$ cup lemon juice, fresh

6 Tbsp. granulated sugar
$^3/_4$ cup beef au jus
1 Tbsp. flour

In a heavy sauce pan, melt the butter until it turns a dark brown, almost burnt look. Turn the heat to medium and stir in the flour and mix well. Add the sugar and lemon juice and be very careful, the butter is very hot and when the lemon juice is added it will produce a very hot steam. Add the au jus and mix well, continuing to cook the mixture until it becomes thick.

Lightly coat the tuna steaks with just a little melted butter and season lightly with seasoned salt. Charcoal grill on both sides until medium rare to medium. Remove and top with the lemon butter sauce and serve immediately.

PEPPERED SALMON
WITH FRESH FRUIT SALSA

Serves 4

PEPPERED SALMON

4 7-oz. salmon filets
$^1/_2$ cup Louisiana hot sauce
1 cup corn starch
$^1/_3$ cup olive oil

FRUIT SALSA

$^1/_4$ cup kiwi, diced
$^1/_4$ cup pineapple, diced
$^1/_4$ cup cantalope, diced
$^1/_4$ cup honey dew, diced
$^1/_3$ cup red bell pepper, cored, seeded and diced
5 Greek pepperocinis or 2 jalapeños, cored, seeded, diced
$^1/_8$ cup juice from Greek pepperoncinis
1 tsp. chili powder
1 tsp. ground cumin
a pinch of ground red pepper

In a medium sized bowl, mix all the fruit salsa ingredients together, cover and refrigerate for 3 hours. Place the salmon filets in a plastic square container in a single layer. Cover the filets with the Louisiana hot sauce, be sure each filet is completely covered. Let marinate for three to four minutes.

While the salmon is marinating, heat a large, non-stick skillet over a medium heat with the olive oil. Place the corn starch in a small bowl. Remove the salmon from the Louisiana hot sauce without shaking off the marinade. Place the salmon in the bowl with the corn starch, one at a time, and lightly pack the corn starch around the fish. Place the fish in the skillet and cook for 3 minutes on each side, depending on the thickness of the filets. Serve the salmon topped with the fruit salsa. The salsa can be either cold or room temperature.

New England Clam Chowder

Willard Scott's favorite! The same recipe has been used for almost 20 years at The Mucky Duck

1 medium onion, chopped
celery, equal amount as the onion, chopped
2 lg. potatoes, washed and cut into ¹/₂-inch
  cubes
2 lb. frozen chopped clams in juice
1 8-oz. clam juice in a bottle
1 gal. milk

³/₄ lb. butter
flour
Seasonings needed are white pepper, salt,
  whole thyme, McCormick's Seafood
  Seasoning®

In a large pot mix together the clam juice, the 2 lb. of clams in their juice, the onions, celery and the diced potatoes. Simmer on a medium-low heat until the potatoes are soft. Add the l gallon of milk and let simmer on a low heat for about 15 minutes.

During this time prepare a butter roux. Melt the butter in a sauce pot, add flour slowly, whipping all the time until the roux becomes thick like a milk shake, but smooth.

Now season the chowder. Add a good shot of white pepper, a little salt, cover almost half of the top of the chowder with whole thyme and a smaller amount of the McCormick's Seafood Seasoning.

Now add the butter roux slowly, stirring constantly until thick. Take off the stove completely. If the clam chowder becomes too thick when you are ready to serve, then thin the chowder with some warmed milk.

CHARCOAL GRILLED TURKEY BURGERS

This is a great recipe for the backyard barbeque when you are tired of the same old burgers.
Your family will fall in love with the garlic sauce - it is great!
Serves 8

GARLIC SAUCE

2 lb. turkey breast, ground
$^1/_2$ tsp. poultry seasoning
2 heaping tsp. of bread crumbs
1 egg
$^1/_2$ tsp. seasoned salt

$^1/_3$ cup yogurt, plain
$^1/_4$ cup tomato ketchup
2 tsp. mayonnaise
2 tsp. white wine
2 tsp. garlic, granulated
$^1/_2$ tsp. Old Bay Seasoning®
$^1/_2$ tsp. Worcestershire Sauce

Combine all the ground turkey, egg, seasoned salt, poultry seasoning and bread crumbs and mix well. Make into patties and when ready, cook on the charcoal grill. It is very important, you must cook the turkey burgers all the way through! NO medium rare turkey burgers allowed.

To make the garlic sauce, just mix all the ingredients together and chill for 1 hour before serving.

Since rice and pasta continue to absorb liquids, add more water or broth to thin the leftovers of soups with these ingredients.

PETER'S LA CUISINE

2224 Bay Street • Fort Myers, Florida 33901 • (941) 332-2228

A native of Nuremberg, Peter Schmid opened his restaurant doors in 1988 in a renovated brick warehouse in downtown Fort Myers. Today, Peter's La Cuisine is recognized throughout Florida for dining excellence.

Peter's style blends classic continental with all its rich sauces, nouvelle with its lighter touch and artistic presentation, along with European regional. The menu at Peter's changes every 6 months, with the lighter sauces of summer giving way to the more traditional sauces during the winter months.

With Manager Thomas Hoccheim, Peter's has earned the coveted Golden Spoon Award for 5 consecutive years. Additionally, the second floor Jazz Bar is the best in town.

OVEN ROASTED PORK LOIN
WITH PEPPERCORN PORT WINE GLAZE & FRESH RASPBERRIES

At Peter's they use this preparation with both the pork loin as well as South Texas antelope.
With either meat the dish is superb.
Serves 4

20 oz. pork loin
4 tsp. vegetable oil
salt and pepper to taste
3 cups veal stock

1¹/₂ cups Port Wine
4 tsp. green peppercorns
8 Tbsp. fresh raspberries

Season the loin with salt and pepper to taste. Heat the oil in a heavy skillet and sauté the loin until golden brown. Put aside to rest.

Reduce the Port Wine in a sauce pan to about 4 ounces. Add the peppercorns and the veal stock and simmer for 1 minute. Salt and pepper to taste, add the raspberries and serve immediately with the pork loin.

For the presentation, slice the pork loin into medallions and fan on a plate. Spoon the sauce around the medallions of pork. Serve with parsley potatoes and caramelized carrots.

A traditional Southern favorite, Fried Green Tomatoes. This delicious version with Shrimp & Mozzarella Cheese is a favorite at The Ritz-Carlton on Amelia Island.

Shrimp, Tomatoes & Angel Hair Pasta from The Ritz-Carlton, Amelia Island.

Chef-owner Johnny Earles' exciting fusion of Caribbean and Creole cuisines has earned Criolla's a handful of Golden spoon awards as one of Florida's top twenty restaurants.

The Caramelized Onion Soup with Thyme Crostini from The Ritz-Carlton on Amelia Island.

The Crispy Scallops at Atlantic's Edge in the Florida Keys. Chef Dawn Sieber's award winning interpretation of Florida's tropical cuisine is one of our favorites.

In addition to being a perennial Golden Spoon Award winner as one of Florida's finest restaurants, Armani's in Tampa has the best antipasto bar in the state.

Yellowtail Snapper with Watermelon, Anatto & Lemon Thyme as served in The Restaurant at the Four Seasons Resort. Like many Florida Chefs, Hubert Des Marais maintains his own herb garden on the resort property.

The Ritz-Carlton in Naples was voted the finest resort in America by the readers of Conde Nast Traveller *magazine. The tradition of high tea takes place in the hotel's luxurious lobby.*

THE SPECIAL TASTE OF FLORIDA

*A stacked presentation of Jumbo Lump Crab, Plantains, Avocado & Passion Fruit Vinaigrette
from the Four Seasons Resort in Palm Beach.*

The presentations range from the elaborate to straightforward at Chef's Garden in Naples. Grilled Pompano is a simple and delicious preparation of this delicate fish.

The exquisite cuisine of The Dining Room at Little Palm Island is no longer a secret. It's first Golden Spoon Award as one of Florida's top twenty restaurants has spread the word that this lovely tropical resort is very special.

Shrimp Scampi from Atlantic's Edge at Cheeca Lodge.

Allen Susser, a national figure and the driving force behind New World Cuisine. Chef Allen's in Aventura features exquisite food and the finest exhibition kitchen in Florida.

THE SPECIAL TASTE OF FLORIDA

The Seared Grouper at King's Crown, South Seas Plantation. The restaurant is housed in the original commissary building of this former working plantation, now a world class destination resort.

And you thought Disney World was just for kids. Disney's Grand Floridian Beach Resort is a detailed dreamland of Rococo architectural style and grace. From the uniforms worn by employees to the vintage automobiles parked at the resort entrance, guests are surrounded by the elegant ambiance of the 1920's.

Champagne Scampi from Café Arugula in Lighthouse Point.

The Far East meets the Southwest with Chef Dick Cingolani's Thai Shrimp Taco at Café Arugula.

The Salmon with Dill & Chive Beurre Blanc from Darrel & Oliver's Cafe Maxx is a statement of elegance in simplicity.

Brooks in Deerfield Beach is a truly beautiful restaurant that serves regional American cuisine with a French flair.

The setting for the Maritana Grille in Tampa is appropriate for some of the Bay Area's finest seafood.

Sarasota may have as many fine restaurants per capita as any city in Florida. Chilled Shrimp with Gazpacho Dipping Sauce (lower right) and Duck Confit with Rice Pilaf (lower left) from Michael's on East.

Veal Tenderloin
with Wild Mushroom Sauce

One of the best veal dishes we tasted.
Serves 2

2 5-oz. veal tenderloins
salt and pepper to taste
8 oz. fresh wild mushrooms cut into bite-
    size pieces (morels, Portobello,
    shiitakes)
2 Tbsp. butter

4 Tbsp. minced onion
1 Tbsp. minced garlic
1 cup white wine
1 cup veal glaze
2 cups heavy cream
fresh parsley & chives

Salt and pepper the veal tenderloins and sear both sides in a hot skillet. Bake in a preheated oven at 350°F. until medium rare.

Melt the butter in a sauce pan and add the onion and garlic, sauté until clear. Add the mushrooms and sauté 3 minutes. Add the wine and reduce until almost gone, then add the veal glaze and the heavy cream. Reduce until the sauce thickens. Finish off with freshly chopped parsley and chives. Salt and pepper to taste.

Slice the veal into medallions and serve with the mushroom sauce.

Yellowtail Snapper
with Herb Tomato Caper Butter

Use fresh, ripe tomatoes for this incredible dish.
Serves 4

4 6-oz. yellowtail snapper filets
2 skinless tomatoes, seeded and cubed
8 Tbsp. unsalted butter
1/2 cup plus 2 Tbsp. fish stock

4 Tbsp. capers with juice
2 garlic cloves, minced
Fresh herbs: equal amounts of chives,
    parsley, dill, basil, garlic chives, sage

Combine the above fresh herbs, finely chop and measure 1/3 cup of the mixed herbs for the sauce.

Heat a sauté pan and melt the butter, add the garlic and tomatoes, capers and fish stock.

Bring to a boil and simmer for 30 seconds. Add the fresh herbs, simmer another 30 seconds, salt and pepper to taste, and serve the sauce over the lightly broiled snapper.

Note: This dish works wonderfully with chicken. Simply use chicken stock in lieu of the fish stock, and use chicken breasts rather than the snapper.

Fried Apples & Strawberries
in White Wine Dough, Tossed in Cinnamon Sugar

This dessert is as good as it is interesting.

Serves 2

1 Granny Smith apple, cored and peeled
6 fresh, ripe strawberries, caps removed
2 eggs
1 cup flour
⅓ cup white wine

1 tsp. vanilla
1 Tbsp. granulated sugar
1 cup sugar
1 Tbsp. cinnamon

In a mixing bowl, whip the eggs until well combined, then add the flour. It will be very pasty. Next, add the wine, vanilla and sugar. If you want the dough to be thinner, add a little more wine. Cut the apples into quarters. Roll the apples and strawberries in flour, then dip in the batter.

Deep fry in 350°F. vegetable oil for about 5 minutes, or until golden brown. Roll in a mixture of 1 cup sugar and 1 tablespoon cinnamon and serve immediately.

Never allow knives to soak in water as it may damage the handle. Do not put your good knives in a dishwasher, as the extreme heat may ruin the structure of steel blades.

The Special Taste of Florida

THE TIMBERS

703 Tarpon Bay Rd. • Sanibel Island, Florida 33957 • (941) 395-2722

The Timbers on Sanibel Island could be called a seafood paradise on an Island Paradise. A perennial selection by Florida Trend Magazine as one of the finest restaurants in the state, Co-owner Matt Asen is also extremely proud of being voted Sanibel Island's "Best Seafood" restaurant for an amazing 12 consecutive years. Their secret is simple, and it's what we look for in a seafood restaurant; the freshest seafood prepared to perfection on a consistent basis.

The Timbers is similar to its sister restaurant in Fort Myers, The Prawnbroker. The staff is extremely friendly and you may occasionally have a short wait for a table in the "season," but the fare is well worth the wait. Matt's enjoyment of his work and appreciation of fine seafood is readily apparent. At any time you may see him rolling up his sleeves to filet fresh fish for his guests or the on-site seafood market, handling the broiling chores in the kitchen or greeting guests.

CHAR-BROILED DOLPHIN Á LA TIMBERS WEST

This is a sure fire method for excellent fish on the grill. Also ideal for halibut and swordfish.
Serves 4

4 8-oz. dolphin filets
¹/₄ cup soy sauce

¹/₂ cup orange juice
¹/₂ cup melted butter

Mix the soy sauce, orange juice and the melted butter thoroughly. Dip the dolphin filets in the mixture and then immediately place the filets on the hot grill. Be careful, as this mixture will cause the grill to flare. Cook about 3 to 4 minutes, baste with the marinade and then turn and baste again. The exact cooking time will depend on the thickness of the fish and the heat of the grill.

SNAPPER ALMONDINE

Serves 4

4 7- or 8-oz. snapper filets
¹/₂ cup slivered almonds
¹/₂ cup flour
¹/₄ cup dry white wine

¹/₄ cup olive oil
1 lemon, juice only
salt and pepper to taste
2 Tbsp. fresh parsley, chopped

Pat the filets dry and sprinkle with salt, pepper and lemon juice. Coat the filets with the flour on both sides. Sauté in heated oil about 4 to 5 minutes each side, depending on the thickness of the fish. Remove to heated serving dish.

Add the almonds to the remaining olive oil and sauté until golden. Add the white wine and reduce. Pour the almonds and the wine mixture over the filets and garnish with chopped parsley.

Absolut® Citrus Tuna au Poivre

This dish is both easy and fun to prepare. A wonderfully exotic taste which works extremely well with tuna.

Serves 4

4 6-oz. tuna steaks (³/₄ to 1 inch thick)
¹/₂ small lemon
1 orange
2 Tbsp. canola oil

coarse ground pepper
4 Tbsp. Absolut Pepper Vodka® (Citrus Vodka may be substituted for a milder taste)

Using a lemon zester, cut 1 inch strips of orange peel, being careful to take only the peel and not the white of the skin. Reserve the peels for later use.

Squeeze the juice from the orange and the ¹/₂ lemon into a shallow dish. Place the tuna steaks into the dish of juice. Allow them to marinate for up to an hour at room temperature, or up to 3 hours in the refrigerator.

Remove the tuna steaks from the marinade and cover them with the coarse ground pepper. Heat the oil in a skillet large enough to hold the tuna steaks. When the oil is hot, place the orange peels in the skillet and stir continuously until they curl up and brown slightly (not black). When they are done, drain oil and add the citrus marinade to the pan of orange peels. When the marinade starts to bubble, place the tuna steaks in the pan and cook for about 30 seconds, then flip the steaks over and cover with more coarse pepper, amount will depend on your taste and cook for another 30 seconds, then add the vodka.

At this point you may remove the pan from the heat and flambé the pan as the vodka will burn. Remove the steaks from the pan and pour the peels and citrus vodka sauce over the fish. Serve with your choice of rice or pasta. Garnish with lemon and orange slices.

Timbers' Pineapple Salsa

2 cups fresh pineapple, peeled, cored & diced
¹/₄ cup red bell pepper, diced fine
1 Tbsp. jalapeño pepper, minced fine
1 Tbsp. fresh cilantro, chopped

1 Tbsp. kosher salt
1 tsp. black pepper
1 Tbsp. red wine vinegar
1 Tbsp. granulated sugar

Mix in a non-reactive bowl and store overnight in the refrigerator. If the pineapple is very ripe, add slightly more vinegar. If the pineapple is very firm, add slightly more sugar.

THE VERANDA

2nd Street at Broadway • Fort Myers, Florida 33901 • (941) 332-2065

The two houses which comprise The Veranda were built in 1902 and 1912 by a young Captain Manuel Gonzalez, one for his mother and the other for his wife and their family. The houses were joined by Peter Pulitzer, son of the publisher, in the early 1970's for his long-time fishing buddy, Fingers O'Banion. "Fingers" ran a restaurant and bar, as did Cloyde Pate after him. Paul Peden bought the buildings in 1979 and transformed them into what is now The Veranda.

Since Peden opened the Veranda, it has been consistently honored as one of the best restaurants in Southwest Florida and Fort Myers. The Veranda's high quality cuisine emphasizes fresh local seafood and prime beef, with many dishes reflecting a Southern influence. All dinners feature the fragrant hot oatmeal-honey-molasses bread. The desserts include a special Chocolate Paté, an incredible Peanut Butter Fudge Pie (like a half-pound peanut butter cup turned inside out) and excellent Pecan Pralines. The entertainment at the piano bar provides a great backdrop for an after-dinner drink.

PECAN PRALINES

A great Southern tradition.

SHORTBREAD CRUST

$^1/_2$ *cup plus 1 Tbsp. sugar*
$^1/_2$ *lb. butter*
$^3/_4$ *cup flour*
1 egg
1 lb. pecans, chopped

CARAMEL TOPPING

1 cup plus 2 Tbsp. brown sugar
$^1/_2$ *lb. butter*
$^1/_2$ *cup honey*
$^1/_2$ *cup sugar*
$^1/_4$ *cup heavy cream*

Make the shortbread crust like a pie crust, adding the eggs last, instead of ice water. Press the dough in a half sheet pan that's been greased. Place 1 lb. of chopped pecans on the dough evenly.

Before starting the dough, place the ingredients for the caramel topping in a sauce pan and cook until bubbling, while making the shortbread.

Pour the caramel over the pecans and be sure to spread very even. Bake at 300°F. until the pecans are toasted and the crust is light brown.

THE VERANDA BOURBON STREET FILET

Serves 2

2 Tbsp. olive oil
2 Tbsp. butter
2 6-oz. beef tenderloin filets
1/2 cup fresh mushrooms, quartered
1/2 tsp. garlic, minced
1/2 tsp. shallots, minced

1/2 cup green onions, chopped
cracked black pepper to taste
pinch rosemary
pinch thyme
3 Tbsp. Kentucky sour mash bourbon
2 Tbsp. butter

Cut each filet into 2 medallions. In a sauté pan over medium heat, sauté the medallions, mushrooms, garlic, shallots, green onions, pepper, rosemary and thyme in the olive oil and butter. Add the bourbon and flambé carefully, then finish with the remaining 2 Tbsp. butter to smooth the sauce. Do not allow the sauce to boil. Medium rare should require about 8 minutes of total cooking. Serve the medallions on a plate and top with the sauce.

PORTOBELLO MUSHROOMS

This is an excellent recipe for this delectable mushroom.
Serves 6 as an appetizer.

6 4-inch Portobello mushrooms
10 oz. boursin cheese
2 cups blended oil

1 tsp. salt
2 tsp. pepper
1 Tbsp. garlic, crushed, chopped

Remove the stems and wash the mushrooms. Combine the oil, salt, pepper and garlic. Marinate the mushrooms bottom side down for at least 12 hours, but no more than 36 hours. Remove the mushrooms and bake in a 400°F. oven until soft in the center (8 - 10 minutes).

Top with boursin cheese and place back in the oven until the cheese is lightly golden (5 minutes). Remove from the oven and cut mushrooms into 4 sections and place on a plate. Serve immediately.

CASHEW ENCRUSTED GROUPER MEUNIÈRE

Serves 4

4 6-oz. grouper filets
1 1/2 cups cashews, medium ground
1/4 cup clarified butter

4 Tbsp. whole butter, salted
1 Tbsp. each chopped parsley and chives
1/2 lemon, juice only

Place the grouper filets flesh side down in crushed cashews. In medium hot sauté pan, add the clarified butter, let the butter get hot, but not to the smoking point. Place the grouper cashew side down in the sauté pan until you achieve a nice golden brown.

Flip the grouper over and cook an additional 2 minutes on low heat. Remove the grouper filets from the heat and place on a sheet pan and cook in a 375°F. oven until done.

In a separate sauté pan, place 4 Tbsp. butter on medium-hot heat and allow to melt. Add the parsley and chives, turn off the heat, squeeze the lemon, the butter should foam. Spoon onto fish, serve with fresh vegetables and rice.

If you are upgrading your utensil collection, first invest in a good chef's knife or paring knife. You can perform almost any task with these two knives.

CHARDONNAY

2331 North Tamiami Trail • Naples, Florida 34103 • (941) 261-1744

There is no doubt about it, the French have a special way with food. At Naples' best French restaurant, Chardonnay, this special way is elegantly displayed with both a sense of taste and style, with traditional French cuisine that is executed to perfection. The combination of Owner René Nicolas handling the front room and Chef-Owner Jean-Claude Martin articulating the kitchen, exemplifies the finest of a professional, owner-operated restaurant.

The wonderful blend of Chardonnay's professional service and consistently outstanding food keeps this beautiful restaurant at the top of the list when discerning Neapolitans think French cuisine.

CHARDONNAY'S SCALLOP PANCAKE

This dish is outstanding with many of the beurre blanc sauces in this book.
For best results use extremely fresh fish.
Serves 4

6 oz. filet of sole
4 oz. salmon
8 oz. scallops

1 cup heavy cream
1 Tbsp. chopped chives
salt, pepper, nutmeg to taste

Grind the sole, salmon and scallops in a processor. Mix together in a bowl with a wooden spoon. Add the heavy cream slowly. Season to taste and add chives.

Make any shape you wish with the mixture, keeping it a uniform 1-inch thick. Poach in hot, salted water for 10 minutes (do not boil). Serve immediately with favorite vegetables and rice.

ESCARGOT WITH ANGEL HAIR PASTA

If you enjoy escargot, you will love this dish. Its beauty lies in its simplicity.
Serves 4

3 dozen snails
3 cloves garlic, chopped very fine
1 pt. heavy cream

½ lb. angel hair pasta
6 Tbsp. butter

Drain the number of snails desired. Sauté in the garlic and the butter. Drain the butter and deglaze the pan with heavy cream. Reduce the consistency of the cream to thoroughly coat the snails.

When the pasta is cooked al dente, mix with some of the garlic butter. Serve the snails on the pasta, using your artistic talent to decorate the plate.

CHOCOLATE TRUFFLES CHARDONNAY

These are just plain sinful. We recommend using the optional praline paste.
Yield is approximately 75 truffles

FOR THE GANACHE

1 pint heavy cream
2 lb. semi-sweet Belgian dark chocolate
6 oz. praline paste (optional)

FOR THE COATING

1 lb. semi-sweet Belgian dark chocolate
4 oz. Drosti cocoa powder-unsweetened

For the ganache, coarsely chop 2 lbs. of chocolate and place in a bowl. Bring the heavy cream to a boil, then transfer to the bowl holding the chocolate. Stir this mix with a wooden spoon until smooth, then add the praline paste. The praline paste is used in fine French pastry preparation as it offers a delicate, nutty flavor which is favored by French Chefs. Remember to never expose chocolate to excess heat, since fine quality chocolate has a perfume about it. High heat will destroy both its aroma and flavor.

Once the ganache is made, cover the bowl with plastic wrap and refrigerate. The next day, prepare the truffles by scooping out with a Parisienne Scoop in little balls. Refrigerate the balls on cookie sheet pans which are lined with waxed paper.

Melt the remaining chocolate in a bowl over a double boiler until at body temperature. Dip truffles into chocolate using a fork, then place into a bowl with the cocoa powder and dust. At this time you can either refrigerate or freeze until needed.

Chocolate truffles are supposed to resemble the "black diamonds" of French cuisine - the highly aromatic, dense, dark brown fungus that sometimes grows underground near oak trees. These wild truffles are more or less round, and are covered with earth when dug up, so we dust chocolate truffles with cocoa in imitation.

When boiling potatoes, always ADD new potatoes to boiling water. Old potatoes should be placed in cold water and brought to a boil.

TERRA

1300 Third Street South • Naples, Florida 34102 • (941) 262–5500

Prior to a complete remodeling, this was The Chef's Garden, a restaurant that earned an incredible thirteen Golden Spoon Awards. Owners Beirne Brown and Tony Ridgway wanted to make a change to a Mediterranean influenced cuisine that has become so popular in much of Florida and California. The two feel that Terra is a timely response to the wishes of their customers and it's hard to argue with their decision. The two have a keen understanding of the Naples dining scene, a product of 24 years of experience with their other excellent restaurants, Villa Pescatore, Plum's Café and Bayside.

Terra enjoys the inviting look and feel of a fine Tuscan restaurant, a wonderful setting that truly compliments the food. The cuisine combines the expected with the unexpected, presenting a delicious mixture of lighter and traditional Mediterranean dishes with fresh seafood from the Gulf of Mexico. Kudos to Terra for having a quality bar menu whose fare is as exciting and delicious as its dinner menu. Top off your meal with a stroll along the exquisite stores of Naples' fashionable Third Street shopping district.

SKILLET ROASTED MUSSELS

A marvelous appetizer that takes only minutes to prepare
Serves 4-6 as an Appetozer

2 lb. fresh mussels
1/2 lb. plum tomatoes, peeled
2 Tbsp. olive oil
¼ cup chopped shallots
2 tsp. chopped garlic

1 cup dry white wine
2 tsp. mixed fresh herbs, finely chopped
(thyme, basil & oregano)
1 lemon, juice only

Preheat your oven to 425°F. Clean and rinse the mussels, set aside. Blanch the tomatoes in boiling water for 15 to 30 seconds, remove and allow to cool. Peel and roughly chop the tomatoes.

Place an oven–proof skillet over high heat and add the olive oil, shallots, garlic, tomatoes and mussels. Stir well and add the wine and fresh herbs. Bring to a boil and allow to simmer for 1 minute. Add the lemon juice and stir again. (The liquids will create a broth for dipping the mussels.) Cover the skillet and place in the oven until all the mussels have opened, approximately 5 to 7 minutes. Discard any unopened mussels. Serve Immediately in individual bowls.

Note: For a special treat, slice a French baguette and coat with some olive oil and minced garlic. Toast under the broiler until golden. Use this to capture all of the broth from the mussels.

Bronzed Swordfish Caesar Salad

We love recipes that are both delicious and flexible. In addition to the swordfish, we had excellent results with fresh tuna and chicken. This was also outstanding prepared on the grill.

Serves 4-6

1 lb. swordfish
2 Tsp. Mediterranean spice
2 Tbsp. olive oil
1 head Romaine lettuce
6 anchovie filets
2 eggs
2 Tbsp. mixed fresh herbs, finely chopped
  (thyme, basil, oregano)

1 tsp. chopped garlic
1/2 cup extra virgin olive oil
2 Tbsp. red wine vinegar
salt & freshly ground pepper to taste
1 lemon, juice only
1/4 cup croutons
1/2 cup freshly grated Parmesan cheese

Cut the swordfish into the number of servings desired. Dust the fish with Mediterranean spice. (Mediterranean spice is easily found in gourmet shops or most grocery store gourmet sections. Substitute Cajun spice.) In a hot, non–stick pan add 2 Tbsp. olive oil and sear the swordfish on both sides to desired doneness and set aside.

Roughly chop the Romaine lettuce and clean under cold running water. Drain and set aside.

In a food processor or blender, blend the anchovies (use more or less, according to taste), eggs and fresh herbs for 30 seconds. Add the garlic, oil, red wine vinegar and lemon juice. Blend until the mixture thickens. Adjust the seasoning to taste with salt and pepper.

Toss the Romaine lettuce with the dressing and croutons. Add the Parmesan cheese to taste and top with the swordfish. You may top the salads with either the whole portions of swordfish or sliced on the bias, according to your preference.

Sun Dried Tomato Encrusted Chicken
with Shitake Mushrooms

The concentrated flavor of the sundried tomatoes is perfect with the mushrooms and chicken.

Serves 2

2 5-oz. chicken breasts, skinless, boneless
2 Tbsp. flour
2 eggs
4 sundried tomatoes, chopped very fine
4 Tbsp. virgin olive oil
1 clove garlic, chopped

1/4 cup shiitake mushrooms, chopped
1 sprig fresh oregano, chopped fine
1 cup dry white wine
1/4 lb. angel hair pasta
Parmesan cheese

Preheat your oven to 400°F. Beat the two eggs in a bowl. Dust the chicken with flour and dip into the eggwash. Press the sundried tomatoes into both sides of the chicken.

Place the olive oil into a hot non-stick, ovenproof pan and sear the chicken on both sides. Place the pan in the oven for 3 to 4 minutes to finish the chicken until done. Remove the chicken from the pan and set aside.

Place the pan over medium–high heat and add the garlic, chopped shiitake mushrooms, fresh oregano and salt and pepper to taste. Add the white wine, stir and reduce for 3 or 4 minutes.

Serve the chicken and the shiitake mushroom mxture over angel hair pasta with freshly grated Parmesan cheese.

Note: We recommend the purchase of quality Parmesan and Romano cheese at your local Italian delicatessen or gourmet store. They will grate the cheese for you. Store it in appropriate plastic containers in your freezer.

The flavor is substantially better than the product purchased in the green cans at your grocery. Additionally, the stronger flavor means you will use less of the quality product. In the long run, you will end up spending less for the quality product with substantially improved flavor.

CORSICAN SUMMER SALAD

Wonderful with garlic bread and iced tea. We highly recommend using fresh mozzarella "rounds" from an Italian delicatessen. The Corsican Summer Salad is excellent with many of the vinaigrette dressings in this book.

Serves 4 to 6

1 package baby field greens
2 eggplant, sliced into ¹/₂-inch rounds
2 rounds fresh mozzarella cheese
6 plum tomatoes

¹/₂ cup virgin olive oil
salt to taste
balsamic vinaigrette

Wash and dry the field green greens, then set aside. Cut the tomatoes and mozzarella cheese into wedges and set aside.

Slice the eggplant and sprinkle with salt to taste. Brush each side with the olive oil and grill over medium-high heat until tender. Cut the eggplant slices into quarters and set aside to cool.

Toss the field greens with the balsamic vinaigrette and place on individual plates. Arrange the tomato, cheese and eggplant according to your preference. For those of you who love onions, try adding grilled red onion slices.

BALSAMIC VINAIGRETTE

¹/₄ cup balsamic vinegar
³/₄ cup extra virgin olive oil

¹/₂ tsp. Dijon mustard
salt and pepper to taste

THE GRILL

The Ritz-Carlton, Naples
280 Vanderbilt Beach Rd. • Naples, Florida 34108 • (941) 598-3300

In 1995, the Ritz-Carlton in Naples was voted the number one U. S. resort by the readers of *Condé Nast Traveler* magazine. Winning awards is nothing new to this magnificent beachfront resort, which also earned the Mobil Guide Five-Star Award and the AAA Five-Diamond Award. It's no wonder that The Ritz-Carlton's well-traveled guests say the resort's service and cuisine rank with the finest in the world.

The resort has two gourmet restaurants, The Dining Room and The Grill, with The Grill being open every night throughout the year. The Grill has also won its share of prestigious awards as one of Florida's finest restaurants, including top honors from The Wine Spectator, *Florida Trend* magazine, *Gulfshore Life* magazine, and has earned the AAA Four-Diamond Award. The Grill features a handsome mahogany paneled dining room reminiscent of a private English gentlemen's club, with romantic touches such as glittering chandeliers, fresh roses and a marbled fireplace ablaze the year-round. The cuisine is classic and hearty, with specialties such as Oysters Rockefeller, Seafood Mixed Grill, Dover Sole and Prime Rib of Beef with Yorkshire Pudding. We highly suggest one of The Grill's famed soufflés to complete a memorable meal.

ONION SOUP
WITH BRIE CHEESE GRATINE

A great variation on a traditional favorite. The brie gratine is the ideal finish.
Serves 12

5 lb. Vidalia onions, thinly sliced	**$^1/_2$ tsp. fresh thyme, chopped**
6 Tbsp. butter	**1 pt. heavy cream**
$^3/_4$ cup dry white wine	**salt and pepper to taste**
2 qts. chicken stock	**1 loaf of French bread**
1 bay leaf, remove after cooking	**8 oz. brie cheese**

In a large, heavy bottomed pot, brown the butter. Add the sliced onions and cook until the onions are brown, constantly stirring so as not to burn. Add the wine and reduce volume by $^1/_3$. Add the chicken stock, thyme and bay leaf. Add the cream and salt and pepper to taste. Simmer for 10 minutes.

In a bowl, top the soup with a crouton of French bread which has been liberally topped with brie cheese. Melt cheese under broiler and serve immediately.

SMOKED BREAST OF DUCK
WITH ORANGE WALNUT VINAIGRETTE

Serves 4 as an appetizer

2 duck breasts (12 oz. each)
1½ cups fresh orange juice
½ cup vegetable oil
1 tsp. fresh parsley, chopped

1 small shallot, diced
⅓ cup walnuts, finely chopped
salt and white pepper to taste
2 apples - 1 red, 1 green

Cold smoke the duck breast with skin on for one hour. Remove the duck from the smoker and place in a preheated 400°F. oven, skin side up for 10 minutes. Remove the skin and refrigerate the duck. When the duck is chilled, split the breasts in half and slice each breast on a bias.

In a mixing bowl, mix the orange juice, parsley, shallot and walnuts. With a wire whip, slowly blend in the oil until the vinaigrette is emulsified. Add salt and pepper to taste.

Toss mixed greens in the vinaigrette and place in the center of a plate. Arrange slices of green and red apples above the greens and place the sliced duck breast on top of the greens with some vinaigrette.

CORNISH GAME HEN AND FLORIDA LOBSTER
WITH COGNAC & GREEN PEPPERCORN SAUCE

Truly an elegant dish worthy of a special occasion that is quite easy to prepare. Have your butcher bone the game hens for you.
Serves 4

4 cornish game hens (16 -18 oz. each)
4 Florida lobster tails (8 oz. each)
¼ cup white wine
1 Tbsp. shallots, chopped
¼ cup Cognac

1 Tbsp. butter
2 Tbsp. green peppercorns
3 cups veal stock
salt and pepper to taste

Remove bones from hens. Shell the lobster tails, ensuring to keep whole. Heat some vegetable oil in a sauté pan. Season the hens and lobster tails with salt and pepper. Place the hens skin side down in the pan to make the skin crisp. Next, place the lobster tails in the same pan. Add the white wine. Turn both the hens and the lobster tails over and place the sauté pan in a 400°F. preheated oven .

After 2 minutes, remove the lobster tails and place aside. Continue cooking the hens for another 8 minutes. Remove the hens from the oven and place to the side with the lobster. Slice the lobster tails into 4 pieces.

Arrange the hens in a "V" in the center of plates, with the lobster medallions in the "V". Finish with sauce on top of both.

For the Cognac sauce, sauté shallots in the 1 tablespoon butter. Add Cognac and burn off the alcohol. Add the green peppercorns and veal stock. Reduce volume by $^1/_3$ and season to taste with salt and pepper.

Seafood Mixed Grill with Florida Beurre Blanc

A mixed grill, whether meat or seafood, is always a special treat. The Florida citrus beurre blanc is the perfect accompaniment.
Serves 4

12 oz. salmon filet
12 oz. mahi mahi filet
12 oz. grouper filet
8 jumbo shrimp, peeled and deveined

Cut each filet into 3 oz. portions. Season the fish and shrimp with salt and pepper. Brush lightly with olive oil. Place on a grill, rotating to obtain "X" markings, being careful not to overcook the fish or the shrimp. Arrange seafood on plates with rice of choice, and serve sauce on the side.

Florida Beurre Blanc

6 Tbsp. mango purée
$^1/_2$ cup orange juice
1 Tbsp. lime juice
1 Tbsp. garlic, minced
2 Tbsp. shallots, chopped

1 tsp. fresh tarragon, chopped
1 Tbsp. butter
$^1/_2$ lb. butter
$^1/_4$ cup dry white wine
salt and pepper to taste

Sauté shallots and garlic in 1 Tbsp. butter. Add the wine, mango purée, orange juice and lime juice. Simmer for 1 minute. Add chopped tarragon and salt and pepper to taste. Whisk in butter a little at a time to finish. Serve immediately with the seafood.

LAFITE

The Registry Resort
475 Seagate Drive • Naples, Florida 34108 • (941) 597-3232

Lafite is the signature restaurant in the luxurious Registry Resort in Naples. This award-winning restaurant is actually a combination of seven intimate dining areas and two private dining rooms, with each providing the comfort and luxury of an affluent home. In addition to seasonal menu changes, Lafite also features special dishes which include fresh regional products and the creativity of Chef de Cuisine Wilhelm Gahabka.

Even though Lafite's cuisine is Regional American, everything else is designed to impart haute French style, with the presentations being works of art. Put simply, Lafite is an elegant restaurant with outstanding cuisine. Lafite is perennially listed by Florida Trend Magazine as one of Florida's finest restaurants and a winner of the Golden Spoon Award as one of the state's top 20 restaurants.

ROASTED ORIENTAL DUCKLING

A wonderful and exotic Oriental flavor
Serves 4

2 4-5 lb. ducks

FOR MARINADE

5 cups soy sauce
$^{1}/_{2}$ cup oyster sauce
4 cups water
1 cup honey

$^{1}/_{2}$ cup sesame oil
3 Tbsp. wasabi
3 Tbsp. powdered ginger
1 tsp. chopped garlic

Rinse ducks with cold water. Mix ingredients for marinade well. Marinate ducks for 24 hours. Preheat oven to 225°F. and roast ducks for 1$^{1}/_{2}$ hours.

BLOOD ORANGE SAUCE

1 onion, sliced
1 carrot, sliced
1 cup duck drippings
3 cups blood orange juice

$^{1}/_{2}$ cup brown sugar
2 cups duck or veal stock
$^{1}/_{4}$ cup red wine vinegar
2 tsp. ginger, chopped, pickled

When the ducks are done, transfer to a warm platter and keep warm. Sauté onions and carrots in drippings. Add sugar and allow to caramel lightly. Add vinegar and then orange juice; reduce by half. Add stock and cook liquid down to 3 cups. Strain into a small pan and add pickled ginger and simmer for 2 minutes. Serve duck on a platter with the sauce separately. *Note: If you are unable to find blood oranges, substitute Valencia oranges..*

SAUTÉED RED SNAPPER
WITH LOBSTER SUCCOTASH

The lobster succotash is a superb companion to the snapper & beurre blanc.
Serves 6

INGREDIENTS FOR THE SNAPPER

6 6-oz. red snapper filets, skin on
2 Tbsp. olive oil
salt & pepper to taste

FOR BEURRE BLANC

3 shallots
1 bay leaf
4 white peppercorns
2 cups Chardonnay
$^{1}/_{4}$ cup heavy cream
$^{1}/_{2}$ lb. butter
salt & pepper to taste

FOR THE LOBSTER SUCCOTASH

2 tsp. olive oil
3 shallots, peeled and chopped
$^{1}/_{2}$ lb. shiitake mushrooms
1 cup cooked lima beans
1 cup cooked corn kernels
1 cup lobster meat, cleaned and diced
1 cup lobster bisque
2 tsp. chopped chives
salt & pepper to taste

FOR THE SUCCOTASH

Heat olive oil in a sauce pan, add shallots and sauté until transparent. Add mushrooms and cook until just softened, add cooked beans, corn and lobster. Heat and stir. Add lobster bisque and chives, season to taste. Set aside and keep warm.

FOR BEURRE BLANC

In sauté pan, place shallots, bay leaf, wine and peppercorns; reduce by half. Add heavy cream, reduce by half. Fold in raw butter. Season to taste with salt and pepper.

FOR THE SNAPPER

Heat olive oil in large sauté pan; season snapper filets, place them skin-side down in hot pan and brown. Turn filets over and finish cooking. To serve: place a filet in center of plate, skin side up; rim snapper with succotash and drizzle beurre blanc on plate around the fish. Garnish with dried fennel leaves.

Roasted Colorado Rack of Lamb
with Sunflower Seeds, Opal Basil & Garlic Crust
Serves 6

For Rack of Lamb

3 racks of lamb, split, shin & feather bone removed
salt & pepper to taste
2 tsp. olive oil

For Crust

1 cup sunflower seeds, roasted (option -
  pine nuts)
3 tsp. peeled, chopped garlic
1/2 cup sundried tomatoes
2 cups opal basil (or regular fresh basil)

2 tsp. tomato paste
3/4 cup olive oil
1/3 cup Parmesan cheese
bread crumbs to thicken
salt & pepper to taste

Heat large sauté pan with oil, season lamb and sear until brown. Finish roasting in oven at 325°F. until medium rare. Remove from oven and let rest.

In food processor, combine sunflower seeds, garlic, sundried tomatoes, opal basil, tomato paste and purée until smooth. Add olive oil, parmesan cheese and bread crumbs to thicken. Season with salt and pepper.

Evenly spread mixture on rack of lamb at least 1/4 of an inch thick. Pack firmly and finish under broiler until golden brown. Slice between the bones and serve immediately.

Red Tomato Vinaigrette

A wonderful, versatile dressing.

3 tomatoes, blanched, skinned and puréed
2 egg yolks
1 cup olive oil
1 cup vegetable oil
2 Tbsp. Champagne vinegar

1/2 cup balsamic vinegar
2 cloves finely chopped garlic
1 tsp. Dijon mustard

Put 2 eggs yolks and 1 tsp. Dijon mustard in bowl. Slowly whisk in 1 cup olive oil, 1 cup vegetable oil and the balsamic vinegar. Add purée of red tomatoes and Champagne vinegar. Season with chopped garlic, salt and pepper.

Baked Wild Mushrooms & Yucca Root Strudel
with Pinot Noir Sauce

3 tsp. butter
8 oz. shiitake mushrooms, sliced
8 oz. oyster mushrooms, thinly sliced
8 oz. chanterelles, sliced
1 tsp. garlic, minced
4 tsp. shallots, diced
2 tsp. each, chopped thyme, rosemary and
    parsley and chives
$^{1}/_{2}$ cup Chardonnay

2 Tbsp. Cognac
$1^{1}/_{2}$ cups heavy cream
$^{3}/_{4}$ cup yucca root, diced, steamed
$^{3}/_{4}$ cup boursin cheese
salt & pepper
phyllo dough
$^{1}/_{2}$ cup soft butter
$^{1}/_{2}$ cup toasted bread crumbs

Sauté shallots and garlic in butter until transparent. Add mushrooms, herbs and flambé with Cognac; deglaze with wine. Reduce to half, add heavy cream and yucca. Cook mushrooms to creamy texture; fold in boursin cheese until melted. Chill mushroom mixture.

Take phyllo dough sheet, brush with butter and sprinkle with bread crumbs. Repeat twice. Take mushroom mixture and place on phyllo dough and roll into a log; brush with butter and chill. Cut log in six diagonal pieces. Place on a cookie sheet and bake at 400°F. for about 6 minutes until golden brown.

Pinot Noir Sauce

1 tsp. olive oil
2 shallots, chopped
1 carrot, chopped
1 tsp. tomato paste
4 tsp. butter
4 cups demi glace (veal stock or brown
    sauce)

1 sprig fresh thyme
4 black peppercorns
2 stalks celery, chopped
2 cups Pinot Noir wine
salt & pepper to taste

Sauté chopped shallots, carrot and celery in olive oil; add tomato paste, cook until golden brown. Deglaze with wine and add peppercorns. Reduce by half, then add demi glace. Let simmer for about one hour. Strain, fold in butter, season to taste. Place sauce in center of plate and put strudel on top of it. Garnish with fresh thyme and whole oyster mushrooms.

MAXWELL'S ON THE BAY

4300 Gulfshore Blvd. North • Naples, Florida 34103 • (941) 263-1662

The tradition of fine waterfront dining at Maxwell's on the Bay is rooted in the organization's sister operation, the century old Harborside Inn on Block Island, Rhode Island. However, the elegant yet tropical atmosphere of Maxwell's is pure Florida. The restaurant's location is appropriately complemented by floor to ceiling windows, with virtually every table having breathtaking water views of Venetian Bay. Maxwell's is indeed a pleasant spot for both lunch and dinner, and its Sunday brunch is a Naples favorite. After dinner, enjoy a stroll through the exclusive shops of Venetian Village.

Fresh Florida seafood is the specialty at Maxwell's, and it is perfectly prepared in a variety of ways, from the simplest grilled fish to the most elaborate of presentations. Maxwell's does retain some of its northern heritage as it uses the same recipes for the award winning New England Clam Chowder and Maine Lobster as they use at the Harborside Inn. In addition to seafood, Maxwell's does an excellent job with aged steaks, chicken, veal and creative pasta dishes.

CHICKEN ROULADE WITH APPLE VINAIGRETTE

A great party dish. You may do all the preparation in advance. Simply pop the chicken into the oven when ready. We also loved this with Swiss cheese.
Serves 2

2 5-oz. chicken breasts   **4 leaves fresh spinach**
4 slices prosciutto   **4 oz. brie cheese**

Preheat oven to 350°F. Trim any excess fat from the breasts. Place the breasts between pieces of Saran Wrap and pound with a tenderizer or other object until the breasts are uniformly ¼-inch thick.

Place 2 leaves of fresh spinach on each breast, then add 2 slices of prosciutto on the spinach leaves. Cut the brie into 6 slices. Place 3 slices on each breast, directly on the prosciutto. Roll the breasts up, making sure the stuffing remains inside. Secure with moistened tooth picks. Bake the chicken for approximately 9 to 10 minutes, or until done. Serve with Granny Smith Apple Vinaigrette.

Granny Smith Apple Vinaigrette

1 Granny Smith apple
$^1/_4$ cup apple juice from concentrate
$^1/_2$ cup white vinegar
$^1/_4$ tsp. salt

$^1/_4$ tsp. freshly ground pepper
$^1/_2$ tsp. Dijon mustard
1 cup vegetable oil

Remove the core from the apple. Place in a juicer or food processor and run for 2 minutes to liquify the apple. Use a strainer to recover only the juice from this mixture and set aside.

In a small mixing bowl, add the vinegar, mustard, salt and pepper. Slowly add the vegetable oil in a steady stream and whisk until emulsified. Slowly add the juice from the apple and the juice from concentrate while continuing to whisk. Refrigerate until ready to use. Shake well before using.

Grilled Portobello Mushroom & Eggplant
with Tomato Basil Binaigrette

Serves 4 as an Appetizer

1 medium eggplant
4 medium portobello mushroom caps
1 cup seasoned bread crumbs
2 Tbsp. chopped parsley
$^1/_2$ tsp. freshly ground pepper

$^1/_2$ tsp. salt
$^1/_2$ tsp. garlic powder
$^1/_2$ tsp. onion powder
8 oz. goat cheese
plum tomatoes for garnish

Remove the stems from the mushrooms. Place the mushrooms in an air tight container with the gills facing up. Cover with the Tomato Basil Vinaigrette for 24 to 36 hours.

Remove mushrooms from marinade and grill for 2 to 3 minutes on each side, or until tender. Set aside.

Find an evenly shaped eggplant and remove all the skin. Cut 4 $^3/_4$-inch slices. Add the spices to the bread crumbs. Moisten the eggplant with some water and dredge in the bread crumb mixture. Heat the oil over medium-high heat in a non-stick pan. Sauté the eggplant slices for 2 to 3 minutes per side, or until golden brown. Remove from pan and drain on paper towels.

Preheat oven to 350°F. Place the eggplant slices on a baking dish. Arrange the goat cheese on the eggplant and heat in the oven until the cheese melts. Top each slice of eggplant with a grilled mushroom cap and place on a plate. Drizzle with Tomato Basil Vinaigrette. Garnish with arugula and plum tomatoes.

Tomato Basil Vinaigrette

1 extra large egg
½ cup olive oil
1 Tbsp. balsamic vinegar
1 Tbsp. red wine vinegar
½ Tbsp. salt
1 Tbsp. honey

1 tsp. chopped garlic
2 Tbsp. fresh basil, chopped
2 Tbsp. sugar
3 plum tomatoes, peeled
1 Tbsp. tomato juice
1 tsp. white pepper

In a blender, add the oil and egg, blend well. Add the vinegars and mix well. Add the honey, sugar, garlic, basil, plum tomatoes and tomato juice, blend well again. Add salt and pepper to taste. Use as a marinade for the portobello mushrooms. Warm in a pan and drizzle over the eggplant and mushroom appetizer.

Salmon with Absolut® Citron

Serves 2

2 6-oz. salmon filets
2 Tbsp. Spanish paprika
4 Tbsp. olive oil
1/2 cup Absolut Citron Vodka

1 Tbsp. butter
1/2 tsp. salt
1/2 tsp. pepper
sliced lemons for garnish

Preheat oven to 400°F. Heat the olive oil over medium-high heat in a non-stick pan. Dredge one side of each salmon filet in the paprika, shaking to remove excess paprika. Place the filets in the pan with the paprika side down and saute for 2 minutes. Remove to an oven safe pan and place in the oven for approximately 10 minutes, or until cooked as desired.

Deglaze the sauté pan with the Absolut Citron Vodka and reduce by one half. Season with salt and freshly ground black pepper to taste. Whisk in butter and pour over salmon filets.

MICHAEL'S CAFÉ

2950 Ninth St. North • Naples, Florida 34103 • (941) 434-2550

Keith Parker believes he must be the one in the kitchen doing the cooking in order to be creative and make certain every detail is correct for his customers. This European trained Chef likes to incorporate flavors of the Caribbean and Florida with a decidedly French style as he blends his classical French background with the flair of today's American cooking. French purists will not be disappointed as traditional dishes are still given equal time with an outstanding Ossu Bucco and Steak au Poivre.

Michael's second floor location is a study in contrasts with its pastel walls and black lacquer tables and chairs, a look which conveys a sophisticated but friendly and relaxing atmosphere. Michael's is consistently recognized by Florida Trend Magazine as one of the state's top 200 restaurants.

HAZELNUT CRUSTED GROUPER
WITH RASPBERRY BEURRE BLANC

A great way to serve grouper.
Serves 2

2 5-oz. grouper filets	eggwash (1 egg, 1 oz. water)
1 cup hazelnuts, ground fine	4 Tbsp. olive oil
½ cup flour	4 Tbsp. butter
pinch salt and pepper	

Mix the hazelnuts and flour together. Salt and pepper the grouper filets. Place the grouper filets in the eggwash, then the hazelnut mixture. Place the olive oil and butter in a large, heavy sauté pan over medium heat. Sauté until brown and turn over and place in a 350° F. oven for 10 minutes. Serve with Raspberry Beurre Blanc.

RASPBERRY BEURRE BLANC SAUCE

1 cup dry white wine	³/₈ cup raspberry purée
½ cup raspberry vinegar	¾ cup cream
1 sprig fresh thyme	1 stick plus 2 Tbsp. butter
1 tsp. shallots	

In a heavy saucepan reduce the wine, vinegar, shallots and thyme by ¾. Add the cream and reduce again by ¾. Add the raspberry purée and simmer for 5 minutes. Remove from the heat and add the butter a little at a time, stirring constantly. Serve over the hazelnut grouper immediately.

Osso Bucco Braised in Port Wine Sauce

An absolutely wonderful, rich flavor which everyone will love.
Serves 2

4 veal shanks, 2 oz. to 3 oz. each
$^1/_2$ cup flour for dredging
3 Tbsp. olive oil
2 celery stalks
2 medium carrots
2 leeks

1 tsp. minced garlic
sprig fresh thyme
$^1/_2$ cup Port wine
3 cups beef or veal stock
salt and pepper to taste

Dust the veal shanks in flour. Season to taste with salt and pepper. Sauté in a heavy pan in olive oil until golden brown. Remove from the pan and place in a roasting pan. Add the Port wine to the sauté pan and reduce by half, then add the beef or veal stock and bring to a simmer and pour over the veal shanks in the roasting pan. Add the vegetables, thyme and garlic. Cover with aluminum foil and braise for 1 hour and 15 minutes. To serve, place 2 veal shanks on each plate and top with strained sauce.

Jumbo Lump Crab Cakes
with Red Pepper Coulis

The Red Pepper Coulis is an ideal accompaniment to the crabmeat.
Serves 2

$^1/_2$ lb. jumbo lump crab meat
1 small red pepper, diced small
1 tsp. green peppercorns, crushed
1 tsp. shallot, chopped fine
2 cups seasoned croutons, diced small

$^1/_2$ tsp. Old Bay Seasoning®
pinch cumin
salt & pepper to taste
1 tsp. lobster sauce or mayonnaise
2 eggs

In a bowl add the red pepper, peppercorns, croutons and the dry seasonings. Add the eggs and lobster sauce and shallots. Toss gently, then add the jumbo lump crab meat, being careful not to break up the crabmeat.

Make six 2 oz. crab cakes and sauté in a small amount of olive oil until golden brown on each side. Serve plain or with red pepper coulis.

RED PEPPER COULIS

3 small red peppers, diced small
1 small leek, diced small
2 cups chicken stock
1/2 cup cream
salt and pepper to taste

Place the peppers and leeks in a large saucepan, season with salt and pepper, cover with the chicken stock and simmer for 30 minutes.

Purée in a blender, place back in saucepan and add cream, reduce until thick, then strain and serve.

GRILLED MARINATED LAMB LOIN
WITH MARSALA SAUCE

Serves 2

2 Lamb loins, between 6 oz. and 8 oz. each.
New Zealand is preferable, but domestic is fine.

MARINADE

1 cup Dijon mustard
3/8 cup honey
3 Tbsp. balsamic vinegar
1 tsp. garlic, diced
1 tsp. shallot, diced

1 tsp. fresh mint, diced fine
1 tsp. fresh rosemary, chopped fine
1 tsp. thyme, chopped fine
4 Tbsp. olive oil

Mix all ingredients and pour over the lamb loins and marinate for 2 to 3 hours. Brush off the marinade and grill to desired temperature. Slice and serve with Marsala sauce.

MARSALA SAUCE

4 cups veal or beef stock
1 cup Marsala wine
1 tsp. fresh mint
1 tsp. thyme

2 tsp. shallots, chopped
1 bay leaf
corn starch & water mixture (1 Tbsp.
  starch to 3 oz. water)

Place the Marsala wine, the mint, thyme, bay leaf and shallots in a saucepan and reduce by 3/4. Add the beef or veal stock and reduce again by 3/4. Add a little of the corn starch mixture if necessary to thicken, and serve with the sliced lamb loin.

VILLA PESCATORE

8920 North Tamiami Trail • Naples, Florida 34108 • (941) 597-8119

Villa Pescatore was opened in 1984, and immediately received Gulfshore Life Magazine's award for the best new restaurant in Naples. It was only three years later that Florida Trend selected Villa Pescatore as one of the top 100 restaurants in Florida. A great start, but the true test of a restaurant is consistency over time. Towards that end, this fine restaurant has won the industry's coveted AAA Four Diamond Award in each of the last 5 years. So much for the credentials.

While the restaurant's name may indicate to some that Villa Pescatore is a seafood restaurant (and their seafood is exquisite), their culinary thrust is actually Northern Italian. Executive Chef Tony Romeo has a special way with providing exactly what his guests want. While many dishes are in the traditional vein of this cuisine, much of the menu consists of wonderfully creative dishes with lighter sauces that provide the best of both worlds.

My first date with my wife was dinner at Villa Pescatore, and like my wife, this restaurant only gets better with time.

Farfalle "Bowtie" Pasta
with Chicken & Gorgonzola Cheese

A perennial favorite, indicative of the exquisite Italian cuisine at Villa Pescatore.
Serves 1

4 oz. cubed chicken
2 Tbsp. cooked pancetta, diced
1 Tbsp. red onion
2 Tbsp. crimini mushrooms
1/2 Tbsp. garlic
1 Tbsp. tomato concasse
1 Tbsp. fresh basil
2 Tbsp. Marsala wine

2 Tbsp. veal glace
2 Tbsp. Gorgonzola cheese
salt and pepper to taste
2 Tbsp. olive oil
6 oz. cooked farfalle
1 Tbsp. pinenuts and 6 broccoli florets to
 garnish

Heat oil in sauté pan. Add chicken, pancetta, onion, garlic, mushrooms and tomato concasse. Deglaze with Marsala wine and reduce. Add veal glace, basil and Gorgonzola cheese. Add salt and pepper and cooked pasta. Garnish with pinenuts sprinkled over the top and steamed broccoli florets.

CHICKEN ALI-OLI

Serves 1

4 oz. chicken breast, cut into half-inch cubes
2 artichoke hearts, quartered
¼ cup sliced black olives
4 Tbsp. sundried tomatoes
2 cloves garlic, finely diced
6-7 basil leaves, chopped

1 tomato, peeled, seeded and chopped
¼ cup white wine
salt and pepper to taste
3 Tbsp. olive oil
½ lb. angel hair pasta

Pre-heat a large skillet over med-high heat. Add olive oil and cubed chicken until lightly browned. Add artichoke quarters, sundried tomatoes and garlic until soft. Be careful not to burn the garlic. Stir in tomatoes and basil. Finish by adding the white wine and salt and pepper. Toss with the cooked pasta, add black olives and let simmer until pasta is brought to the desired temperature.

CAPELLINI WITH SHRIMP & LOBSTER

A wonderful dish enhanced by the fragrant addition of Pernod®.
Serves 1

6 shrimp (medium to large size)
3 oz. lobster meat
1 Tbsp. fresh fennel
1 Tbsp. red onion
2 Tbsp. tomato concasse
2 Tbsp. sundried tomatoes
1 Tbsp. fresh basil
½ Tbsp. garlic

¼ cup extra virgin olive oil
2 Tbsp. clam juice
2 Tbsp. marinara sauce
salt and pepper to taste
crushed red pepper to taste
1 Tbsp. Pernod®
6 oz. cooked capellini

Heat 2 Tbsp. olive oil in a sauté pan. Add shrimp, garlic, fennel, red onions and tomato concasse. Toss above ingredients quickly in pan.

Add Pernod and flame. Add clam juice, 2 Tbsp. olive oil, sundried tomatoes, basil, marinara sauce and seasonings and cooked lobster meat. Toss pasta with all ingredients and serve with fresh grated cheese.

Roast Quail

with Apple, Walnuts, Sausage, Cheese & Wild Mushroom Risotto

An outstanding stuffing which may be used with any fowl.

Serves 1

2 quail, semi-boneless
1 "tart" cooking apple (Granny Smith)
$^1/_2$ red onion
1 Tbsp. walnuts, chopped
$^1/_4$ Italian sausage, cooked
1 tsp. garlic
2 Tbsp. white wine
$^1/_2$ Tbsp. fresh basil

$^1/_2$ Tbsp. fresh thyme
$^1/_2$ Tbsp. fresh sage
2 Tbsp. grated 4 cheese mix (Fontinella, Parmesan, Fontina and Romano)
3 slices crusty Italian bread
1 Tbsp. dried wild cherries
$^1/_4$ cup chicken stock
1 Tbsp. olive oil

Cube the bread into $^1/_2$-inch pieces, then place in a bowl. Dice red onion, apple, garlic, sausage, cherries and walnuts; sauté together in the olive oil until semi-soft. Add white wine and chicken stock. Pour mixture into bowl with bread cubes.

Add cheese, herbs and salt and pepper to taste. Stuff quail and roast at 400°F. for 25-35 minutes.

Wild Mushroom Risotto

Serves 1

1 cup cooked risotto, al dente
$^1/_2$ Tbsp. red onions
$^1/_2$ Tbsp. garlic
2 Tbsp. each, fresh basil, thyme, rosemary
2 Tbsp. crimini mushrooms, diced
2 Tbsp. morel mushrooms, diced
2 Tbsp. black trumpet mushrooms, diced
2 Tbsp. Portobello mushrooms, diced

2 Tbsp. red wine
2 Tbsp. chicken stock
4 Tbsp. Parmesan
$^1/_4$ cup demi-glace
5 florets broccoli
2 Tbsp. olive oil
salt and pepper to taste

Heat oil in a sauté pan. Add red onions, garlic, mushrooms and risotto. Sauté quickly on high heat and deglaze with wine and chicken stock. Add herbs, cheese and seasonings, cover and bake 10-20 minutes in a pre-heated oven at 400°F. Mold into a small bowl (12-16 oz.) and invert onto a plate. The risotto should hold in the shape of the bowl when inverted onto a plate. Garnish with demi-glace and broccoli.

SINCLAIR'S AMERICAN GRILL

Jupiter Beach Resort
5 North A1A • Jupiter, Florida 33477 • (407) 744-5700

Sinclair's American Grill at the Jupiter Resort has well established credentials as an exquisite restaurant featuring the finest in creative new American and rotisserie cuisine. The tropical ambiance of Sinclair's is the perfect setting for the imaginative dishes and wonderfully fresh seafood of Executive Chef Kevin Durkin.

With the guidance and expertise of Consulting Chef Jean Banchet (formerly with world famous Le Français in Chicago and Ciboullette in Atlanta), Sinclair's features dishes such as Grilled Vegetable Tureen, Caribbean Root Vegetables, Lobster and Mushroom Ravioli and Warm Apple Tart. The attentive service, exhibition kitchen and ocean front location of this wonderful resort all contribute to the casual elegance of Sinclair's.

CARIBBEAN CRAB CAKE WITH TROPICAL FRUIT CHUTNEY

Serves 4

3 green onions
6 medium shrimp, shelled, deveined
1 egg
1 tsp. Dijon mustard
1 dash Tabasco®

3 dashes Worcestershire Sauce®
1 cup whipping cream
1 cup crabmeat, jumbo lump
salt and pepper

Cook the sliced green onions in olive oil until soft on low heat. Process the shelled and deveined shrimp in food processor for 30 seconds. Add 1 egg, process again and place the bowl in a freezer for 5 minutes.

Add green onions, process and add the cup of whipping cream and season lightly. Add mustard, Tabasco and Worcestershire sauce and gently mix in lump crabmeat.

In a non-stick saucepan, cook the crab cakes in a ring (or shaped with a spoon) 2 minutes on each side.

TROPICAL FRUIT CHUTNEY

1 cup fresh pineapple, diced
1 mango, peeled, pitted and diced
1 papaya, peeled, seeded and diced
1 medium-size red onion, diced
2 to 3 cloves garlic, minced
1 Tbsp. minced fresh ginger
1 cup red wine vinegar

$^1/_4$ cup brown sugar
$^1/_4$ tsp. ground cloves
$^1/_2$ tsp. ground cumin
$^1/_2$ tsp. freshly ground black pepper
$^1/_4$ tsp. salt
1 kiwi fruit, peeled and diced

Place all of the ingredients, except the kiwi fruit, in a non-reactive saucepan and cook over medium heat. Simmer for 15 minutes, stirring occasionally. Lower the heat as the mixture begins to thicken. Stir in the kiwi fruit and cook for another 5 minutes.

Allow the chutney to cool to room temperature, then refrigerate. If refrigerated, the chutney should keep for about 2 weeks.

GUAVA TURNOVERS

Quick and easy - great with vanilla ice cream.

1 lb. frozen puff pastry, thawed and cut
    into 4-inch squares
ground cinnamon and nutmeg to taste
1 cup canned guava preserves (not guava
    paste)

1 egg, beaten
butter to grease cookie sheet
parchment paper

Preheat the oven to 350°F. Dust your working surface with flour. Roll out the puff pastry to make a rectangle measuring 8 x 16 inches. Sprinkle cinnamon and nutmeg on the dough. Put 1½ Tbsp. guava preserves in each piece of puff pastry. Brush the edges with beaten egg. Fold over to form a triangle.

Grease a cookie sheet and line with parchment paper. Place the pastries 2 inches apart. Refrigerate for 30 minutes. Bake for 25 to 30 minutes, or until light golden brown. Cool before serving.

MARINATED MAHI-MAHI WITH PAPAYA SALSA

Serves 4

MARINADE

1 16-oz. mahi-mahi filet
½ cup soy sauce
½ cup pineapple juice

1 lime, juice only
2 Tbsp. minced ginger
2 Tbsp. sesame oil

SALSA

1 ripe papaya, diced, peeled and seeded
1 minced red onion
1 garlic clove, minced

½ bunch chopped cilantro
salt to taste
juice of 1 lime

To prepare the marinade, combine the soy sauce, pineapple juice, sesame oil, lime juice and ginger in a shallow glass baking dish. Add the fish and marinate in the refrigerator for 3 to 4 hours.

To make the salsa, combine the papaya, red onion, garlic, lime juice, cilantro and salt in a small mixing bowl. Set aside.

Preheat the oven to 400°F. Place the fish in a greased baking pan and pour the excess marinade over the fish. Bake for 12 to 15 minutes, or until the center of the fish flakes easily with a fork. Serve with salsa.

WARM BITTERSWEET CHOCOLATE CAKE
WITH ALMOND MILK SAUCE

Great with the milk sauce.
Serves 6

1 stick plus 1 Tbsp. butter
7 oz. bittersweet chocolate
1³/₄ cup powdered sugar
⁷/₈ cup pastry flour

4 whole eggs
2 egg yolks
1 oz. Amaretto® di Saronno

Melt the butter and sugar together. Whisk in the eggs and egg yolks. Add broken up chocolate and continue heating until melted. Combine the powdered sugar and pastry flour and whisk into chocolate mixture. Finish with Amaretto. Spoon into 3-inch round, 1¹/₂-inch tall buttered molds. Bake at 425°F. for 7 minutes. Put on plate over almond sauce and cut once down the middle.

ALMOND MILK SAUCE

2 cups milk
¹/₂ cup plus 1 Tbsp. sugar
1 vanilla bean (split)

³/₄ cup almond flour
¹/₄ cup Amaretto® di Saronno

Boil together for 5 minutes, then chill.

To prevent eggs from cracking during hard cooking, poke a tiny hole in the large end of each egg with a pin. Start the eggs in cold water. The hole will allow the normal expansion of the egg during cooking without cracking the shell.

BASIL'S NEIGHBORHOOD CAFÉ

771 Village Blvd. Suite 211 • West Palm Beach, Florida 33409 • (561) 687-3801

Since the husband and wife team of Uwe and Donna Roggenthien opened their restaurant in 1990, Basil's Neighborhood Café has built a devoted following with a menu of fresh grilled specialties such as local and exotic seafood, steaks and poultry, as well as pizza from a wood burning oven and fresh pasta. It is no wonder that the bar and dining room always seem to be crowded with people who have a healthy respect for good food and wine.

Basil's is a result of the Roggenthien's philosophy that they would have a great time serving innovative fresh food and wine in an upscale environment at a relatively moderate cost. Great attitude. Great food. Life is grand.

GRILLED HOISIN BABY BACK RIBS
WITH TROPICAL FRUIT SALSA

These ribs truly taste as delectible as they sound.
Serves 2

SALSA

2 bananas
3 oranges
1 large papaya
2 mangoes
1 pineapple
3 Tbsp. ginger
1/2 cup Morgan's Spiced Rum®
1 Tbsp. coriander
2 Tbsp. rice wine vinegar
3 Tbsp. sugar
2 limes, juice only

MARINADE

2 cups hoisin sauce
1/4 cup black bean paste
2 Tbsp. Chinese 5 spice powder
1 cup white wine
2 racks, baby back ribs
1 cup honey

For the salsa, cut all fruit into a large dice and combine all ingredients in a large glass bowl and chill.

For the marinade, combine all the ingredients except the honey, and marinate the ribs overnight. Steam the ribs for 45 minutes. Bring reserved marinade to a boil and add the honey. Grill the ribs over a medium heat, and brush with marinade for the last 15 minutes. Serve with chilled salsa.

ROTISSERIE DUCK SALAD

An absolutely fantastic dressing - we loved this with duck and chicken.
Serves 2

8 oz. frozen raspberries
1/2 cup apple cider vinegar
1/2 cup honey
2 cloves garlic
2 shallots, diced
1/2 tsp. salt

1 tsp. pepper
2 1/2 cups vegetable oil
1/4 pint fresh raspberries
1 pkg. baby greens
2 roasted duck breasts
3 Tbsp. dried cranberries

Add all ingredients, excluding fresh raspberries, greens, duck, cranberries and oil, into a food processor and purée. Slowly add oil until incorporated. Pull the two breasts off the duck and pull the breast meat into small pieces. Toss the greens, duck and dressing together with dried cranberries, and garnish with fresh raspberries.

CHICKEN RIGATONI

Serves 4

1 cup cream, reduced by half
3 cups marinara sauce
1/2 cup sundried tomatoes
1/2 cup frozen peas

3 Tbsp. cajun spice
2 chicken breasts, poached & chopped
1 pkg. rigatoni

Add 3 cups marinara sauce to the reduced cream, then add peas, sundried tomatoes and cajun spice. Let simmer for 4 or 5 minutes.

Add poached chicken and simmer for another 2 minutes, then toss in rigatoni which has been previously cooked al dente. Serve with grilled garlic bread and freshly grated Parmesan cheese.

ONION PIE

Basil's never ceases to impress with new and traditional dishes. This onion pie is an excellent reason why onion dishes are enjoying such popularity.
Serves 8

8 onions
1 cup white wine
6 Tbsp. butter (herb butter if possible)
1 quart heavy cream
16 eggs

1 Tbsp. salt
1 Tbsp. white pepper
1 Tbsp. granulated garlic
1/2 cup fresh parsley

Peel and chop the onions into coarse pieces. Sauté onions in butter and white wine until limp. Drain the onions and return to room temperature.

Mix the eggs, cream, chopped parsley, salt, garlic and pepper. Add onions and mix until the mixture is uniform. Cover with foil and bake in a casserole dish for 30 minutes in a preheated oven at 400°F. or until center begins to harden. Remove foil and let brown for 15 minutes.

ESPRESSO TOFFEE CUSTARD

Truly decadent!
Serves 6

8 cups half-and-half	1 Tbsp. instant espresso granules
8 egg yolks	12 Heath Bars®
1/2 cup sugar	heat-proof glass or ceramic custard cups
1/2 tsp. salt	

In a saucepan, heat the half-and-half until bubbles form along the edge of the pan, do not let it boil. Remove from the heat and let cool slightly. Add the instant espresso powder and stir gently until dissolved.

Chop the Heath Bars and place 2 in each custard cup. In a bowl beat the egg yolks, sugar and salt. Do not over beat and do not create too many air bubbles. Gradually stir in the half-and-half mixture until smooth.

Strain the custard mixture through a fine sieve, and pour the mixture into custard cups. Place the cups in warm water about halfway up the cups, and bake approximately 45 minutes in an oven that has been preheated to 325°F. Transfer custard to wire racks and serve chilled.

"*Restaurants are to people in the 80's what theater was to people in the 60's .*"
Marie (Carrie Fisher)
When Harry Met Sally

CAFÉ CHARDONNAY

4533 PGA Blvd. • Palm Beach Gardens, Florida 33418 • (561) 627-2662

Café Chardonnay's dedication to creative cuisine and fine wine is apparent the moment you sit down to dine in this Florida art deco restaurant.

The eclectic menu is influenced by a multitude of culinary regions including Italian, Caribbean, French and Pacific rim.

The ever changing menu has been recognized by the Zagat survey and Bon Appetit magazine, as well as receiving the 1994 Di RoNA award for one of the most distinguished restaurants of North America.

As a four time recipient of the Wine Spectator's Award of Excellence, Café Chardonnay's wine bar features 25 wines by the glass. The diligence of a professional staff ensures their guests of a pleasurable dining experience.

MEDALLIONS OF VEAL
WITH ROASTED ARTICHOKES, PLUM TOMATOES & MADEIRA WINE
Serves 4

8 3-oz. slices veal sirloin or top round,
    pounded thin
¹/₄ cup clarified butter
¹/₄ cup safflower or vegetable oil
¹/₂ cup flour seasoned with ¹/₄ tsp. salt and
    pepper
12 baby artichokes, blanched until tender,
    outer leaves removed, cut in half (or 8
    canned artichoke hearts - cut in
    quarters)

3 plum tomatoes, cut in 6 pieces each
¹/₂ small onion, diced
2 Tbsp. extra virgin olive oil
1 tsp. each chopped basil and Italian
    parsley
¹/₂ cup Madeira wine
1 cup veal stock
salt and pepper

Toss artichoke hearts, tomatoes and onions with olive oil and half the herbs, season with salt and pepper. Roast in 375°F. oven for 20-30 minutes until lightly browned. In skillet, heat butter and oil. Dredge veal in flour. Sauté on 1 side until brown, turn and sauté one minute. Remove from pan, drain most of the oil.

Add garlic and sauté 15 seconds, do not brown. Then add wine and bring to a boil. Add veal stock and herbs and reduce by ¹/₃. Add artichoke mixture and simmer for one minute. Season with salt to taste. Place veal over polenta or risotto and top with artichoke mixture and sauce.

MACADAMIA CRUSTED YELLOWTAIL SNAPPER
WITH TROPICAL FRUIT SALSA
Serves 4

TROPICAL FRUIT SALSA

4 8-oz. yellowtail or other snapper filets, skin and bones removed
1/2 cup crushed macadamia nuts
1/4 cup flour
salt and white pepper
1/2 cup milk
1/2 cup vegetable oil, or clarified butter
1/4 cup white wine
1/4 cup fresh squeezed orange juice
1 tsp. chopped fresh chives

mango, papaya, kiwi, starfruit, pineapples, blackberries, oranges, watermelon or any sweet tropical fruits
1 lime for juice
2 Tbsp. chopped cilantro
1 tsp. sugar
1/4 cup fresh orange juice
1/2 hot chili pepper, such as serrano, jalapeño or scotch bonnet, finely diced, seeds and membrane removed
salt and pepper
1/2 small red pepper, diced fine
1 scallion, sliced into thin rounds

For the snapper, heat oil in a sauté pan to medium heat. Mix nuts with flour, salt and pepper. Dip filets in milk and dredge in nut mixture. Place flesh side down in pan and sauté until lightly browned. Turn fish and sauté for 2 minutes. Pour out most of the oil and add wine and orange juice.

Reduce by half and add chives. Remove filets to a plate. Spoon a Tbsp. of sauce over fish and top with 2 Tbsp. of fruit salsa. Serve with basmati rice.

For the salsa, dice enough fruits of your choice to have 2 cups. Place in a non-reactive mixing bowl. Add lime and orange juice, cilantro, sugar, peppers and scallion. Season with salt and pepper. Let sit for 1/2 hour and serve.

Note: Red bell pepper and scallion are optional.

Tiramisu with Espresso Sabayon

A very special dessert which is well worth the time and effort!

1 pkg. Italian lady fingers
15 amaretto cookies - crumbled
1 cup Italian mascarpone cheese mixed
   with 6 Tbsp. sugar
1 cup pastry cream
1 cup sweetened whipped cream

$^1/_2$ cup Amaretto di Saronno®
1 cup brewed espresso or strong coffee
$^1/_2$ cup sugar
1 small piece of bittersweet chocolate
a shallow decorative bowl
$^1/_2$ pint raspberries or blackberries and
   mint leaves for garnish

In a mixing bowl, blend the Mascarpone, $^1/_2$ of the Amaretto and the pastry cream. Fold in the whipped cream and refrigerate until needed. This can be done up to 3 hours ahead. Put the espresso, sugar and remaining Amaretto in a small pot and simmer for 5 minutes. When the syrup has cooled, layer the bottom of the bowl with half the lady fingers. Brush them with the espresso syrup until they are beginning to soften. Spread a layer of the filling over the lady fingers about $^1/_2$-inch thick. Top this with another layer of lady fingers, syrup and then cream filling.

Smooth the top with a spatula. Sprinkle the top with the crumbled cookies and grate the chocolate over the top. Set in the refrigerator for 3 hours before serving. To serve, place a Tbsp. of sabayon on a plate. Spoon a piece of tiramisu from the bowl and place on the sauce. Garnish with the berries and mint leaves. Dust the plate with confectioners' sugar or cocoa powder if desired.

Espresso Sabayon

6 egg yolks
$^1/_2$ cup sugar
3 oz. espresso syrup
1 cup whipped cream

Place eggs, sugar and syrup in a stainless steel bowl. Place the bowl over a pot of simmering water. Whip the mixture with a thin wire whisk until it is thick and you can see the bottom of the bowl while whipping. While whipping over the hot water, you must be whipping constantly or the eggs will cook too quickly. If you must stop, remove the bowl from the heat. Cool over a bowl of ice, stirring occasionally. When cool, fold the whipped cream into the eggs.

Angel Hair Pasta
with Shrimp, Fire Roasted Sweet Peppers & 3 Basil Pesto

A delightful dish which is served as an appetizer at Café Chardonnay.
Serves 2

10 large shrimp, peeled and deveined
8 thin slices roasted red bell peppers
2 Tbsp. herb olive oil
4 Tbsp. pesto
³/₄ cup seasoned fish stock
2 appetizer portions of angel hair pasta

3 basil pesto

1 bunch sweet basil
1 bunch purple basil
¹/₂ bunch lemon basil
1 bunch Italian parsley
4 garlic cloves
salt and pepper to taste

Place oil in small sauté pan, heat and add shrimp. Sauté for 1 minute. Add the peppers and fish stock. Simmer for 1 minute and add the pesto and seasonings. Toss with hot pasta and serve on a 9-inch appetizer plate. Garnish with grated Parmesan cheese and a purple basil sprig. (Sea scallops may be used to replace shrimp.)

For the 3 Basil Pesto, wash and pick the leaves from all herbs. Place in food processor and thouroughly mix with the garlic. Salt and pepper to taste. Store in refrigerator until needed.

To ensure your whipping cream will whip in warm weather, use very cold cream and chill the bowl as well as the beaters.

RENATO'S

87 Via Mizner • Palm Beach, Florida 33480 • (561) 655-9752

Renato's is tucked away in the lovely, historic Via Mizner, a charming walkway that opens into flower gardens, art galleries and boutiques. Somehow the visitors and residents have had no trouble finding Renato's, as it has become one of Palm Beach's most popular restaurants in just seven years. The Mediterranean ambiance features views of wrought iron balconies with climbing flowers and a great patio area for dining "al fresco" when weather permits.

The cuisine at Renato's includes both French and Italian dishes which are beautifully presented in classic French style, with specialties such as Terrine of Fresh Seafood, Penne alla Caprese and Snapper Livornese. The lunches are the perfect way to break up a day of shopping on Worth Avenue, and the intimate piano bar is the perfect ending to an excellent meal.

YELLOWTAIL SNAPPER WITH FRESH FENNEL EN PAPILLOTE

So easy and fun to make, the fennel adds a touch of perfection to the yellowtail.
Serves 6

6 6-oz. snapper filets
¾ cup scallions cut into small julienne
¾ cup shiitake mushrooms
3 medium size tomatoes
6 Tbsp. unsalted butter

juice of one lemon
salt and freshly ground pepper
3 fennel bulbs diced
6 Tbsp. chopped shallots
½ cup dry white wine

Preheat oven to high. (500°F.) Spread a large sheet of heavy duty aluminum foil or parchment paper on a flat surface. Invert a 12-inch round cake pan on the foil and trace around the pan with a sharp knife to make a 12-inch circle. Make 6 of them.

Cut tomatoes in small cubes. Cut off and discard the stem of each mushroom and cut the cap into thin slices. Heat 2 Tbsp. of butter in a frying pan over medium high heat. Add the mushrooms and lemon juice. Cook, shaking the pan and stirring for one minute. Add the scallions, fennel and salt. Then cover and cook for 7 to 8 minutes. Set aside.

Melt the remaining butter in a small saucepan. Place the foil rounds on a flat surface and brush them with the melted butter. Spoon equal portions of the mixture on each disk, slightly below the center, leaving a margin large enough to fold over. Lay one fish over each mound of vegetables. Sprinkle each serving with a tablespoon of shallots, a ½ tomato cut in cubes, a Tbsp. of white wine and salt and pepper. Fold the foil to completely enclose the contents, while leaving some room for expansion. Crimp the seal as tightly as possible. Arrange the papillotes on a baking sheet and bake for 8 minutes.

Sautéed Salmon Steaks

with Orange Butter Sauce

Serves 6

6 6-oz. salmon steaks, skinless
¹/₂ cup freshly squeezed orange juice
6 Tbsp. unsalted butter at room temperature
³/₄ cup tomatoes, diced, peeled and seeded
salt and freshly ground pepper

2 Tbsp. olive oil
4 finely chopped shallots
steamed baby zucchinis or boiled mini potatoes with dill
¹/₄ cup chopped fresh coriander or parsley leaves

Put orange juice and shallots into a saucepan and reduce it by half over high heat. Add the butter and tomatoes and cook just until the combination is well blended. Season with salt and pepper to taste. Heat two Tbsp. of olive oil in a large, non-stick frying pan. Season the salmon steaks with salt and pepper. Place the steaks in the pan and cook over high heat until they are lightly browned, about 1¹/₄ minutes on each side. The time will vary depending on the thickness of the fish.

Transfer the steaks to warm plates, pour the sauce over them and garnish with the steamed zucchini or boiled mini potatoes with dill. Top with chopped coriander or parsley.

Salmon Marcchiaro

The essence of simplicity, this is a must for seafood lovers.
Serves 1

8 oz. salmon filet
3 mussels and 3 clams (cleaned)
1 oz. scallops
¹/₄ cup white wine

¹/₄ cup clam juice
olive oil
pinch salt, pepper, basil
¹/₂ cup crushed tomatoes

Sauté salmon, shellfish and scallops in sizzling olive oil. Reserve cooking juice. Deglaze cooking pan with white wine and add clam juice, salt, pepper, fresh basil, and fresh crushed tomatoes. Reduce for approximately 5 to 10 minutes to create a very light sauce. Serve at once.

CHOCOLATE CARAMEL TART

This dessert is so easy to make, a pleasure to look at and a joy to eat!
Serves 8

7 oz. sweet pie pastry
1⅓ cups heavy cream
3½ oz. semi sweet chocolate (3½
   squares), melted

¾ cup sugar
1½ Tbsp. corn syrup
3 Tbsp. water
1½ Tbsp. lemon juice

Bake a 9-inch circle of pastry in a 350°F. oven for about 15 minutes or until golden brown. Let cool.

In a small saucepan, bring ⅓ cup heavy cream to lukewarm. Remove from heat and stir in the melted chocolate and set aside to cool, stirring occasionally until the mixture is just firm enough to hold its shape.

Spread a layer of chocolate mixture over the pastry circle. Scrape the remaining chocolate mixture into a pastry bag with medium star tip, and pipe the chocolate around the rim of the pastry to form a border. Then, starting at the center of the pastry, pipe the outline of 8 tart wedges. Refrigerate for 30 minutes.

In a heavy saucepan, combine the sugar, corn syrup and water to make the caramel. Bring to a boil over medium heat and cook until lightly golden. Remove from the heat and stir in the remaining cream. Bring the caramel to a boil over medium high heat, stirring constantly. Remove from heat and stir in lemon juice. Let the caramel cool to room temperature. When caramel is cool, spoon it into the 8 outlined tart sections. If you desire, the tart can be finished with another layer of chocolate.

Most raisins come from the Thompson seedless grapes, with the dark ones sun dried and the light ones mechanically dehydrated and treated with sulphur dioxide to retain their golden color.

THE RESTAURANT

Four Seasons Ocean Grand
2800 S. Ocean Blvd. • Palm Beach, Florida 33480 • (561) 582-2800

The Four Seasons Ocean Grand is a beachfront resort epitomizing the relaxed luxury of Palm Beach and Florida's Gold Coast. The signature dining room is simply referred to as The Restaurant, although it is anything but simple. Recognized as one of the finest dining establishments in Florida, The Restaurant is an enclave of grace, style and faultless service. The Restaurant is a most deserving winner of Florida Trend's Golden Spoon Award as one of Florida's top 20 restaurants.

The culinary artistry of Executive Chef Hubert Des Marais has earned recognition from many of the food world's most exacting critics, including Gourmet Magazine, The James Beard Foundation and most recently named one of America's 10 Best New Chefs by Food & Wine Magazine. A graduate of the Culinary Institute of America, Chef Hubert has created a cuisine which is characterized by an inspired blend of the traditions and flavors of the deep south, the Caribbean and South and Central America. As a strong believer in freshness of ingredients, Chef Hubert grows his own herbs, citrus and exotic fruits. Additionally, The Restaurant's menu features several deliciously healthy "Heart Smart" selections.

INDIAN RIVER JUMBO LUMP CRAB
WITH CRISP PLANTAIN, AVOCADO & CAVIAR

This recipe was a favorite among our test group. It's not difficult to make, the taste is outstanding and the presentation is especially attractive. The passion fruit vinaigrette really brings this dish together.
Serves 1

¹/₂ green plantain
¹/₄ cup avocado
1 Tbsp. Bermuda onion, medium dice
¹/₂ tsp. fresh cilantro, chopped
1 tsp. crème fraiche
¹/₂ cup jumbo lump crab
1 Tbsp. fresh chives, chopped
1 Tbsp. Osetra caviar

1 Tbsp. mango purée
2 Tbsp. olive oil
1 Tbsp. confetti of zucchini, red & yellow pepper
¹/₈ tsp. scotch bonnet pepper, finely diced
1 key lime, juice only
3-4 Tbsp. passion fruit vinaigrette

Slice the plantain into ¹/₈-inch thick rounds. Place 6 rounds together in a circle and press together to adhere. Make two such circles and fry in olive oil until crisp. Drain on paper towel and set aside.

Dice the avocado with the Bermuda onion. Add $1/2$ of the key lime juice, the scotch bonnet pepper, cilantro and season with salt and pepper to taste. Set aside.

Combine the crab with $1/2$ of the chopped chives, $1/2$ of the key lime juice and 1 tablespoon mango purée. Mix gently and set aside.

Place the avocado mixture in the center of a plate and place one of the plantain "circles" on top. Then the crab mixture and another plantain "circle." Ladle the passion fruit vinaigrette around the stack and top with crème fraiche and caviar. Sprinkle the confetti of vegetables on top for the final touch.

PASSION FRUIT VINAIGRETTE

1 cup passion fruit purée
3 Tbsp. Champagne vinegar
4 Tbsp. hazelnut oil
1 cup olive oil
1 Tbsp. Dijon mustard

$1/2$ cup sterling oil
1 Tbsp. salt & cracked black pepper
1 Tbsp. shallots
1 tsp. garlic, minced
1 pinch of cinnamon

Combine the purée, vinegar, salt, pepper, cinnamon, mustard, shallots and garlic in a blender until mixed well. Slowly add the oils while continuing to mix.

YELLOWTAIL SNAPPER
WITH WATERMELON, ANNATO AND LEMON THYME

This dish is especially good in the summer when cantaloupe, honeydew and watermelon are at their peak.
Serves 1

1 whole yellowtail snapper
1 slice seedless watermelon, 1-inch thick
$1/2$ cup assorted melons, diced (cantaloupe,
    honeydew, etc.)
2 tsp. red bell pepper, small dice
2 sprigs lemon-thyme, fresh

1 sprig cilantro, fresh
6 Tbsp. orange vinaigrette
1 tsp. chives
2 Tbsp. annato oil
6 Tbsp. peanut oil

Take the whole yellowtail snapper and remove the scales with the back of a knife or by using a scaler. Using a sharp knife, make an incision down the back of the snapper from the head to the tail following the vertebrae. Do this on both sides of the fish, then cut over the rib cage down to the tail, making sure not to remove the filets from the tail area. Cut the spine of the snapper at the tail base, removing all the bones. You should be left with two filets attached to the tail (butterfly cut).

Remove any pin bones with a pair of pliers. Brush the filet (meat side) with one tablespoon of olive oil and place the sprig of cilantro and one sprig of thyme on the filets and place the filets together.

Using a sharp knife, score the skin side of the filets, making a ¼-inch deep incision in two separate directions, making an "X". This prevents the fish from buckling during cooking. Brush the fish with olive oil and season with salt and pepper to taste.

Use a large sauté pan over high heat and sear the snapper until brown on both sides in the three ounces of peanut oil, being careful not to burn the tail.

Cut the slice of watermelon using a round cutter 5 inches in diameter. Place the watermelon off center on a plate. On one side of the plate place the orange vinaigrette. Sprinkle the diced melons and red pepper around the plate. Sprinkle the leaves of a lemon thyme sprig around the melon on the plate. Place the snapper on top of the watermelon and brush the snapper with annato oil. Sprinkle the fish with chopped chives and garnish with a sprig of lemon thyme.

Note: Annato oil may be made by heating annato seeds in olive oil for a few minutes, then straining the seeds out.

CASHEW CRUSTED KEY LIME PIE
WITH ORANGE ZEST MERINGUE
For a 9-inch pie

½ lb. ground graham cracker crumbs
½ roasted cashews, finely ground
⅜ cup granulated sugar
⅜ cup melted butter
16 oz. can sweetened condensed milk
   (2 cups)

4 egg yolks
½ cup Key lime juice
½ cup egg whites
½ cup plus 1 Tbsp. granulated sugar
water
zest of ½ orange

Mix the first three ingredients and then add the melted butter. Press into a lightly buttered 9" pie tin and bake in a 350°F. oven for 5 minutes before filling. Place the egg yolks in a bowl, whip and gradually add sweetened condensed milk, then the key lime juice. Pour into the pre-baked pie crust and bake at 350°F. for approximately 20 minutes. Do not allow the filling to boil. Remove from oven and allow to cool or chill in refrigerator before topping with meringue.

To make meringue, place egg whites in a mixing bowl and set aside. Pour sugar into a very clean pot. Add enough water just to cover the sugar. Bring sugar and water to a soft ball stage.

In a mixing bowl, on high speed, whip egg whites to a soft peak, then carefully pour sugar syrup into the mixture. Mix until the sides of the bowl are cool. Add the chopped zest and fold into the meringue. Top the pie with meringue and bake at 450°F. approximately 3 minutes, or until the meringue is golden in color. Allow to cool before serving. The pie is best served chilled.

THE RESTAURANT

The Ritz-Carlton, Palm Beach
100 South Ocean Boulevard • Manalapan, Florida 33462 • (561) 533-6000

This luxurious Mediterranean style beachfront resort is located just eight miles from the world renown shops of Worth Avenue. The resort offers two gourmet dining outlets, The Grill and The Restaurant. While the names of these two fine restaurants may not be very creative, their cuisine is wonderful.

The Restaurant is the perfect choice for fine dining, Florida style, as it overlooks the Atlantic Ocean with outdoor terrace seating available. Traditional in decor, its beige wood paneling and pastel accents result in an elegant, yet relaxed ambiance. A Mobil Four-Star Award winner, The Restaurant features the freshest of seafood, in addition to creative meat and poultry dishes. All fruits and vegetables used in The Restaurant are produced organically, with the emphasis on fresh, local ingredients. The impeccable quality of service is what we have come to expect from restaurants in The Ritz-Carlton organization throughout Florida.

SEARED SEA SCALLOPS WITH CITRUS VINAIGRETTE
Appetizer for 2

6 sea scallops
1 Tbsp. walnut oil
1 orange, juice and zest
1 lemon, juice only
1 lime, juice only

1 grapefruit, juice only
1 Tbsp. walnut oil
salt and freshly ground pepper
lettuce, any variety

Heat a non-stick saute pan over high heat. Season the scallops with salt and pepper to taste on both sides. Add the walnut oil to the pan and add the scallops. After 2 minutes, reduce the heat and turn over with a pair of tongs. Cook an additional minute and remove the pan from the heat. Allow to sit for 1 minute before serving.

For the citrus vinaigrette, whisk the citrus juices with the walnut oil. Julienne the orange zest and add to the juice mixture. Add salt and pepper to taste.

To serve, arrange lettuce leaves in the center of each plate. Place 3 scallops for each serving on the lettuce. Drizzle with the vinaigrette. Garnish with wedges of fresh citrus.

Note: Use fresh juices for this recipe. Especially important is the use of fresh grapefruit juice. Additionally, ask your fish monger to provide scallops that do not contain tripolyphosphate sodium, a preservative that adds water weight to the scallops.

Swordfish with Eggplant & Goat Cheese Crostini

A wonderful seafood dish with a Mediterranean flair. The goat cheese crostini is a treat.
Serves 4

6 8-oz. swordfish steaks
4 slices eggplant, ¼-inch thick
1 Tbsp. olive oil
¼ cup olive oil

1 tsp. minced garlic
1 tsp. fresh oregano, chopped
1 tsp. fresh basil, sliced
1 cup basic tomato sauce

Coat the eggplant with the ¼ cup olive oil, garlic and fresh herbs. Allow to marinate for 20 minutes.

Grill the eggplant or cook in the oven at 350°F. until tender.

Preheat the oven to 300°F. Sauté the swordfish in 1 Tbsp. olive oil in a non-stick pan on high heat for 2 minutes on each side. Place a slice of eggplant on each swordfish steak and finish baking in the oven for 5 to 7 minutes, or until the fish is firm to the touch.

To serve, drizzle warmed tomato sauce in a circle around the plate. Place the swordfish and the eggplant in the center. Arrange the Goat Cheese Crostini around the perimeter of the plate. Spoon the Marinated Tomato Confit between the Crostini.

Goat Cheese Crostini

12 thin slices of French baguette
6 oz. goat cheese
4 Tbsp. pesto

Toast the slices of French bread. Top with goat cheese and a dab of the pesto. Just before serving place the crostini under the broiler to melt the cheese.

Marinated Tomato Confit

15 red plum tomatoes, chopped
15 yellow plum tomatoes, chopped
¾ cup balsamic vinegar
¾ cup olive oil

¼ tsp. minced shallots
¼ tsp. minced garlic
¼ tsp. fresh oregano, chopped
¼ tsp. fresh basil, sliced

Add 2 Tbsp. olive oil to a non-stick pan over high heat. Add the tomatoes and saute for 5 minutes, or until well done. Add the remaining ingredients and allow all to sit for ½ hour.

Maine Lobster Salad with Blood Orange Vinaigrette

Serves 6

1 gallon court bouillon
6 1-lb. lobsters
1 lb. green beans
1 lb. sun chokes
3 blood oranges (substitute Valencia)

1 red bell pepper, diced
1 green bell pepper, diced
1 yellow bell pepper, diced
salt and freshly ground pepper

Bring the court bouillon to a rapid boil. Add the lobsters and cook for 5 minutes. Allow the lobsters to cool and remove the tail meat. Chop into bite sized pieces.

Blanch the green beans and sun chokes in boiling salted water until al dente. Toss in a bowl with the orange vinaigrette, salt and pepper to taste.

To serve, place the green beans and sun chokes on a plate and top with a layer of lobster meat. Spoon over the Blood Orange Vinaigrette and sprinkle with the diced peppers. Segment the oranges by cutting between the sections with a sharp knife. Place these segments on top of the salad. Garnish with scallions and fresh cilantro.

Court Bouillon

1 gallon water
1 cup vinegar
$^1/_4$ cup salt

1 bay leaf
1 chopped onion
1 Tbsp. black peppercorns

Bring all the ingredients except the peppercorns to a boil and simmer for $^1/_2$ hour. Add the peppercorns and turn off the heat. Allow to sit for $^1/_2$ hour before cooking lobsters.

Blood Orange Vinaigrette

2 tsp. Dijon mustard
3 tsp. rice vinegar
2 cups hazelnut oil

2 cups fresh blood orange juice
salt and freshly ground pepper

Whisk the mustard, vinegar and orange juice in a bowl. Gradually add the hazelnut oil while whisking continuously. Salt and pepper to taste.

Note: Substitute Valencia oranges if unable to find blood oranges.

ARTURO'S RISTORANTE

6750 N. Federal Hwy. • Boca Raton, Florida 33487 • (561) 997-7373

Arturo's Ristorante, owned and operated by Joseph and Vincent Gismondi, was founded by their father, Arturo Gismondi. Arturo owned his first restaurant in Rome and now enjoys two locations, in New York and Boca Raton. Now with four generations involved in the restaurant, Arturo's is not resting on its reputation. Arturo's cuisine is classic, no-nonsense Italian, and it is excellent. As always, all breads, desserts and pasta are homemade daily on the premises.

Located in a stately Mizner-style building, the restaurant continues the Italian tradition of providing both private and public dining areas. Additionally, special windows provide excellent views of the kitchen to display the quality of ingredients as well as preparation. There is also a superb wine cellar where you can not only select the perfect wine to complement your dinner, but you may also have your dinner served in the very same room. When you dine with the Gismondi family it is truly like being in Italy.

FILET OF SNAPPER AL BRODETTO

This flavorful seafood dish is easy, quick and absolutely out of this world! If you use red snapper, we suggest the American product rather than the imported snapper.
Serves 4

4 6-oz. snapper filets	4 fresh basil leaves
4 Tbsp. olive oil	8 little neck clams, scrubbed, rinsed
1 garlic clove, finely chopped	8 mussels, scrubbed, bearded
1/2 cup dry white wine	1 lb. ripe tomatoes, peeled and coarsley
1 tsp. Italian parsley, chopped	chopped
1/4 tsp. oregano	salt and pepper to taste

Heat the oil in a large, heavy skillet over medium heat and sauté the filets, skin side up, for about 2 minutes. Turn them over carefully using a spatula.

Add the garlic, clams and mussels. Add the wine, tomatoes, basil, oregano and salt and pepper to taste. Cover the pan and cook for 10 minutes.

Arrange the filets, clams and mussels on a hot serving platter. Pour the remaining sauce over the filets and serve at once.

VEAL CHOP MODENESE

Too often the veal chop is overlooked in favor of lamb and pork chops. This is a very tasty cut of meat which is extremely flexible. The Veal Chop Modenese is a specialty of Arturo's. Serve this with risotto or spaghettini… it is great!

Serves 4

4 loin veal chops, cut 1-inch thick
$^1/_2$ cup flour
4 Tbsp. oil
4 Tbsp. butter
1 cup dry white wine

1 clove garlic, sliced
1 clove shallot, sliced
1 cup clear broth
$^1/_2$ tsp. rosemary, chopped
$^1/_2$ lemon, juice only

Dry the chops thoroughly with paper towels, then dust with flour. Heat the oil in a large, heavy skillet and add the chops. Brown on each side for 3 minutes.

Add the garlic, shallots and rosemary. Add the wine and simmer till it evaporates. Add $^1/_2$ cup cooking broth and 2 Tbsp. butter. Turn the chops over once during the cooking period and baste with the juices in the pan. Cover the pan tightly and simmer over low heat for about 10 minutes.

The chops are fully cooked when their juices run clear yellow when pierced with a fork. Transfer the chops to a hot serving platter and keep warm.

Add the remaining broth and the butter to the sauce in the pan. Simmer over high heat until the sauce thickens. Remove from the heat, add the lemon juice and pour the sauce over the chops. Serve immediately.

TIRAMISU

This is one of two Tiramisu desserts we selected for The Special Taste of Florida. A classic presentation, Arturo's version features a combination of Amaretto di Saronno, Strega and triple sec.

Serves 6

$7^1/_2$ oz. mascarpone cheese
3 egg yolks
$1^5/_8$ cup powdered sugar
3 Tbsp. cocoa powder
3 cups espresso coffee

$^1/_4$ cup Strega Liqueur®
$^1/_4$ cup Amaretto di Sarono®
$^1/_4$ cup triple sec
24 lady finger cookies

In a small bowl, mix the mascarpone cheese with the egg yolks and the sugar until smooth. Set aside.

In another bowl, mix the liqueurs with the espresso.

In a long serving plate, arrange 12 lady fingers which have previously been dipped in the liqueur mixture. With a long, narrow metal spatula, smooth over the lady fingers with $^1/_2$ of the mascarpone cheese mixture.

Dip the remaining lady fingers in the liquor and form a second layer. Cover this layer of lady fingers with the remaining mascarpone mixture. Sprinkle the dessert with the cocoa powder. Refrigerate for 2 hours before serving.

Arturo's Caesar Salad

Serves 4

2 cloves garlic, crushed
3 anchovies, crushed
$^1/_4$ cup extra virgin olive oil
$^1/_2$ lemon, juice only
2 dashes Worcestershire Sauce®
2 egg yolks

1 Tbsp. Grey Poupon Mustard®
4 Tbsp. Parmesan cheese, freshly grated
fresh ground pepper
fresh croutons
1 head romaine lettuce, hearts

Rinse the romaine well, drain well or pat dry, and set aside.

In a large wooden bowl, mash the garlic and anchovies together into the bottom of the bowl with a fork. Add the egg yolk and mustard, then mix well. Add the Worcestershire and lemon juice, again mix well.

Add the romaine, croutons and Parmesan cheese. Toss well and add the olive oil along with the pepper. Continue to toss for another minute.

When marinating fish, be careful not to over-marinate, as this may cause the fish to dry out during cooking.

DAMIANO'S AT THE TARRIMORE HOUSE

52 North Swinton • Delray Beach, Florida 33444 • (407) 272-4706

Anthony Damiano and his wife Lisa are both the owners and chefs of this exquisite restaurant situated in the historic Pineapple Grove district of Delray Beach. The Tarrimore House was built in 1924, and has been beautifully restored into three separate dining rooms, each with a different theme.

Anthony's background includes an internship at Maxim's in Paris, and Executive Chef at New York's Russian Tea Room. Lisa developed her considerable pastry skills at New York's River Cafe, Montrachet, and the Russian Tea Room, where she and Anthony worked with consulting chef Jacques Pepin.

Together they have created an absolute gem of a restaurant, rated by the Zagat Survey as one of the finest in Palm Beach County. The wide variety of ethnic influences in their cuisine includes Russian, French, Italian, Oriental and American. Many dishes feature Anthony's "Florasian" cuisine, combining his passion for Oriental flavors and techniques with Florida's bounty of fresh seafood and produce.

For sweet endings, don't pass up dessert! Lisa works magic in the kitchen to create a range of spectacular desserts that are legendary. As a special bonus, many of Damiano's dishes and desserts are amazingly low in fat.

ASIAN CHICKEN SAUSAGE
WITH WILD GOOSE AMBER AND ASIAN VEGETABLES

Serves 2

12 oz. chicken or turkey sausage
1 cup red, yellow and red bell peppers,
   cut into strips
2 tsp. garlic, minced
$^1/_2$ cup vidalia onion, sliced
$^1/_2$ cup Wild Goose Amber,
   or any dark beer you prefer

$^1/_2$ cup bok choy, chopped
$^1/_2$ cup chopped cabbage, red or green
2 Tbsp. ginger, minced
$^1/_4$ cup light soy sauce
2 Tbsp. hoisin sauce

In a non-stick pan, sauté the sausage over medium heat until golden brown. Remove from pan and set aside.

To the same pan add the peppers, onions garlic and ginger, soy sauce and hoisin sauce. Cook for about 30 seconds and then pour in the beer. Simmer on low heat for a minute and then add the cabbage and bok choy. Continue to cook until the cabbage and bok choy are thoroughly warmed through but still crisp. Serve with rice or cous cous.

LOBSTER, SHRIMP & BLACK BEAN BURRITO

This is a delightful blend of seafood, black beans and saffron.

Serves 6

6 fat free flour tortillas
12 oz. lobster meat, raw
1 lb. large shrimp, cleaned, deveined
1/2 cup Vidalia onions, julienne
2 red bell peppers, julienne
1/4 cup zucchini, julienne
3 tsp. roasted garlic
1/2 tsp. chili powder

1/2 cup rice
1 cup water
1/2 cup black beans, cooked
1/4 tsp. saffron (French or Spanish)
salt & freshly ground pepper to taste
1 cup reduced fat sour cream
1/4 bunch fresh cilantro, chopped

Bring the water to boil in a pan, add the saffron, salt and pepper to taste, rice and black beans. Cover and simmer until rice is done.

Prepare the vegetables and set aside.

Cut the lobster meat into bite sized pieces. In a 10-inch non-stick pan, lightly coat with olive oil and sauté the onions, garlic and chili powder for about 30 seconds. Add the peppers and the zucchini. Cook for another minute. Add the shrimp and lobster meat and salt and pepper to taste. Cook until the lobster meat is just translucent.

To assemble the tortillas, spread the rice and bean mixture on a tortilla, add the shrimp and lobster mixture. Roll into a burrito and garnish with sour cream mixed with cilantro. Repeat with remaining tortillas.

Note: Chef Damiano suggests adding a little tequila to the cilantro sour cream for an interesting taste. We agree.

AMARETTO CRUSTED RICOTTA PUMPKIN PIE

Lisa Damiano prepared this pie at a demonstration for Bon Appetit Magazine at Bloomindale's in New York to rave reviews. Here's a recipe that will be the hit of your holiday season ... easy, delicious and with less than 1 gram of fat per serving.

One 8-inch Pie

7 oz. Amaretto cookies
2 tsp. vanilla extract
1 lb. non fat Ricotta cheese,
1 cup canned pumpkin
3/4 cup brown sugar

1 tsp. ground cinnamon
1/2 tsp. ground nutmeg
1/2 tsp. ground cloves
1 tsp. vanilla extract
6 egg whites at room temperature

Pre-heat your oven to 350°F. Fine grind the cookies, add the 2 teaspoons of vanilla extract and mix well. Press into a pie pan sprayed with Pam®. Set aside.

Process the Ricotta cheese with a food processor or rotary mixer until it is smooth. Add the pumpkin, brown sugar, spices and 1 teaspoon vanilla. Blend the mixture for several minutes. Whip the egg whites to stiff peaks and fold into pumpkin mixture. Place the filling into the Amaretto pie crust and bake for 40 minutes, or until center is set.

CARAMELIZED BANANAS FOSTER CHOCOLATE TOSTADA
Serves 6

6 fat free flour tortillas
1 egg white
1/3 cup granulated sugar

1 tsp. cocoa
1 tsp. cinnamon
1 tsp. nutmeg

For the tortillas, preheat oven to 400°F. Brush each tortilla with egg white, then sprinkle each side with sugar. Mix the spices and brush both sides with the mixture. Spray a baking sheet with Pam®, place the tortillas on the sheet and bake for 5-7 minutes.

2 cups skim milk
3 Tbsp. corn starch

1/3 cup granulated sugar
3/4 cup Hershey's Cocoa

To make the custard, in a heavy bottom sauce pan add 1½ cups of skim milk. Pour the remaining ½ cup milk into small bowl and add the corn starch and stir well to mix. Pour the corn starch mixture into into the milk and add the sugar and cocoa. Cook on medium heat, stirring constantly with a wooden spoon until scalding. Remove from heat to cool.

2 bananas, cut in half lengthwise, then crosswise
  into thirds to provide 6 pieces per banana
1 cup granulated sugar

1 ¼ cup water
1 tsp. lemon juice

To caramelize the bananas, heat a heavy bottom skillet (cast iron is great) over high heat and add the sugar, stirring constantly until sugar caramelizes, approximately 10 minutes. Add the water and let the mixture reduce into a sauce. Add the lemon juice and stir to combine. Placed the sliced bananas into the skillet and reduce the heat to low and allow to cook the bananas, basting occasionally, until soft and tender.

To assemble the tostadas, begin by spooning the chocolate custard onto the crisp tortillas. Place 2 caramelized banana pieces on each tortilla.

For the crowning touch, sprinkle 1 teaspoon of granulated sugar on each tostada, then use a household propane torch to caramelize this sugar with the flame until it turns a dark amber color. Refrigerate no longer than 30 minutes to set this caramel crust.

LA FINESTRA

171 E. Palmetto Park Rd. • Boca Raton, Florida 33432 • (561) 392-1838

It hardly seems possible that La Finestra has been open for over 10 years, but then again time flies when good things are happening. Chef Antoine Pepaj has developed a large following of dedicated customers with a light cuisine which he introduced with the opening of the restaurant, long before lighter cuisine became so popular.

Maitre d' Glen Perry and a friendly, knowledgeable staff provide the perfect complement to Chef Antoine's interpretation of Northern Italian cuisine in this most intimate setting. As the Palm Beach Post says, "Beyond the exquisite work of the chef, this little bit of Northern Italy can pride itself on impeccable service." The following recipes are excellent examples of the light cuisine of Chef Antoine.

Salmon Tuscana
A wonderful way to prepare salmon.
Serves 4

4 8-oz. Norwegian salmon filets
1 cup hazelnuts, toasted and chopped
2 medium tomatoes, pealed, seeded,
  chopped

2 shallots, diced fine
6 fresh basil leaves, sliced
1 bunch of arugula

Brush salmon with virgin olive oil and dredge in hazelnuts. Grill one minute on each side (for a medium rare portion). Toss concasse of tomato, shallots and basil leaves quickly in skillet over high heat for approximately 30 seconds.

Place the salmon filets on a bed of arugula and top with concasse. Optionally, toss the arugula in a balsamic vinaigrette.

Tuna Oriental
One of the best tuna dishes we had the pleasure of trying.
Serves 4

4 8-oz. tuna steaks (shashimi quality)
³/₄ cup sesame seeds (black and white)
¹/₄ cup sesame oil
1 bunch watercress

4 Tbsp. wasabi
4 Tbsp. pickled ginger
3 cups seaweed salad
¹/₂ cup punza sauce (Oriental markets)

Marinate the tuna steaks in sesame oil for five minutes. Dredge in sesame seeds and sear the steaks in a hot skillet for 20 seconds per side. Remove each steak and slice into six pieces.

Place on a bed of watercress and top with 2 Tbsp. of punza sauce per serving. Garnish with wasabi, ginger and seaweed salad. Can also be served as an appetizer using four ounce portions.

CAPELLINI CON FRUTTI DI MARE

A light twist on this classic Italian seafood dish.
Serves 4

1/2 lb. capellini pasta
3/8 cup virgin olive oil
2 cloves garlic, diced
12 basil leaves, chopped
12 pear tomatoes, peeled

8 large shrimp, peeled and deveined
8 oz. calamari, cleaned and sliced
8 oz. sea scallops
12 little neck clams, rinsed and washed

Heat the oil in a saucepan and add the garlic until light brown. Add the basil and then the tomatoes. Add the clams, calamari, shrimp and scallops a minute apart, in this order. Season sauce with salt and pepper. Cook the capellini in boiling water and place in serving bowls. Top with sauce, dividing the individual seafood into equal portions. Garnish each serving with fresh basil leaves.

POLLO ALLA SANTA MARGHERITA

Serves 4

4 6-oz. chicken breasts, skinless and
    boneless
1/2 cup virgin olive oil
1 Tbsp. lemon juice, fresh squeezed

1 Tbsp. crushed black pepper
1 bunch arugula, chopped
1 medium head of radicchio, chopped
1/2 cup balsamic vinaigrette

Marinate the chicken breasts in the oil, lemon juice and pepper for 10 minutes. Grill chicken for three minutes on each side over high heat. Toss arugula and radicchio in vinaigrette and divide equally over each portion of chicken.

TOP OF THE TOWER -
THE ITALIAN RESTAURANT

Boca Raton Resort & Club
501 East Camino Real • Boca Raton, Florida 33431 • (561) 395-3000

Dining at The Boca Raton Resort & Club is a culinary experience above all others, literally, thanks to Top of the Tower - The Italian Restaurant. Located on the top floor of the acclaimed Resort & Club's majestic 27-story Tower, the restaurant features spectacular views of the Atlantic Ocean, Florida's Intracoastal Waterway and the historic resort grounds.

Top of the Tower - The Italian Restaurant is managed by Nick Nickolas, the well-known restauranteur who owns and operates award-winning restaurants in Chicago, Honolulu and Miami. Nickolas describes his cuisine as "regional Italian fare that is hearty, delicious and comforting." Top of the Tower - The Italian Restaurant's menu includes a selection of fresh pastas and entrées of seafood, chicken, veal and lamb, as well as homemade breads served tableside.

Located in the heart of Palm Beach County on Florida's Gold Coast, the Boca Raton Resort & Club is one of the country's premier destination resorts. Set in a backdrop of casual elegance, Boca's amenities include two 18-hole championship golf courses, 34 tennis courts, several pools, state-of-the-art fitness centers, a half-mile stretch of private beach and a full-service marina.

ROASTED BELL PEPPER SALAD
Serves 8

5 green peppers
5 red peppers
5 yellow peppers
¹/₄ cup extra virgin olive oil
¹/₄ cup balsamic vinegar
3 Tbsp. garlic, minced
1 Tbsp. oregano

Herbamare Spice to taste (health food
  stores)
salt to taste
Tuscan bread, toasted
garnish: Belgian endive and red oak leaves

Roast peppers on a grill until the skin begins to blacken, but not burn. Place peppers into sealed plastic containers (or a Zip Lock bag) to create a steaming effect which will assist in peeling the peppers. Peel when cooled and cut into 1-inch strips.

Heat the extra virgin olive oil in a sauté pan and add garlic and oregano, then sauté for 1 minute. Add balsamic vinegar, then finish with the Herbamare and salt to taste.

Place a slice of toasted Tuscan bread on a plate and top with the roasted pepper salad, garnish with the Belgian endive and red oak leaves. Then top with the balsamic vinegar dressing.

SWORDFISH ROMANO

This is a great recipe for firm fish such as wahoo, marlin, halibut and swordfish.
Serves 2

2 8-oz. swordfish steaks
$1/2$ cup ripe tomatoes, peeled, seeded, diced
$1/2$ cup feta cheese, crumbled
2 scallions, chopped

6 calamata olives, pitted, sliced
$1/4$ cup virgin olive oil
salt and pepper to taste

Grill the swordfish to preferred doneness. Mix all of the remaining ingredients in a bowl and place on the cooked fish.

FRUITTI DI MARE

Serves 2

$3/4$ stick unsalted butter
2 Tbsp. shallots, chopped
$1/4$ cup scallions, chopped
$3/4$ cup mushrooms, sliced
6 extra large shrimp, peeled, deveined
8 sea scallops

4 clams
4 small pieces of fish (any firm textured fish)
$1^1/2$ cups Lobster Cream Sauce*
8 oz. linguine, not quite cooked al dente

Heat sauté pan and add butter, all vegetables and seafood. Cut muscles of clams to open with a knife, and place the clam with the meat side down into the sauté pan to cook. Add the cream sauce and cooked pasta. Simmer for 5 minutes.

Remove the clams and place on either side of the plates. Place the pasta and seafood in the center of the plate, with the seafood on top.

LOBSTER CREAM SAUCE

2 cups heavy cream
2 Tbsp. lobster sauce or reduced lobster stock
2 drops Tabasco® sauce
2 tsp. Worcestershire Sauce®

2 tsp. fresh lemon juice
salt, white pepper, cayenne pepper and paprika to taste (roughly 2 pinches of each)

Mix all ingredients together. Simmer for 5 minutes with the Fruitti Di Mare.

Bolognese Sauce

Bolognese is truly a meat-lover's sauce - this traditional recipe is excellent with a bold red wine and crusty garlic bread.

Serves 6

2 Tbsp. unsalted butter
3 oz. prosciutto ham, finely chopped
1 oz. dried porcini or Chilean mushrooms
1 medium onion, coarsely chopped
2 medium carrots, coarsely chopped
2 medium stalks of celery, coarsely
   chopped
8 oz. lean ground beef
8 oz. lean ground veal
8 oz. ground Italian sausage
2 cups dry red wine
$^1/_4$ cup chopped Italian parsley, plus more
   for garnish

1 Tbsp. marjoram
fresh ground black pepper to taste
2 tsp. ground nutmeg
$^1/_2$ cup flour
2 large tomatoes, peeled, seeded, diced
3 cups canned beef stock
12 oz. radiatori (or other spiral pasta)
$^1/_2$ cup heavy cream
$^3/_4$ cup fresh grated Parmesan cheese,
   divided

Cover the mushrooms with warm water and soak for 30 minutes. Drain and coarsely chop. Heat butter in skillet over medium heat, then sauté the prosciutto until brown. Add the onion, carrots, celery, parsley and mushrooms, then sauté for 3 minutes. Add the ground meats and sauté until brown. Make sure all the meat is broken up finely, not left in lumps. Add wine and spices, then simmer until the wine is reduced 80%, approximately 20 minutes.

Stir in the flour and mix well. Add the beef stock and tomatoes, then simmer approximately 45 minutes. Meanwhile, cook the pasta according to package directions.

Stir the cream and half of the Parmesan cheese into the meat sauce. Cook over medium heat to reduce the sauce, about 1 minute.

Divide the pasta and sauce among 6 serving plates. Toss to combine. Garnish with additional chopped parsley and pass the remaining cheese to guests.

Use a ZipLoc®-type baggie to marinate your food. It is easy to shake and easy to clean up.

MAXALUNA

5050 Town Center Circle • Boca Raton, Florida 33486 • (561) 391-7177

Maxaluna first opened its doors in 1986, and has since remained one of Boca Raton's most popular and highly acclaimed restaurants. Dennis and Patti Max did their research in Tuscany prior to opening Maxaluna, incorporating venerable Tuscan features such as the wood burning stove, exposed brick and a comfortable, informal atmosphere.

Formally educated in French Cuisine at Ecole Hotelliére du Québec in Canada, Chef Pierre Viau found that interpreting the grilled food of Tuscany was more interesting and creative than traditional French fare. His food is based in Italian tradition, but is influenced by product availability in Florida and his own French background. Dennis Max and his wife Patti also own Max's Grill in Boca Raton.

GAZPACHO VERDE

Serves 24

4 lb. grilled tomatillo
4 roasted jalapeño (skinless & seedless)
6 bunches Italian parsley
3 bunches scallions
12 bunches arugula
5 lb. fresh spinach leaves
2 bunches fresh thyme

2 bunches fresh oregano
3 bunches fresh cilantro
2¼ cups lime juice
3 cups extra virgin olive oil
32 oz. reduced chicken stock or fondblanc
* (white veal stock)*
salt and pepper to taste

Combine all ingredients in food processor. Strain with large hole strainer. Garnish with grilled corn, finely diced celery, cucumber, avocado, red and yellow pepper, crème fraiche or sour cream and grilled shrimp or sea scallops. Recipe may be halved or quartered.

SPINACH FETTUCINE WITH SQUAB BREAST

This dish takes only minutes to make - it is among our favorites.
Serves 2

2 oz. olive oil
2 tsp. shallots
1 tsp. garlic
1 cup wild mushrooms
2 tsp. sundried tomatoes, puréed
pinch fresh thyme, chopped
1 cup squab stock (or chicken stock)

salt and pepper to taste
1 oz. balsamic vinegar
2 tsp. butter
2 squab breasts, grilled and sliced thin
thyme twig
4 oz. spinach fettuccine

Sauté shallots, garlic, wild mushrooms and sundried tomatoes in olive oil. Cook 2 minutes. Add squab stock and cook another minute. Finish with balsamic vinegar and fresh thyme. Add 1 tsp. butter and salt and pepper to taste. Add cooked spinach fettucine and toss. Garnish with squab breast and thyme twig.

TIRAMISU CUSTARD

An elegant dessert for entertaining. Everyone will love it.
Serves 12

8 oz. cream cheese
$^1/_8$ cup dark rum
$^1/_2$ cup coffee liqueur (Tia Maria® or Kahula®)
5 egg yolks
$^1/_2$ cup sugar

$^1/_2$ oz. water
$1^1/_4$ lb. imported mascarpone
4 egg whites
$^1/_4$ cup sugar
1 cup heavy cream

Place the mascarpone in one large stainless steel or glass bowl. Set aside. Place cream cheese in another bowl and with electric mixer on low, slowly add rum and coffee liqueur, and mix until thoroughly creamed together. Set aside. In a heavy sauce pan combine $^1/_2$ cup sugar and water and heat it until it reaches 242°F.

Meanwhile, place the egg yolks in a bowl and beat with electric mixer at medium speed until light and fluffy. Then, gradually add the sugar water mixture to the yolks and continue to beat until pale (white), thick ribbons form and the mixture is cool.

Fold the cream cheese mix into the mascarpone, careful not to over mix. Then fold the yolk mixture into this, again careful not to over mix.

Whip the egg whites with the mixer until soft peaks form, then add $^1/_4$ cup sugar and mix briefly. Fold $^1/_3$ of the whites into the cream mixture to blend and lighten the custard, then add remaining whites and incorporate completely. Whip the cream in a bowl until firm peaks form, and gently fold into custard until evenly distributed. Use immediately or refrigerate to use as needed. Serve with ladyfingers.

"Only the first bottle is expensive."

French Proverb

LA VIEILLE MAISON

770 E. Palmetto Park Rd. • Boca Raton, Florida 33432 • (561) 391-6701

Dining in grand style had its origins at La Vieille Maison, for sixteen years the only Mobil Guide Five-Star Restaurant in the Southeastern U. S. The ambiance and charm of this antique-filled mansion is the perfect setting for superior food, wine and professional service. Intimate dining areas with private rooms for special parties, garden dining alcoves and a profusion of exotic flowers create a Mediterranean ambiance that echoes the Palm Beach of a bygone era.

This year Chef Richard has introduced the cuisine of the Provencale to South Florida for the first time. As one would expect from Leonce Picot, managing partner of La Vieille Maison as well as The Down Under in Ft. Lauderdale, the extensive wine list complements the thoroughly French menu. When weather permits, dining outdoors at La Vieille Maison is especially enjoyable.

GRATIN OF ESCARGOT WITH FENNEL & PISTACHIO NUTS
This layered dish is wonderful; the sauce with vanilla is a delight!
Serves 2

ONION LAYER

2 Tbsp. white onions, chopped
1 tsp. sugar
1 tsp. butter

1 tsp. beef marrow or Marmite® (available in most grocery stores)

Sauté onions in butter with sugar and beef marrow or Marmite until caramel in color. Add salt and pepper to taste and set aside.

FENNEL LAYER

1 fennel bulb, thinly sliced
1 Tbsp. olive oil

¹/₂ tsp. Pernod®
salt and pepper to taste

Sauté fennel slices in olive oil until crunchy and finish with Pernod and olive oil to taste. Set aside.

OYSTER MUSHROOM LAYER

3 oyster mushrooms, thinly sliced
1 Tbsp. olive oil

¹/₂ tsp. crushed garlic
salt and pepper to taste

Sauté mushrooms in olive oil with garlic until soft but not brown. Add salt and pepper to taste and set aside.

Escargot Layer

6 large snails
2 Tbsp. sweet butter

1 Tbsp. fine herbs or Herbes de Provençe (McCormick® - available in most supermarkets. A blend of basil, fennel seed, lavender, marjoram, rosemary, sage, summer savory and thyme.)

Sauté the snails with butter and garlic and herbs until slightly browned.

Sauce

2 Tbsp. shallots
2 Tbsp. roasted pistachios
2 Tbsp. sweet butter
2 Tbsp. white wine

$1/4$ cup veal stock or chicken consommé
$1/2$ vanilla bean
$1/2$ cup whipped cream

Combine shallots and pistachios with butter and wine in sauce pan. Add veal stock or consomme and bring to a boil. Add vanilla bean and reduce by half.

To assemble: In a terrine, place the layers of onions, fennel, oyster mushrooms, snails and sauce. Put in a warm oven where it will hold up to four hours before serving.

Immediately before serving, whip cream and drizzle snail mixture with butter, then top with dollops of whipped cream. Then put entire dish into broiler for two minutes and serve.

FLOURLESS CHOCOLATE CAKE
WITH MILK CHOCOLATE MOUSSE AND RASPBERRY COMPÔTE

The raspberry compôte makes this a very special dessert.
Makes 4-6 portions in muffin pans

4 oz. bittersweet chocolate (preferably Lindt Courante®), chopped or shaved
2 large eggs

1 Tbsp. sugar
$1/4$ cup unsalted butter
Pam® non-stick vegetable spray

Preheat oven to 325°F. Spray 6-cup muffin pans with non-stick coating such as Pam. Combine chocolate with butter in a double boiler. When chocolate is almost melted, remove from heat and let chocolate continue to melt in hot butter. Combine eggs and sugar in a separate bowl and place over double boiler until mixture is warm. Then put eggs and sugar mixture in a food processor or blender on the high speed and process until stiff peaks form. Add the egg and sugar mixture to the chocolate and butter mixture and fold with whisk until smooth. Fill muffin pans $1/4$ full and bake until firm, approximately seven minutes. Remove from oven and set aside to cool.

CHOCOLATE MOUSSE

8 oz. milk chocolate (Lindt Special®),
chopped or shaved
3 large eggs, separated

³/₄ tsp. Knox® unflavored gelatin
1 cup heavy whipping cream

Whip cream until stiff and place in refrigerator. Sprinkle gelatin in two tablespoons water and stir until it dissolves. Let stand (it will thicken naturally). Separate yolks from whites in two different mixing bowls. Gently melt chopped chocolate over a double boiler and remove from heat when almost melted. Place bowl with gelatin mixture over double boiler to melt completely. Whip the egg yolks vigorously until they double in volume. Whip egg whites vigorously until they reach medium soft peaks. Fold gelatin into yolks, then add one half at a time to the chocolate mixture. Fold in beaten egg whites, one-third at a time, and beat gently until there are no streaks. Fold whip cream in gently. Take muffin pans with Flourless Chocolate Cake in them, and spray sides again with non-stick spray to ensure that the mousse will release easily. Pour mousse over cake into prepared molds and refrigerate for 4-5 hours (freezer may be used to speed set-up time).

To serve, run a knife around the edges of muffin tins and invert. Serve immediately with raspberry compote.

RASPBERRY COMPÔTE

In a small sauce pan, simmer 3 cups raspberries, 1 cup sugar and ¹/₄ cup water over medium heat until the raspberries are soft, approximately five minutes. Cool and serve on top of mousse.

BASIL OIL MASHED POTATOES

1 lb. cubed potatoes
1 tsp. salt
1 cup heavy cream
¹/₄ pound butter
2 Tbsp. basil oil

(Purée 1 tsp. fresh basil and 1 tsp. fresh
spinach—add 3 Tbsp. olive oil and
strain through a sieve or cheesecloth)
¹/₄ tsp. ground white pepper

Start with the potatoes in cold water. Boil until thoroughly cooked. Strain.

Bring heavy cream to boil with butter, basil oil and white pepper. Add heavy cream mixture in three steps to potatoes and thoroughly blend each time (for best results, use electric mixer at medium speed). Adjust seasoning to taste.

BROOKS RESTAURANT

500 S. Federal Highway • Deerfield Beach, Florida 33441 • (954) 427-9302

According to Frenchman Bernard Perron, he became enamored with contemporary cooking when his children, Lisa Howe and Marc Perron, returned from American culinary schools. He proceeded to change his menu from the traditional French to regional American, and his restaurant has become more popular than ever.

The menu may have changed, but the ambiance remains gracefully French. Consistency of quality and service is paramount, with family members in both the kitchen and the dining rooms to ensure an intimate evening meal. The effort has obviously paid off, with Brooks receiving the Golden Spoon Award 4 consecutive years and named "Best Restaurant" in South Florida Magazine. Brooks is a gem of a restaurant.

SHRIMP TEMPURA FRITTER
WITH GINGER SCALLION MAYONNAISE

Serves 6

peel and devein 24 shrimps
half an hour before cooking, marinate in:
¹/₄ cup olive oil
juice of two limes

¹/₄ tsp. of crushed red pepper
¹/₄ cup of chopped cilantro
pinch of salt

After dipping in the tempura batter, cook in a hot vegetable oil at 350-360°F. for about 5 minutes or until golden brown.

TEMPURA BATTER

1 cup all purpose flour, sifted
1 Tbsp. baking soda
1¹/₄ cups cold water

salt and pepper to taste
¹/₄ cup cilantro chopped

Whisk the flour and baking soda in the water until the batter is smooth. Add the seasoning and cilantro.

GINGER SCALLION MAYONNAISE

To a cup of preferably homemade mayonnaise add:

3 Tbsp. chopped scallions
2 Tbsp. minced fresh ginger
juice of 1 medium lime
1 dash of Tabasco® sauce

Use the ginger scallion mayonnaise as a dipping sauce.

Individual Rack of Colorado Raised Lamb
Caribbean Mustard Coated

No doubt about it, the French have a way with food. This is an outstanding example. Do not lose this mint sauce recipe!

Serves 4

2 trimmed and Frenched domestic racks of lamb (ordered from your butcher)
salt and pepper

Coating Mix (combine in a bowl)

2 cups Dusseldorf mustard
3 Tbsp. sweet sherry wine
1/4 cup Myers's® Rum

1/2 cup light brown sugar
2 tsp. garlic crushed

Breading Mix (combine in a bowl)

2 cups bread crumbs
3 Tbsp. rosemary, chopped

Preheat your oven to 400°F. Season your rack of lamb with salt and pepper, place on a roasting pan side up and blanch it for 10 minutes. Let it rest for 5 minutes. Take the rack by the bones and dip the side in the mustard coating, then in the bread crumbs and shake the excess. Place the racks back in the roasting pan with water removed. Turn your oven down to 375°F. and roast 5 to 7 minutes for medium rare. Remove lamb from the oven, let it rest 5 minutes and carve it into portions.

Mint Sauce

1/2 cup Cabernet Sauvignon
2 sliced shallots
2 cups veal stock

2 Tbsp. fresh chopped mint
2 Tbsp. soft butter
salt and pepper to taste

In a small pan, combine the Cabernet Sauvignon and shallots over high heat. Reduce by half. Pour in veal stock and continue to reduce till 2/3 cup remain. Remove from the heat and add the fresh mint. Let stand for 1/2 hour, then strain. Bring back to a boil and whisk in butter. Season to taste.

SAUTÉED FLORIDA CRAB CAKE

WITH CHARDONNAY LOBSTER SAUCE

Yields approximately 12 crabcakes

2 Tbsp. olive oil
1 cup minced celery
1/2 cup red bell peppers, diced
4 cups bread crumbs
2 eggs, whipped
2 Tbsp. chopped parsley
1 tsp. Tabasco® sauce
salt and white pepper to taste

1 1/2 lb. blue crab meat, shells removed
1 cup minced onions
1/2 cup green bell peppers, diced
4 egg yolks
2 Tbsp. chopped dill
flour
1 Tbsp. soy sauce

Lightly sauté in olive oil, bell peppers, onions and celery until tender. Transfer and let it cool. Gently whip egg yolks, soy sauce and Tabasco. In a bowl combine crabmeat, bell peppers mixture and herbs. Then fold in the egg mixture and three cups of bread crumbs. Check the seasoning and chill. Divide the crab cake mixture and form the cakes. Then lightly flour both sides, dip it into the whole eggs and coat with remaining bread crumbs.

Place on a tray in the refrigerator.

CHARDONNAY LOBSTER SAUCE

2 lobster heads, shells cut into pieces, or
   shrimp shells
1/2 cup minced shallots
3 oz. tomato paste
1 1/2 cups heavy cream

1 Tbsp. olive oil
1 Tbsp. minced garlic
3 cups Chardonnay
1 small bouquet garni
salt and white pepper to taste

Sweat the shells in olive oil until they turn red. Then add the shallots and garlic for 3 minutes. Add the tomato paste.

Deglaze with the Chardonnay and reduce to 1/2 cup. Add the heavy cream and reduce by half. Strain the sauce through a fine mesh and season. Keep warm.

SET UP AND SERVE

Melt 1 Tbsp. of butter with 2 Tbsp. of olive oil over medium high heat and sauté the crab cakes until golden brown on each side, then drain on a paper towel. Ladle the sauce on a warm plate and arrange 2 crab cakes on the center of each plate. Serve immediately.

Rum Basted Baked Bananas
with Coconut Ice Cream

One of the best desserts we had. Also wonderful with vanilla ice cream. By the way, Brooks makes their own coconut ice cream for this dessert.

Banana Rum Mixture

¹/₄ lb. unsalted butter
¹/₄ cup light brown sugar
¹/₄ cup dark brown sugar

Bring to a boil in a sauce pan, whisking constantly. Add two bananas sliced at an angle. Heat throughout.

Add

1 oz. Barbados rum
¹/₂ oz. banana liqueur

Keep cooking for one minute. Have 4 goblets half-filled with coconut ice cream. Spoon the banana rum mixture on top. An excellent addition to this recipe is a spoonful of whipped cream and a sprinkle of toasted macadamia nuts.

To obtain a clear bouillon (chicken or fish), put all the ingredients in a pot and start with cold water.

CAFÉ ARUGULA

3150 N. Federal Hwy. • Lighthouse Point, Florida 33064 • (954) 785-7732

Dick Cingolani is the dynamic owner of Café Arugula, as well as its sister restaurant, Arugula Grill in West Palm Beach. Originally from Cape Cod, Dick was brought up harvesting mussels, digging clams, lobstering and collecting wild berries and mushrooms from local woods. From this background came a love of cooking, eating and freshness of ingredients. Cingolani's passion for fresh foods results in everything possible being homemade on the premises, including breads, sun-dried tomatoes, mozzarella cheese, ice cream and desserts.

To say the Café Arugula is eclectic is conservative. His ever changing menu features local Florida foods with the flavors of the Mediterranean, Southwest and the Orient. This intimate restaurant has received every major award, including the readers' choice for overall Favorite Restaurant in South Florida Magazine for 1995, as well as Florida Trend's Golden Spoon Award as one of Florida's top 20 restaurants. A special tip of the hat to Dick and his wife, Carolann, for spearheading numerous events benefitting both local and national charities.

Thai Shrimp Tacos

This is so good! The Far East meets the Southwest in this special fusion that won first place in the Ft. Lauderdale Museum of Arts culinary competition.
Serves 6 as an Appetizer

Taco Shells

6 egg roll skins   *4 cups peanut oil for deep frying*

Cut egg roll skins into 3-inch circles. Place in a taco frying mold (available at oriental stores) and deep fry for a minute or so, until crisp. Remove and continue to fry the rest of the shells. Pre-made taco shells may be used, but the flavor will be totally different.

Taco Filling

24 medium shrimp, shelled and deveined   *2 Tbsp. finely chopped garlic*
3 Tbsp. butter   *3 cups shredded lettuce*
1 1/4 cups Thai chili sauce   *1 cup diced tomatoes*

In a saute pan large enough to hold all the shrimp, heat butter and garlic, add the shrimp and cook two minutes. Add the chili sauce and cook another minute or so, until the shrimp are done. To serve, place a little chopped lettuce in the taco shell, top with diced tomato and lay on a plate. Place the shrimp so it spills out of the shell. Drizzle with chili sauce from the pan and spoon a little Coconut Curry Sauce on the side of the shrimp. Garnish with shredded carrots and black sesame seeds if desired. All ingredients are available at Oriental stores.

COCONUT CURRY SAUCE

2 16-oz. cans unsweetened
   Thai coconut milk
1/2 tsp. turmeric

1 1/2 Tbsp. Thai fish sauce
1 tsp. Thai red curry paste (or to taste)

In a sauce pan, reduce the coconut milk until it coats the back of a spoon. Whisk in all the remaining ingredients and taste for seasonings.

THREE BERRY PECAN CRISP

This is one of our favorite desserts. The selection of berries depends on the seasons and availability, use what is available and fresh. This can be made with just blueberries or strawberries or any combination.

Serves 8 to 10

6 cups assorted berries, blueberries,
   strawberries and raspberries
1/2 cup sugar, (depending on sweetness of
   berries)

3 Tbsp. of instant tapioca
1/4 cup flour
juice and zest of one lemon

Mix all together in a bowl, tossing gently to mix without breaking berries. Pour berries in a 9x9 inch pan.

TOPPING

1 1/2 cups flour
1/2 cup brown sugar
1/2 cup granulated sugar
1/2 cup pecan pieces, toasted in oven until
   crisp, about 3 minutes

1 1/2 sticks cold butter, cut into 1/4-inch
   pieces
1/2 tsp. allspice
1/2 tsp. cinnamon

Mix all dry ingredients in a bowl, add butter cubes and break up with your fingers, or use a pastry cutter to mix flour and butter into a pebble consistency. Do not over mix, when you take some of the mixture in your hand and squeeze, the mixture should stick together. Top berries with mixture by squeezing together in small lumps no bigger than one inch, continue until all of the berries are covered and you use all the topping. Bake in 350°F. oven for 30 minutes until top is brown and berries are bubbly.

Serve warm with your favorite ice cream. This crisp can be made ahead, just refrigerate and when ready to serve, pop it in the microwave for a minute or two.

MEDITERRANEAN BAKED SHRIMP

Everybody loves shrimp, and when they're combined with cheese, tomatoes, prosciutto and pasta, a good thing just got better.

Serves 6

24 large shrimp	1 lb. mozzarella, shredded
flour to dust shrimp	3 cups marinara sauce
6 Tbsp. olive oil	salt and pepper to taste
6 thin slices of prosciutto	1 lb. linguine, cooked al dénte

Peel shrimp, leaving tail shell on, and cut all the way through, up the back to the shell. Wash out sand vein and dry. Dredge in flour and sauté in olive oil, and place in pan uniformly so the shrimp looks like a "w" with the tip of the tail in the middle. Cook one minute on each side until they just turn pink. Season with salt and pepper, remove from heat and drain off oil. Wrap each shrimp in a piece of prosciutto, stand up in an individual casserole or baking sheet, lining up shrimp in a row, cover with marinara sauce and then the cheese. Bake in a 375°F. oven until all is hot and bubbly, about 5 minutes. Serve over pasta with more sauce if desired.

CHAMPAGNE SCAMPI

Here is an unusual version of the traditional scampi - it uses champagne instead of white wine and is seasoned with fresh rosemary. We thoroughly enjoyed this.

Serves 4

24 large shrimp	1½ cups champagne
½ cup flour	1 Tbsp. fresh lemon juice
2 Tbsp. butter	2 Tbsp. chopped fresh Italian parsley
2 Tbsp. olive oil	1½ cups chopped fresh tomato, peeled and
2 Tbsp. garlic, chopped	seeded
2 Tbsp. rosemary, chopped	salt and pepper to taste

Shell and devein the shrimp, leaving tail shell on. Put butter and oil in sauté pan over medium high heat, dust shrimp in flour and sauté until just pink, one or two minutes, add garlic and rosemary, cook one minute, do not brown. Remove shrimp from pan, turn heat on high, add champagne, lemon juice, tomatoes, parsley and reduce until thick. Return shrimp and heat through, season to taste and serve over pasta.

World's Best Bread Pudding

Instead of bread, the Arugula Grill uses pecan cinnamon rolls or cinnamon-style rolls. Use the kind that is available to you. This is a very rich, "company's coming" dessert.

Custard

4 cups of half-and-half
2 cups of cream
3 cinnamon sticks

2 star anise
2 Tbsp. of lemon zest
2 Tbsp. of orange zest

Bring these ingredients to a boil, remove from heat and let steep for two hours, reserve.

about 2 or 3 pounds of cinnamon rolls
8 egg yolks
1 cup sugar

2 tsp. vanilla
1 Tbsp. of Grand Marnier®
$^1/_4$ tsp. of nutmeg

Whisk egg yolks, sugar and flavorings until well mixed, then add the cooled custard mixture. Cut cinnamon rolls into quarters if very large and put in a 8x13 two-inch deep pan or similar size, use two pans if need be. Pour custard mixture over rolls, straining out zests etc. If all of the custards do not fit at one time, let pudding rest 15 minutes and add more custard if necessary. Bake in 350°F. oven for 35 to 45 minutes until custard is set and firm. Serve warm or cold. Chef Cingolani serves his pudding with a creme anglaise sauce spiked with Jamaican dark rum.

To avoid burning milk when boiling, first wet the pan with cold water.

DARREL & OLIVER'S CAFÉ MAXX

2601 E. Atlantic Blvd. • Pompano, Florida 33062 • (954) 782-0606

Darrel Broek has an academic degree in Hospitality and Food Service, and Oliver Saucy has a solid classical culinary background and is a graduate of the prestigious Culinary Institute of America in Hyde Park, New York where his father is a Chef/Instructor. When these two joined forces and purchased the Café Maxx in 1988, they had already established a tradition of excellence and a reputation as influential leaders in creating what has evolved into the distinctive South Florida regional cuisine. The two have continued to extend the legacy of Café Maxx by moving beyond the primary California cuisine to create an eclectic blend of Oriental, Creole, Caribbean, Southwestern and classic European.

Although many local and national tributes have been paid to Chef Oliver's accomplishments, perhaps his most significant achievement was being invited in 1993 to create a dinner at the James Beard House in Manhattan; he was then named one of the nation's top five finalists for the coveted 1993 "Rising Star Chef" award by the James Beard Foundation.

It is sufficient to say that Darrel & Oliver's Café Maxx has won numerous awards, including the celebrated Golden Spoon by *Florida Trend Magazine*, Best of Award of Excellence from the Wine Spectator and a DiRoNA as one of the Distinguished Restaurants of North America. One of the primary reasons there is so much interest in Florida's cuisine is the tremendous amount of culinary talent the state has attracted. These two are outstanding examples of this talent.

SWEET ONION CRUSTED SNAPPER
WITH MADEIRA SAUCE

*The thin layer of sweet, caramelized red onions is perfect
with the snapper and Madeira sauce.*
Serves 6

6 8-oz. yellowtail snapper filets	1 Tbsp. lemon juice
2 lbs. red onions, peeled and sliced	1 tsp. garlic, chopped
2 Tbsp. olive oil	1 tsp. shallots, chopped
1/4 cup plus 1 Tbsp. balsamic vinegar	1/2 tsp. tomato paste
2 Tbsp. plus one tsp. light brown sugar	2 tsp. heavy cream
salt and pepper	3 tsp. butter
1/4 cup Madeira wine	1 tsp. olive oil

For Onions

In a large shallow pan, heat 2 tablespoons of olive oil over medium to high heat. Add onions. Cook onions until browned, but not crisp. Add vinegar, brown sugar and salt and pepper to taste; reduce heat and continue to cook until all liquid has evaporated from pan and onions are well browned and caramelized. Remove from heat and cool thoroughly. This can be done a day or two ahead and the onions refrigerated.

For the Fish

Prepare snapper, removing skin and bones; rinse. Arrange filets on cookie sheet and lightly season with salt and pepper as desired. Using carmelized onions, pack on a light crust, (approximately ⅛ inch) dividing mixture between filets. Do not allow crust to get too thick at any one area. Can be done two hours in advance.

For the Sauce

In a heavy sauce pan over medium heat, cook wine, garlic, shallots, tomato paste, lemon and cream until mixture is reduced. It should be half or two-thirds of the starting volume. Whisk in the butter to form an emulsion. Strain and season with salt and pepper. Keep warm until needed. Cook snapper, onion side down, in a hot skillet with 1 tsp. olive oil. When onions are browned and crisp, turn carefully. Place in a baking pan and bake in 375°F. oven for 4 - 6 minutes or until filets are done. Serve sauce on plate with fish on top.

SEAFOOD FETTUCCINE WITH TOMATOES

Sautéed marinated gulf seafood with garlic and tomatoes. The types of seafood and type of pasta can be interchanged with what is available at the given time.
Serves 6

12 large shrimp	*salt and pepper, as needed*
2 spiny lobster tails	*6 to 8 ripe tomatoes*
6 oz. lump crab meat	*¼ cup onions, chopped*
6 sea scallops	*2 Tbsp. chopped garlic*
1 Tbsp. chopped shallots	*1 bunch chopped basil*
1 Tbsp. lemon juice	*2 Tbsp. chopped parsley*
2 Tbsp. white wine	*2 Tbsp. butter*
2 Tbsp. olive oil	*12 oz. fresh fettucine*

Peel, seed and chop tomatoes.

Clean shrimp, dice lobster similar to size of shrimp. Marinate with scallops, shrimp, oil, wine, shallots and lemon juice for 30 minutes. Make certain no shell fragments remain in the crabmeat.

In a hot skillet, sauté marinated seafood in olive oil. When half cooked add onion and garlic, sauté briefly. Add tomatoes and cook until seafood is tender. Add the crabmeat, butter, herbs and seasonings. Toss with fettucine and divide onto plates. Garnish with green beans.

GRILLED SHRIMP BROCHETTE
WITH BANANA LIME SAUCE

The banana lime sauce gives this superb dish a great tropical flair.
Serves 3

FOR THE SHRIMP

18 large shrimp, peeled and deveined
1 tsp. shallots, chopped
1 tsp. garlic, chopped
1 Tbsp. olive oil
1 Tbsp. white wine
1 lime, juice only
salt and pepper, to taste

FOR THE SAUCE

3 ripe bananas, peeled
1/4 cup low fat mayonnaise
1/2 cup plain lowfat yogurt
1 Tbsp. Dijon mustard
1 lime, juice only
1/4 tsp. cayenne pepper, or more to taste
1 Tbsp. chives, chopped
salt and pepper, to taste

THE SHRIMP

Marinate the shrimp in the shallot, garlic, oil, wine, lime juice and seasonings and place on skewers for ease of grilling. Let stand in refrigerator for 30 minutes to 4 hours prior to grilling.

THE SAUCE

Place all ingredients except chives in the food processor and purée until smooth. Fold in chives and reserve until ready to serve. Can be prepared up to 8 hours in advance. Grill shrimp over high heat in order to lightly caramelize, and then turn skewer and baste with banana mixture as you would BBQ. Be careful not to over cook the shrimp. The shrimp should be cooked 2 to 3 minutes on one side, then for another 1 to 2 minutes after turning. If using a gas grill, leave the lid down to hold the heat. Serve immediately with remaining banana sauce for dipping.

FLORIDA GOLDEN TOMATO GAZPACHO
WITH GULF SHRIMP

A chilled soup of Florida-grown yellow beefsteak tomatoes (recipe also works very well with red tomatoes). Served with jumbo shrimp . . . absolutely wonderful.
Serves 10

FOR THE SOUP

*4 to 6 ripe tomatoes, 2 cups of pulp needed
    after peeled, seeded*
1 European seedless cucumbers, peeled
1 yellow bell pepper
1 celery stalk
1 small red onion
1 tsp. finely garlic, chopped
1 tsp. finely shallots, chopped
1 to 2 tsp. finely chopped jalapeño pepper
1 Tbsp. opal basil, or green basil
1 Tbsp. parsley or cilantro, chopped
1 oz. light wine vinegar
2 to 3 oz. extra virgin olive oil
salt and pepper, to taste
sugar, to taste

FOR THE SHRIMP

20 to 30 jumbo shrimp
1 Tbsp. garlic, chopped
1 Tbsp. shallots, chopped
1/2 cup white wine
2 cups water
1 lemon, juice only
salt and pepper, to taste

Peel and seed tomatoes by removing core and scoring an "X" on the bottom of each tomato. Plunge into boiling water for 30-60 seconds and immediately shock in ice water. Remove peel and discard. Cut tomato in half and squeeze pulp into fine strainer to separate liquid from seeds, reserve any of this liquid to finish soup later. Cut cucumber into pieces that will fit into meat grinder attachment or food processor. Remove seeds and core from the bell pepper and jalapeño and roughly chop.

Purée tomatoes, cucumber, celery, onion & peppers by passing through the meat grinding attachment into a medium bevel. Use a piece of plastic wrap on the end of the grinder to prevent splattering of vegetables. If meat grinder is not available, utilize a food processor using the pulse option; purée in 2 or 3 parts to evenly grind vegetables. Be careful not to over process, mixture should be a little chunky. Can be made 8 hours in advance up to this point.

Finish the soup by adding to the tomato mixture the garlic, shallots, herbs, vinegar, oil, reserved tomato juice, water and season to taste with salt, pepper and sugar. Can be made 1-2 hours in advance at this point. Let stand at least 30 minutes before serving in order to marry all the flavors.

To prepare the shrimp, in medium-large sauce pan heat garlic, shallots, white wine, lemon juice, salt and pepper to a boil. Add shrimp and cover sauce pan, bring back to simmer stirring occasionally. Be careful not to overcook shrimp, should take 3-5 minutes depending on size of shrimp. Strain and immediately shock in ice water. Peel and devein shrimp and reserve until service. Can be prepared 8 hours in advance.

To serve, on medium sized plate or soup bowl, cover plate with gazpacho and top with poached shrimp. To enhance presentation, also top with a colorful assortment of mixed baby greens (optional).

CONCH FRITTERS
WITH MANGO & HABAÑERO SALSA

Conch fritters are leavened with beaten egg whites then pan fried "pancake" style, served with mango salsa. Lobster, shrimp, lump crab or salmon may be substituted if conch is not available.
Serves 24

1 cup conch, cleaned, diced in 1/8" cubes	1 Tbsp. sliced scallions
1 Tbsp. corn	1 Tbsp. chopped cilantro
1/4 cup red bell peppers	1/4 cup yellow corn meal, or semolina
1 Tbsp. red onions, diced	1 1/2 cups all-purpose flour
1 tsp. chopped garlic	1 Tbsp. baking powder
1 tsp. chopped shallots	1 tsp. salt
1 tsp. chopped Scotch bonnet pepper	1 Tbsp. black pepper
2 Tbsp. lime juice	1/2 to 3/4 cup milk
2 Tbsp. olive oil	
4 eggs, separated	

In a medium bowl combine conch and vegetables with garlic, shallots, lime juice, olive oil and Scotch bonnet peppers (you may substitute jalapeño). Season to taste with salt and pepper. Marinate for 1 - 3 hours.

Separate eggs and reserve whites, then combine yolks with marinating conch mixture. Sift remaining dry ingredients and mix carefully by adding 1/2 of the flour to the egg and conch mixture. Then stir in the milk and add remaining flour at the same time in order to achieve a thick batter (adjust with additional milk if necessary). Let conch batter rest for 1 hour.

Whip egg whites to soft peaks. In order to keep the "air" in the beaten egg whites, fold whites gently into the conch batter one-third at a time, leaving small "streams" of egg whites throughout the mixture (mixing all the way loses the "air" necessary to lighten the fritters). Immediately fry heaping tablespoon size pancakes in a medium hot black steel skillet with peanut oil until golden brown on both sides. Be careful the pancake doesn't get too thick for it will not cook enough in the middle without requiring oven time. Drain on paper towels and season with salt and pepper. Serve dolloped with ripe mango salsa.

Mango & Habañero Salsa

Serves 6
3 mangos, depending on size, diced small
1/2 cup red bell peppers, diced small
2 Tbsp. habañero pepper, chopped fine,
*   or to taste*
2 Tbsp. chives
2 Tbsp. cilantro, optional
2 Tbsp. virgin olive oil
salt and pepper, to taste
1 tsp. red wine vinegar
1/2 cup lime juice
salt and pepper to taste

In a medium bowl, combine all ingredients and season to taste with salt and pepper. Chill for two hours prior to serving to allow flavors to mature.

Add a pinch of salt when beating egg whites to make them firmer.

BON GUSTO! RISTORANTE

5640 N. Federal Hwy. • Ft. Lauderdale, Florida 33308 • (954) 771-9635

Born in Italy, Chef/Owner Antonio Cerone attended culinary school in Rome and worked as an apprentice in some of that cities finest restaurants. Chef Cerone's culinary style reflects his classical training, with superb creations of classic Italian and Continental Cuisine. In 1988 Chef Cerone joined forces with his wife, Ann, as hostess and opened Bon Gusto!

The menu and cuisine of Bon Gusto! embodies exactly what is so appealing in a quality restaurant where a couple handles the purchasing, cooking and management, and handles it with an absolute commitment to quality and the enjoyment of its guests.

LINGUINE AL BON GUSTO

This dish is so easy to make and absolutely out of this world!

Serves 4

$1^1/_2$ lb. linguine pasta
4 Tbsp. olive oil
$^1/_2$ lb. large shrimp, cut in pieces
12 fresh clams, rinsed and cleaned
3 cloves fresh garlic, minced

1 bunch scallions
$^1/_2$ lb. mushrooms, sliced
5 large ripe tomatoes, chopped
$^1/_4$ cup dry white wine
fresh Italian parsley to taste, chopped

In a very hot sauté pan, add olive oil, shrimp, garlic and clams. When garlic is lightly roasted, add scallions, mushrooms and white wine. Cook until wine evaporates, then add tomatoes which have been previously boiled in a separate pan. Cook until clams open. Add cooked linguine to sauce and toss with parsley. Serve immediately.

TORTELLINI ANNABELLA

Serves 4

2 lb. tortellini (meat or cheese)
$^1/_2$ lb. fresh mushrooms
2 oz. prosciutto
2 Tbsp. brandy

$^1/_2$ cup fresh grated Parmesan cheese
4 Tbsp. butter
2 cups (1 pint) heavy cream

In a sauce pan, sauté mushrooms and prosciutto in butter for 5 minutes. Remove from fire and add brandy, flambé if desired. Add cream, cooked tortellini and boil for a few minutes to reduce. Stir in freshly grated Parmesan, and serve immediately.

VEAL CAPRICIOSI

The stuffed scalloppine may be made in advance for easy entertaining.
Serves 4

12 large veal scallopine, well flattened
¹/₂ lb. mushrooms, sliced
2 oz. prosciutto, julienne
1 bunch scallions
8 Tbsp. butter
¹/₂ cup dry white wine

small package fresh spinach (cooked & drained)
1¹/₄ cups fresh mozzarella
4 Tbsp. olive oil
1 cup chicken broth
flour for dredging

To make stuffing, in a pan, sauté mushrooms in 2 tablespoons butter. In a separate pan, sauté scallions and prosciutto with 2 tablespoons butter, then combine with mushrooms and add half of wine. When wine has evaporated, let the stuffing cool.

Squeeze dry and chop the spinach. Add the spinach and the mozzarella cheese to the stuffing mix.

Place 1 tablespoon of the stuffing mix on each piece of veal and roll up to create a sausage shaped rollatini. Close with a tooth pick and then roll each one in flour. Sauté in olive oil until browned.

Drain oil. Add remaining wine and butter, and sauté until evaporated. Add the broth, cover and cook slowly for 10 minutes, making sure the broth does not evaporate. Serve immediately with pasta.

PRANZO DEL PESCATORE

It's amazing what can be performed with a large sauté pan, fresh seafood, a few friends . . .
and a recipe from Bon Gusto!
Serves 4

2 lobster tails, split into 4 total pieces
20 fresh clams, rinsed, cleaned
20 fresh mussels, cleaned, bearded
4 thick pieces of fish (tuna or swordfish)
1 lb. calamari, sliced
1 Tbsp. diced garlic

3 oz. dry white wine
1 Tbsp. Italian parsley, chopped
¹/₄ cup olive oil
28 oz. peeled, diced tomatoes
flour for dredging

Put a large pan on the burner. When hot, pour in olive oil and add lobster and fish which has been lightly dredged in flour. When golden, turn over and add garlic and continue to cook for 2 minutes, then add remaining seafood ingredients and cook for another 2 minutes.

Add wine. When almost evaporated, add tomatoes and parsley and cook until clams and mussels open. Serve immediately with pasta. If sauce is too liquid, remove seafood and reduce until desired texture is reached.

EAST CITY GRILL

505 North Atlantic Boulevard • Fort Lauderdale, Florida 33304 • (954) 565 5569

The 1996 New Year was ushered in with a bang in Fort Lauderdale with the opening of the wildly anticipated East City Grill, owned and operated by Darrel Broek and Oliver Saucy, the people behind Darrel & Oliver's Cafe' Maxx in Pompano. The timing could not have been better, with Cafe' Maxx recently receiving the respected Zagat Guide award as Broward County's top restaurant.

East City Grill is located in the center of Fort Lauderdale's refurbished beach front, just one mile north of fashionable Las Olas Blvd. The menu and atmosphere is completely different than Cafe' Maxx, featuring the intriguing Caribbean, Asian and Southwest flavors, combined with the best of South Florida's tropical influence. In addition to indoor dining, East City Grill features a spacious open-air dining terrace overlooking the Atlantic Ocean.

Saucy is noted as one of the region's premier masters of New World cuisine. His "right on" instincts for ingredients that work perfectly together, combined with his classical training, produce distinctive recipes with wonderful flavor.

SALMON WITH DILL CHIVE BEURRE BLANC

There is a special magic that exists between salmon and dill. The simple elegance of the dill chive beurre blanc makes this dish very special.

Serves 4

4 6-oz. salmon filets	3/8 cup white wine
3 Tbsp. virgin olive oil	1/2 lemon, juice only
3 Tbsp. fresh dill, chopped	1/8 cup heavy cream
3 Tbsp. fresh chives, chopped	1/4 tsp. shallots, chopped
1/4 tsp. salt	1/4 tsp. garlic, chopped
1/4 tsp. white pepper	6 Tbsp. butter

Mix together the chopped dill and chives. Brush the filets with olive oil and lightly coat with half of the dill and chives mixture, reserving the other half for the beurre blanc.

In a hot sauté pan place the remaining olive oil and sear the salmon on both sides. If needed, finish the salmon in a 350°F. oven until done to taste.

For the Dill Chive Beurre Blanc, combine the salt, white pepper, wine, lemon juice, cream, shallots and garlic in a sauce pan and reduce by half. Whisk in the butter a tablespoon at a time to achieve a smooth consistency. Do not bring to a boil. Add the remaining dill and chives. Serve over the salmon filets.

Asparagus & Warm Goat Cheese Salad
With Lemon & Hazelnut Vinaigrette
Serves 4

4 ¹/₂-inch slices of goat cheese
1 egg white
1 Tbsp. water
¹/₂ cup toasted hazelnuts, ground
¹/₂ cup bread crumbs

24 asparagus
¹/₂ cup toasted hazelnuts for garnish
3 small heads mixed baby field greens
3 Tbsp olive oil
Lemon & Hazelnut Vinaigrette

In a small bowl, beat the egg white and water with a fork. In another small bowl, combine the ground hazelnuts and bread crumbs. Coat the slices of goat cheese with the egg white mix, then coat the slices with the nut mixture, applying pressure with your fingers to make certain the breading sticks. Reserve the breaded goat cheese in the refrigerator until ready to use. This can be prepared up to 6 hours in advance.

In a medium saucepan or steamer, add asparagus to boiling water and cook for 2-5 minutes, depending on the size of the asparagus. Remove and plunge into ice water to stop the cooking process. The asparagus should be firm and vibrant green.

In a non-stick sauté pan over medium-high heat, add the olive oil. Add the goat cheese and sauté quickly on both sides until golden brown. Arrange the asparagus on each plate, top with the mixed field greens and top with the warm goat cheese. Drizzle the Lemon & Hazelnut Vinaigrette over the greens and asparagus. Garnish with ¹/₂ cup whole toasted hazelnuts and slices of lemon on the rim of the plate if desired.

Lemon & Hazelnut Vinaigrette

1 egg yolk or 1 Tbsp. mayonnaise
1 tsp. Dijon mustard
1 tsp. honey
1 Tbsp. fresh lemon juice
1 tsp. lemon zest

1 tsp. white wine vinegar
6 Tbsp. hazelnut oil
1 Tbsp. chopped chives
salt & freshly ground pepper to taste

In a small bowl, whisk the egg yolk, Dijon mustard, honey, lemon juice, lemon zest and vinegar until thoroughly incorporated. Add the hazelnut oil 1 Tbsp. at a time, whisking in between to ensure a smooth dressing. Fold in the chives and season to taste with salt and pepper. Thin with a little cold water if too thick. Cover and reserve in the refrigerator until ready to serve. This can be prepared up to 6 hours in advance.

East City Grill Cioppino

This West Coast classic is adapted by Oliver Saucy to Southern Florida. Almost any combination of seafood in this recipe would be delicious. However, Oliver recommends that the clams and/or mussels remain in the dish because the "liquor" they release is integral to the flavor. Our test group fell in love with this dish.

Serves 4

1 Tbsp. garlic, chopped
1 small onion, diced
³/₈ cup olive oil
³/₄ cup white wine
8-12 clams, depending on size
4-6 stone crab claws, cracked
2-3 Florida lobster tails, cut in half
8-12 mussels, depending on size

8-12 shrimp, depending on size
8-12 sea scallops, depending on size
1 cup tomatoes, seeded, peeled &
   chopped
1 cup tomato sauce
1 tsp. orange zest
¹/₈ tsp. saffron threads, or to taste
4 Tbsp. fresh basil, chopped
1 Tbsp. fresh tarragon, chopped

In a medium-large stock pot, sauté garlic and onion in the olive oil over medium heat for 1-2 minutes. Add clams, stone crabs, lobster and white wine. Cover tightly and bring to a boil for 2 minutes, allowing seafood to steam. Stir and add the mussels, shrimp, scallops, tomatoes, tomato sauce, orange zest and saffron. Cover tightly and simmer until seafood is cooked, approximately 5 to 6 minutes, stirring occasionally. Discard any of the clams or mussels that do not open Add basil, tarragon and season with salt and freshly ground pepper as desired.

Serve the steamed seafood and its broth arranged in a large bowl with pasta or steamed rice.

IL PORCINO

8037 West Sample Road • Coral Springs, Florida 33065 • (954) 344-9446

Il Porcino celebrates its name by specializing in sumptuous dishes prepared with Porcino and other wild mushrooms. Chef/Owner Filippo Ascione agrees with the Ancient Romans who proclaimed mushrooms "Food of the Gods." "The earthy, woodsy aroma," says Chef Ascione, "reminds us that food is not just nourishment - it is a source of pleasure for the senses."

At Il Porcino everyone is treated like they are guests in the Ascione's home. There is a warm feeling the moment you step in the door and are greeted by Filippo's wife, Victoria. Intimate, with only 50 seats, guests are pampered with warm hospitality and gracious service. The chef's Northern Italian cuisine is classic and consistent, and the ingredients are always the finest and freshest available. At Il Porcino, guests can have their heart's desire, whether or not it is on the menu.

In addition to Florida Trend's Top 200 Award, the readers of the South Florida Magazine have voted Il Porcino the "Best Italian Restaurant in Broward County" for three consecutive years.

WILD MUSHROOMS OVER MOZZARELLA

A wonderful dish with a savor rich mushroom flavor.
Serves 2

$^1/_2$ cup fresh shiitake mushrooms	2 cloves garlic, finely chopped
$^1/_2$ cup fresh oyster mushrooms	1 tsp. fresh parsley, chopped
$^1/_2$ cup fresh Portobello mushrooms	2 medium plum tomatoes, chopped
$^1/_2$ cup dry porcini mushrooms	salt
4 medium slices mozzarella cheese, $^1/_8$-inch thick	pinch crushed red pepper flakes
	1 Tbsp. dry white wine
4 Tbsp. extra virgin olive oil	1 Tbsp. dry cooking Marsala wine

Soak the dried porcini mushrooms in lukewarm water for 20 minutes to soften them and release the sand particles. When ready, gently lift porcini mushrooms out of the water, but do not disturb any of the sediment at the bottom. Reserve this porcini water.

Wipe the fresh mushrooms (shiitake, oyster and Portobello) with a damp cloth to remove any soil, and slice. Heat the oil in a large skillet. Add garlic and sauté until golden. Add parsley, mushrooms, tomatoes. Season with salt and red pepper flakes. Cook over high heat until moisture evaporates. Add the Marsala wine and cook until it has evaporated. Add the white wine. Stir gently for 3 minutes over medium heat. If mushrooms become too dry, add some porcini water — take a Tbsp. of porcini water from the top, without disturbing the sediment at the bottom of the bowl.

In the center of a platter arrange mozzarella slices overlapping in a circle. Transfer mushrooms over mozzarella. Garnish with fresh chopped parsley. Serve immediately.

LINGUINE AL FRUTTI DI MARE AL CARTOCCIO

Great Fun, Great Flavor. Like a clambake in the kitchen.
Serves 2

10 oz. linguine pasta
3 Tbsp. extra virgin olive oil
2 cloves garlic, chopped
1 Tbsp. fresh chopped parsley
4 fresh plum tomatoes, chopped coarsely
10 littleneck clams, rinse, washed

10 medium mussels, rinsed, washed,
   bearded
4 medium shrimp, peeled, deveined
1 Tbsp. dry white wine
salt
crushed red pepper flakes
2 - 12"x 25" sheets of aluminum foil

Preheat the oven to 450°F. In a large bowl, mix all the ingredients together, except the pasta, and season with salt and red pepper flakes to taste.

Cook the linguine in plenty of boiling, salted water for 3 minutes. Drain while pasta is still "hard." Flatten the sheets of aluminum foil and place half of the pasta in the center of one half of the foil and top with half the seafood mixture. Fold the other half of the foil over the pasta and tightly seal all three sides by pinching together. Repeat this procedure with the second sheet of aluminum foil. This will form a leakproof and steamproof pouch called a "cartoccio," in which the ingredients will cook. Place the two cartoccio in a large oven-proof skillet or baking dish and cover bottom with ¼-inch of water. Place pan in preheated oven and cook for 3½ minutes. Carefully open cartoccio and transfer contents to a plate — serve immediately.

FETTUCCINE WITH PESTO, SUNDRIED TOMATOES & TOASTED PINE NUTS

Serves 2

PESTO SAUCE

2 packed cups of fresh basil leaves, washed
   and thoroughly dried
2 cloves garlic, peeled
1 Tbsp. pine nuts
½ cup freshly grated Parmesan cheese
½ cup virgin olive oil

10 oz. fettuccine pasta
2 Tbsp. unsalted butter
4 Tbsp. pesto sauce
2 oz. sundried tomatoes
1 Tbsp. pine nuts
1 Tbsp. grated Parmesan cheese
salt and freshly ground black pepper
   to taste

To prepare pesto sauce: In a blender or food processor, blend basil, garlic, pine nuts, Parmesan cheese and olive oil into a sauce. Reserve 4 Tbsp. for recipe. Remaining pesto can be preserved.

Place the sundried tomatoes in boiling water for $1^1/_2$ minutes to soften. Drain and dry gently with a paper towel. Chop coarsely and set aside.

Heat a skillet over medium heat. Put pine nuts in a skillet to lightly brown, shaking the skillet every few seconds to prevent burning. When golden in color, add butter. When butter is melted, add sundried tomatoes. Sauté for 15 seconds. Add the pesto, salt and pepper to taste, and stir for 30 seconds. Remove pan from heat.

Cook pasta in plenty of boiling, salted water until al dente. A minute before pasta is ready, add $^3/_4$ cup of the pasta water to sauce and return skillet to heat. Drain the fettucine, then immediately turn into the skillet and mix together with sauce. Transfer pasta to a dish and sprinkle with freshly grated Parmesan cheese.

VEAL CHOP
STUFFED WITH SUNDRIED TOMATOES AND GORGONZOLA CHEESE

*In an authentic Italian restaurant it is impossible to pass up
an excellent veal chop recipe like this.*
Serves 2

2 14-oz. veal chops	*4 Tbsp. dry red wine*
1¹/₂ oz. sundried tomatoes	*1 tsp. Dijon mustard*
¹/₂ cup Gorgonzola cheese	*1 Tbsp. white wine*
1 tsp. black peppercorns, crushed coarsely	*salt to taste*
1 Tbsp. virgin olive oil	
1 Tbsp. unsalted butter	

Place the sundried tomatoes in boiling water for $1^1/_2$ minutes to soften. Drain and dry gently with a paper towel. Chop coarsely and set aside.

Baste veal chops on both sides with olive oil and place under the broiler for 2 minutes on each side. Remove veal chops and butterfly cut across the center to the bone.

Stuff veal chops with the sundried tomatoes and Gorgonzola cheese. Press slightly on top of veal chop. If necessary, secure with a toothpick.

In a bowl, mix the mustard and white wine. Lightly brush this mixture on the top of the veal chops and sprinkle with crushed peppercorns. Place stuffed veal chops on a broiler pan lined with aluminum foil to capture any mixture that may seep out, and return to broiler for 3 minutes.

In a small saucepan, melt butter, add red wine, salt, and reduce to half. Arrange veal chops on a platter, top with sauce and serve immediately.

POLLO AL FUNGHI PORCINI SECCHI

The flavors of sage and porcini mushrooms are divine together.
Serves 2

4 chicken breasts, skinless, boneless
$^1/_2$ cup dried porcini mushrooms
$^1/_2$ cup virgin olive oil
1 cup all purpose flour
$^1/_2$ stick unsalted butter
$^1/_2$ tsp. dried sage

1 tsp. chopped fresh parsley
salt
freshly ground black pepper
$^1/_2$ cup dry white wine
$^3/_4$ cup chicken broth

Soak dried porcini mushrooms in warm water for 20 minutes to soften them and release sand particles. When ready, gently lift porcini mushrooms out of the water, but do not disturb any of the sediment at the bottom. Set mushrooms aside.

Lightly coat chicken breasts in flour. Heat olive oil in large skillet over high heat. Place chicken in skillet and brown on each side for 30 seconds. Transfer chicken to a platter.

In a separate skillet, add the butter and sage, then melt over medium heat. Add mushrooms and parsley to the melted butter, and season to taste with salt and freshly ground pepper.

Place the chicken in sauce and cook over high heat. Add white wine to sauce. When wine evaporates, add chicken broth and reduce heat to medium. Simmer for 10 minutes, stirring sauce to prevent sticking. Transfer to platter and serve immediately.

Never place food too closely to the rim of the plate. Use your rim as a border to create the look of elegance. The rim is the frame for your "work of art."

LE DOME

333 Sunset Drive Ft. • Lauderdale, Florida 33301 • (954) 463-3303

Le Dome's history as a premier restaurant in Ft. Lauderdale spans over 30 years. Originally established in 1963, dinner at Le Dome was French "Haute Cuisine," prepared and served by an all French staff. In 1987, Doug Mackle purchased Le Dome with the commitment to preserve the existing level of elegance and ambience. Consecutive Golden Spoon Awards are testimony to his success.

The 12th floor location of Le Dome provides beautiful views of the Atlantic Ocean and the waterways which make Ft. Lauderdale the "Venice of America." Le Dome features live piano entertainment nightly from Thanksgiving to April, and Friday and Saturday nights in the summer.

SEAFOOD FANTASIA

A distinct French touch to this delicate seafood dish.
Serves 2

8 large shrimp, peeled and deveined, tail
   on
2 oz. sea scallops
2 oz. bay scallops
1 oz. lobster meat (Le Dome uses Maine,
   Florida lobster meat will do)
2 cloves garlic, chopped
4 Tbsp. shallots, sliced
3/4 cup mushrooms, sliced
4 Tbsp. scallions, chopped

2 Tbsp. sundried tomato, chopped
2 Tbsp. tomato paste
1/4 cup dry white wine
1/2 cup chicken velouté
2 Tbsp. olive oil
4 Tbsp. butter, unsalted, cold
salt and pepper to taste
dash paprika
fresh basil to taste

Heat the olive oil in a sauté pan until it is very hot. Sauté the shrimp, sea and bay scallops for a minute or two. Remove from pan. Add to the pan the garlic, scallions, shallots, sundried tomato and mushrooms and sauté for a few minutes. Add to the pan the paprika, tomato paste, white wine and chicken velouté. Let simmer for a minute, stirring occasionally. Return the shrimp and scallops to the pan and add the lobster meat. Add the butter, and season to taste with salt, pepper and basil. Stir slightly to blend colors and ingredients, but not hard enough to break up scallops or lobster meat. Serve over cooked angel hair or fettuccine pasta.

Escargots Au Porto

A low-fat escargot dish that is superb
Serves 4

1 Tbsp. olive oil
24 pieces French snails, drained from the
    can
4 oz. spinach (fresh is best, frozen is okay)
    clean and cut into medium-to-small
    pieces.
3/4 cup fresh mushrooms, cleaned and sliced.
2 pieces shallots, finely sliced julienne
2 cloves garlic, finely chopped

1 ripe tomato, seeded, skinned and sliced
    julienne
2 Tbsp. port wine
3/8 cup veal stock (chicken stock or beef
    stock will do)
nutmeg to taste
salt and pepper to taste

Heat the olive oil in a sauté pan until it is very hot. Sauté the garlic, shallots and mushrooms, frequently tossing or stirring, until the mushrooms start to brown and exude a little moisture. Reduce heat. Add the escargots and sauté 3-4 minutes over low heat. Add the spinach and sauté until heated through. Deglaze the pan with the veal stock, then season to taste with the nutmeg, salt and pepper. Just before serving, add the julienne tomatoes. Serve with toasted garlic bread.

Mushroom Bisque

This classic presentation has a wonderful texture and flavor.
Serves 12

2 lb. fresh white (or wild) mushrooms
1 pint heavy cream
roux (flour and butter), as required
1 gal. chicken stock
1/2 lb. sliced mushrooms for garnish
1/2 cup sherry

1 cup dry white wine
1/4 cup fresh chopped parsley
1/4 cup chopped shallots
1 Tbsp. fresh garlic
salt and pepper to taste

Clean and slice the 2 lb. of fresh mushrooms. Chop the shallots and garlic. Sauté them in a large pot with some butter. Add the sliced mushrooms to the pot and sauté for about 10 minutes. Add the white wine and chicken stock to the pot. Let it reduce on medium heat for 1/2 hour. Use a hand blender or processor to purée this mixture. Add the roux to the pot until the soup is a light, creamy consistency. Strain the soup and return to the cooking pot. Add the 1/2 lb. sliced mushrooms to the soup.

Add the heavy cream. Let it cook on low heat to reduce to desired consistency. Remove from heat. Before serving, swirl in a little butter, sprinkle a little chopped parsley and add a few drops of sherry to each cup.

THE LEFT BANK RESTAURANT

216 SE 6th Avenue • Fort Lauderdale, Florida • (954) 462-5376

Nineteen years of success makes this very popular restaurant a Fort Lauderdale landmark. Owner and Chef Jean-Pierre Brehier, classically trained in France, creates his exciting and innovative "Sunshine Cuisine," also the name of his PBS television cooking show, where he is the host and chef. His contemporary cuisine combines the strong flavors of the Mediterranean — olive oil, vine-ripened tomatoes, garlic, basil and rosemary — and all the fresh seafood, tropical fruits and vegetables available in South Florida.

On the daily menu you'll find dishes such as Sesame-Seared Rare Yellowfin Tuna, Farm-Raised Domestic Venison, Red Snapper with a Confit of Bell Peppers and Vidalia Onions, and Grilled Swordfish with a Ragout of Wild Mushrooms.

Understandably, The Left Bank Restaurant has been selected by Florida Trend Magazine as one of Florida's Best Restaurants for the past nineteen years. Also, Condé Nast Magazine rated The Left Bank as one of "America's Best Restaurants."

YELLOW PEPPER & TOMATO GAZPACHO

Another terrific dish - it's easy to see why Chef Jean-Pierre is regarded so highly.
Serves 8

4 large yellow tomatoes, peeled, seeded and cut into chunks
2 yellow bell peppers, seeded and cut into chunks
2 peeled European cucumbers, peeled, halved lengthwise and seeds removed
3 garlic cloves, minced
¹/₂ white onion, chopped
1 Tbsp. rice wine vinegar
1 Tbsp. lemon juice
¹/₄ cup olive oil
¹/₂ cup chicken stock

1 small yellow Scotch bonnet, or yellow Tabasco®, or yellow habanero pepper (remove the seeds and ribs for less heat)
1 Tbsp. White Wine Worcestershire Sauce®
1 Tbsp. fresh cilantro leaves
Salt and freshly ground white pepper to taste
1 cup Chive Creme Fraiche (see following recipe)

For garnish, reserve ¹/₄ cup each of the tomatoes, peppers and cucumbers into ¹/₄-inch squares. Working in batches, in the blender combine the remaining tomatoes, peppers, cucumbers, lemon juice, garlic, onion, vinegar, olive oil, chicken stock, chili pepper and Worcestershire Sauce, then blend until very smooth. Season with salt and pepper, add the cilantro and blend for 15 to 20 more seconds. Remove from the blender, add the reserved vegetables and chill thoroughly.

After the soup is chilled, you can adjust the seasonings by adding a bit more lemon juice, salt or pepper, or perhaps a touch of Tabasco.

This soup should be served ice cold and should taste slightly spicy.

Note: Use "European" or "English" cucumbers as they are meatier and have fewer seeds. You need to peel them as you do not want the bright green to darken this beautiful soup.

CHIVE CRÈME FRAICHE

Creme fraiche has a slightly tangy, slightly nutty flavor that's wonderful. It's easy to make at home and will keep for a couple of weeks in the refrigerator. Crème fraiche is often used in cooking, because it doesn't separate when heated as sour cream can.

Yields 1 cup

1 cup heavy whipping cream
(for best results, use cream that's pasteurized but not ultra-pasteurized)
1 Tbsp. buttermilk

¹/₄ tsp. salt
1 Tbsp. freshly chopped chives
¹/₄ tsp. ground white pepper

In a large glass bowl, mix together the cream, buttermilk and salt. Cover the bowl with plastic wrap and let stand at room temperature for 24 to 36 hours. The mixture will thicken, become very creamy and develop a smooth nut-like flavor.

Refrigerate for 24 more hours for more texture and flavor. Add the chives and white pepper and mix well.

ROASTED FILET MIGNON
WITH PINOT NOIR AND PISTACHIO SAUCE

Serves 4

STEAKS

4 filet mignon steaks, 6 to 8 oz. each
1 tsp. unsalted butter
1 tsp. olive oil
freshly ground black pepper and salt to
    taste

SAUCE

3 tablespoons unsalted butter, divided
1 Tbsp. olive oil
4 shallots, separated if double, sliced into
    thin rings
2 cups Pinot Noir wine
2 cups beef stock
¹/₂ cup chopped unsalted pistachio nuts
1 tsp. minced fresh parsley
salt and freshly ground black pepper to
    taste

In a sauté pan, heat 1 tablespoon of butter with 1 tablespoon olive oil over medium heat until very hot. Add the shallots. Lower the heat and cook slowly until they begin to soften. When the shallots are translucent, not brown, add the wine and let boil gently until volume is reduced to approximately ³/₄ cup. Add the stock and the nuts and continue to cook until ³/₄ cup is left. Remove from the heat and swirl in the remaining 2 Tbsp. of butter and the parsley. Adjust seasoning with salt and pepper.

In an oven-proof roasting pan on the stove, heat the butter and oil until sizzling, then cook the steaks on both sides until they are a nice, golden brown. Set the roasting pan in the oven and bake for 5 to 7 minutes at 375°F.

To serve, pour 2 tablespoons of sauce on the bottom of each plate and place the filet mignon in the middle. May be served with Parisienne potatoes and fresh green beans.

GRILLED SCALLOPS
WITH YELLOW BELL PEPPER-BLACK BEAN SALSA
Serves 4

SCALLOPS

¹/₂ cup olive oil
1 small Scotch bonnet pepper, chopped and seeded
4 garlic cloves, minced
8 whole black peppercorns
1¹/₂ lbs. jumbo sea scallops
Salt and freshly ground black pepper to taste

SALSA

1 large yellow bell pepper, cored, seeded and roughly chopped
1 Tbsp. Dijon mustard
1 Tbsp. white wine vinegar
¹/₂ cup olive oil
2 Tbsp. hot water
¹/₄ tsp. salt
¹/₄ tsp. pepper
1 Tbsp. fresh cilantro leaves (no stems)
4 cups cooked black beans

Mix the oil, Scotch bonnet pepper, garlic and quartered peppercorns in a glass bowl. Add the scallops, mix well and let rest at room temperature for 1 hour.

Place the chunks of yellow pepper into a processor and add the mustard and vinegar. Blend for 1 minute. Stop and scrape down the sides, if necessary. Strain the purée through a sieve and return the strained liquid to the blender. Turn on the blender and slowly pour in the olive oil. With the motor still running, add the hot water, salt and pepper. Add the cilantro and blend 15 more seconds. Pour the mixture into a serving bowl and stir in the black beans. The salsa will keep for several days, covered, in the refrigerator. Mix well before using.

Prepare the grill for high heat. It is important that the grill be very hot, otherwise the scallops will lose their juices. Grill the scallops for two minutes on each side, or to your liking. Salt and pepper to taste.

Serve the scallops immediately with the salsa; they should be enjoyed while they are still juicy and steaming.

Grilled Mahi-Mahi
With Avocado Salsa and Ginger & Lime Vinaigrette

Three outstanding ways to serve grilled mahi-mahi. You may use either the avocado salsa or the vinaigrette, or you may use both together - either way is delectable.
Serves 4

4 6-oz. mahi-mahi filets

2 Tbsp. olive oil

Preheat the grill to high heat. Brush the fish filets with olive oil and let sit for 10 minutes. Meanwhile, make the salsa or vinaigrette. Then grill fish to preference.

Avocado Salsa

2 cups perfectly ripe avocado, peeled and
   diced into ¹/₄-inch cubes
¹/₂ cup finely diced red onion
1 cup peeled and seeded tomato

¹/₄ cup extra virgin olive oil
¹/₄ cup lemon juice
1 tsp. minced cilantro leaves
salt and freshly ground black pepper
   to taste

In a stainless steel bowl, blend all ingredients carefully so that avocados are not crushed. Pour 3 Tbsp. of the salsa over grilled mahi-mahi.

Ginger and Lime Vinaigrette

1 tsp. finely minced fresh ginger
2 Tbsp. soy sauce
1 Tbsp. Champagne vinegar
³/₄ cup sunflower oil
1 Tbsp. freshly squeezed lime juice

salt and freshly ground white pepper to
   taste
1 Tbsp. warm Chardonnay
   or dry white wine
1 Tbsp. Dijon mustard

Combine all ingredients except the wine in a food processor and blend for 15 to 20 seconds. Add the heated wine and blend for 20 more seconds. Ladle the vinaigrette onto each serving plate, top with the sautéed mahi-mahi. Reserve the rest of the sauce for vegetables or rice.

SHEFFIELD'S

Marriott's Harbor Beach Resort
3030 Holiday Drive • Ft. Lauderdale, Florida 33316 • (954) 766-6100

Sheffield's is intimately tucked away in Marriott's luxurious Harbor Beach Resort. The interior of Sheffield's is a refreshing departure from what we expect in a Florida waterfront resort, with Elizabethan paintings and fine decorative china against stained wood trimmed walls.

Ultimately, the cuisine sparks the highest fascination, combining many contemporary dishes such as Chilled Medallions of Roast Duck with Pinot Noir, Currant and Orange Zest, with universal favorites like Dover Sole. The Roasted Back of Lamb and the Beef Wellington are both exquisite. Superb service by an experienced staff and a wine list receiving the Award of Excellence by the Wine Spectator have helped Sheffield's earn the Chaine de Rotisseurs Five-Star rating.

FRESH TOMATO BRUSCHETTA

Very simple, very traditional. Try this with a generous amount of Parmesan cheese

6 tomatoes, fresh, peeled, seeded, ¹/₂-inch
    diced red or yellow, mix if available
1 cup red onion, ¹/₈ inch diced
3 cloves fresh garlic, minced
¹/₄ cup balsamic vinegar
¹/₂ cup extra virgin olive oil

1 large bunch basil, fresh chopped
2 tsp. black pepper, fresh ground
2 tsp. kosher salt
1 loaf French bread (baguette), sliced at
    an angle, approximately 2 inches thick

Combine the first eight ingredients in a plastic, glass or stainless steel bowl. Let stand at room temperature for an hour, then refrigerate.

Serve chilled over grilled French bread slices which have been brushed with olive oil and garlic.

LOBSTER POMPADOR

Use Maine lobsters for best results in this elegant dish.
Serves 6

6 1¹/₂-lb. lobsters
4 gallons water
8 cups white wine
4 peeled carrots, chopped
4 stalks cleaned celery, chopped
2 cleaned leeks, chopped
¹/₂ bunch cleaned parsley
3 bay leaves

¹/₂ oz. black peppercorns
4 cups heavy cream
2 cups vegetable julienne (such as yellow
    or red bell peppers, carrots, zucchini,
    yellow squash)
3 tsp. Beluga caviar
Beurre manie (2 tsp. butter mixed with 2
    tsp. flour)

Place water, wine, carrots, celery, leeks, parsley, bay leaves and black peppercorns in large pot and bring to a boil. When boiling heavily, put washed lobsters in the pot and let simmer for about 15 minutes. Take the meat out of the shell and save the juice from the lobsters. Place the lobster meat in a small warm sauté pan and cover with a lid. Put the juices in a large sauté pan, add the heavy cream and two cups vegetables julienne. Bring to a boil and thicken with beurre manie. Let cook about five minutes. Add lobster meat and Beluga caviar. Serve hot with rice or angel hair pasta.

CRÈME BRULÉE GRAND MARNIER®

Why do so many restaurants feature a form of creme brulée with their desserts? Simply because everyone loves them and the dessert allows for many variations.
Serves 8

1 cup egg yolks	*2 oz. Grand Marnier®*
1 cup sugar	*2 cups half-and-half*
chopped zest from 1 orange	*2 cups heavy cream*

Wisk together egg yolks, sugar, zest and liqueur. Bring the half-and-half and heavy cream to a boil and slowly add this mixture to the yolk mixture while stirring. Strain and pour into ramekins. Bake in a water bath at 350°F. until set, about 25 minutes, then cool overnight in refrigerator. Sprinkle with sugar and place under a broiler until caramelized. Serve immediately.

Heat lemons briefly in the microwave before juicing to increase the juice yield.

THE DOWN UNDER

3000 East Oakland Park Blvd. • Ft. Lauderdale. FL 33306 • (954) 563-4123

The Down Under enjoys an ideal waterfront location on the Intracoastal Waterway at Oakland Park Blvd., just 2 blocks away from the beach. Now in its 26th year, The Down Under has the distinction of being Broward County's pioneer in fine waterfront dining. Under the guidance of managing partner Leonce Picot and Executive Chef Joe Nalley, The Down Under specializes in the finest dry aged beef and fresh seafood, with stone crabs a seasonal feature. Classic menu selections include Beef Wellington and Brutus Salad, as well as Idaho Rainbow Trout which is flown in daily.

Of special note, The Down Under was one of the first ten restaurants to receive The Wine Spectator Grand Award, and continues to earn this honor year after year in recognition for one of Florida's finest wine lists. The Down Under is also affiliated with another award-winning restaurant, La Vieille Maison in Boca Raton.

BEEF WELLINGTON

A grand presentation everyone should experience at least once a year.
Serves 8

1 7-lb. tenderloin of beef
10 oz. paté de foie gras
2 medium carrots
1 small onion
2 cloves garlic
1 stalk celery
2 lb. mushrooms
pinch of thyme

2 bay leaves
1 Tbsp. beef base*
Salt and pepper to taste
1 stick butter
2 lbs. puff pastry dough
1 egg yolk
2 Tbsp. milk

Preheat oven to 400°F. Trim fat and membranes off tenderloin. Cut two inches off the head and six inches off the tail of the filet. Cut the paté de foie gras into strips the size of an index finger and three inches long. Freeze strips.

For the stuffing, combine carrots, onions, garlic, celery, mushrooms, thyme, bay leaves, beef base, salt and pepper. Chop fine and sauté in melted butter until almost dry. Let cool.

Make a hole lengthwise in the filet with the handle of a wooden spoon. Push in the frozen paté. Cover the filet lightly with the prepared stuffing. Roll out pastry dough to ¹/₂-inch thickness and wrap the filet with the dough. Combine the egg yolk with milk and brush the outside of pastry dough wrapping to form a glaze. Bake at 400°F. for 30 minutes for medium rare (cover with aluminum foil if browning too fast).

* Beef base is sold commercially as Marmite or Kitchen Bouquet.

Madeira Sauce

2 cups good brown sauce
3 cups clear brown stock
3¹/₂ Tbsp. good quality Madeira wine

Make a ²/₃rds reduction of brown sauce and stock (five cups should be cooked down to approximately two cups). Remove from heat and add 3-4 Tbsp. Madeira.

Leftover sauce will keep at least two weeks if covered and refrigerated.

Serve Beef Wellington with Madeira sauce.

Mustard Sauce for Stone Crabs

Whether you like Stone Crab claws hot or cold, this sauce is excellent.

Mix until smooth:
7 Tbsp. of Coleman's® dry mustard
³/₈ cup white wine

Add:
2 cups mayonnaise
1 Tbsp. A-1 Steak Sauce®
2 Tbsp. Nabisco Escoffier Robert Sauce®
¹/₂ cup heavy cream
2 Tbsp. half-and-half (or more to reach creamy consistency)
salt and pepper to taste
(Recipe may be halved.)

Mushroom Ravioli

Ravioli Filling

¹/₄ cup olive oil
2 shallots, finely diced
1¹/₂ cups mixed mushrooms, washed and sliced*

¹/₄ cup fresh basil leaves, finely chopped
salt and pepper to taste

*You may use a variety of mushrooms such as shiitake, Portobello, oyster, porcini or others, depending on market availability.

Combine the shallots, mushrooms and basil together. In a very hot pan, sauté all ingredients quickly and remove from the pan. Season to taste. Set aside to cool.

Assembling the Ravioli

4 ravioli sheets of pasta dough, rolled out
(6 x 6 inches)
1 egg, beaten with 1 Tbsp. water to make
egg wash

Place two ravioli sheets on a clean work surface and use a pastry brush to coat with an egg wash (other sheets should be covered with damp towel to keep them from drying out). Using the first sheet of rolled-out pasta as a sort of checkerboard, place a mound of about 1 teaspoon of the mushroom mixture every 2 inches across and down the pasta (nine mounds per sheet). Dip pastry brush into a bowl of egg wash and make vertical and horizontal lines in a checkerboard pattern on the sheet of pasta, between the mounds of mushroom filling. Be sure to use enough egg wash to wet the lines evenly (the water will act as a bond to hold the finished ravioli together). Carefully spread the second sheet of rolled-out pasta on top of the first one, pressing down firmly around the filling and along the wetted lines.

With a ravioli cutter, a pastry wheel or a small, sharp knife, cut the pasta into squares along the wetted lines. Separate the mounds of ravioli and set them aside on wax paper. In the same fashion, roll out, fill and cut the two other portions of dough. Press edges firmly to ensure a tight seal.

Cooking the Ravioli

To cook, place the ravioli into 6 to 8 quarts of rapidly boiling salted water to which 1 Tbsp. of oil has been added. Stir gently with a wooden spoon to keep them from sticking to one another or to the bottom of the pot. Boil the ravioli for 5-8 minutes or until they come to the top of the water and test for tenderness. Drain thoroughly in a large sieve or colander. Serve the ravioli with the sauce and garnish with fresh basil leaves and diced tomato.

Sauce

¹/₄ cup butter
¹/₂ cup white wine
4 shallots, finely chopped

1 cup heavy cream
1 Tbsp. fresh basil, chopped
salt and pepper to taste

Sauté shallots lightly in butter and add the white wine, reducing to approximately one-half the volume. Add the heavy cream and bring to a boil. Reduce heat to a simmer and add the basil, salt and pepper to taste. Reduce to desired consistency, adjust seasonings and strain.

BANG RESTAURANT

1516 Washington Avenue • South Miami Beach, Florida 33139 • (305) 531-2361

It seems like only yesterday that Bang first began dazzling South Beach customers with its innovative New World Cuisine and exhibition kitchen. That was then and this is now. While Bang has now been totally renovated, the cutting edge cuisine that gave a new definition to New World Cuisine on South Beach is still what makes this restaurant so special.

Over the past five years, Bang has remained on everyone's list as an excellent restaurant that continually serves outstanding food emphasizing the finest of local ingredients. The highly varied and creative cuisine of Bang will satisfy anyone's wishes, including many delicious light menu items that are so popular with late night diners. Bang is still a spot on the South Beach scene that dazzles with excellent food and fine service in a lovely setting.

FRIED GREEN TOMATOES
WITH FRESH TOMATO VINAIGRETTE AND CITRUS VINAIGRETTE

A classic. The citrus vinaigrette brings everything together perfectly.
Serves 4

4 green tomatoes
1 cup cornmeal
1 cup flour
1 cup buttermilk

¹/₂ cup peanut oil for frying
2 cups mixed organic greens
sea salt
fresh ground pepper

Slice tomatoes into ³/₄-inch thick slices. Salt and pepper and marinate in buttermilk for ¹/₂ hour. Mix the cornmeal and flour together. Heat oil in a heavy sauce pan over medium heat. At the last minute before serving, dredge tomato slices in cornmeal mixture and fry in medium-hot peanut oil. Drain on paper towels when golden brown.

FRESH TOMATO VINAIGRETTE

3 very ripe tomatoes
¹/₄ cup apple cider vinegar
¹/₄ cup extra virgin olive oil
2 Tbsp. maple syrup

¹/₄ cup snipped chives
sea salt
fresh ground pepper

Pass tomatoes through food mill and strain to remove seeds. Add vinegar, olive oil, maple syrup and chives. Season to taste with salt and pepper.

CITRUS VINAIGRETTE FOR ORGANIC GREENS

1 cup fresh orange juice
1/2 cup fresh lemon juice
2 Tbsp. chopped tarragon
3 roasted shallots

2 Tbsp. Dijon mustard
1 cup olive oil
sea salt
fresh ground pepper

Combine all ingredients except oil, salt and pepper and purée in a blender. Slowly add oil to citrus mix and blend. Adjust for taste with salt and pepper.

To assemble, toss organic greens with citrus vinaigrette, set aside. On 12-inch plates or oval platters, pour 1/4 cup of fresh tomato vinaigrette on plate. Slice two tomatoes in half per order and stand on edge in center of the plate to form a triangle. Arrange tossed greens in the middle of the sliced tomatoes and serve while fried tomatoes are warm.

MANGO CRÈME BRULÉE

The fresh mango pieces add texture and flavor.
Serves 4

CRÈME BRULÉE MIX

4 large egg yolks
3/4 cup sugar
1 1/2 cups heavy cream

1 tsp. vanilla extract
1 cup mango, diced

Combine egg yolks and sugar and place in a stainless steel bowl. Mix well. In a heavy pan, heat heavy cream until simmering. Add 1/4 of this mixture to the eggs, whipping constantly. Then add the rest of the egg mixture to cream, stirring well. Place in stainless steel or crockery bowl. Cover with aluminum foil and place in a water bath. Cook at 350°F. for 30-45 minutes, or until custard sets. Remove from water bath and chill at least 4 hours or overnight. When cool, mix in the mango.

FOR THE SHELL

1 package frozen puff pastry, or use your
    favorite recipe
parchment paper

pastry beans for baking
3-inch circular molds

This recipe is more technique than anything. The concept is to have a thin, crisp shell to place the creme brulee mixture into.

Two sheets of puff pastry, 10 inch x 10 inch rolled ⅛-inch thick. Dock the pastry with a fork and let rest for 10-15 minutes in the refrigerator. Cut the pastry into a 5-inch diameter and place in a 3-inch diameter ring 1-inch deep. Chill the pastry. Place pastry beans or rice inside of pastry with a piece of parchment paper between.

Bake at 325°F. until light brown and crisp.

To assemble: Fill shell with creme brulée mixture to the brim and smooth with a knife, covering edges of puff pastry shell.

Sprinkle 2 Tbsp. of sugar over the top of creme brulée mixture.

Place under broiler until sugar caramelizes or caramelize with a butane torch. Put on a 10-inch plate and finish with your favorite fruit purée or a sauce. Garnish with mangoes and fresh berries.

CASHEW DUSTED MOLASSES CHICKEN
WITH TANGERINE SALSA AND GINGERED STICKY RICE

Absolutely wonderful. The tangerine salsa has a fresh taste all its own.
Serves 2

2 8-oz. chicken breasts, skin removed
¼ cup molasses
¼ cup pineapple juice
¼ cup diced onion
1 jalapeño chopped, seeds in
1 tsp. chopped thyme
1 tsp. ground coriander
½ tsp. Chinese five-spice powder

½ cup ground cashews
½ cup Chinese bread crumbs (available in Oriental grocery store)
½ cup buttermilk
⅜ cup peanut oil
¾ cup tangerine salsa
½ cup gingered sticky rice
Kosher salt and fresh ground pepper

Combine molasses, pineapple juice, thyme, jalapeño, onion, coriander and five-spice powder in a blender and mix for 15 seconds. In a non-reactive dish, pour molasses marinade over chicken and let sit for 3 to 4 hours or overnight. Remove chicken from marinade and wipe clean, salt and pepper, then dip in buttermilk. Combine Chinese bread crumbs with cashews and bread the chicken by pressing firm to adhere the breading.

In a heavy-bottom skillet, heat peanut oil till hot, but not smoking, brown chicken and remove and place in a 350°F. oven for 10-12 minutes to finish cooking. Remove from oven and let rest for 4-5 minutes before serving.

To assemble the dish: In a 6 oz. coffee cup fill halfway with sticky rice, then 2 Tbsp. of salsa, and then fill to the top with sticky rice.

Invert coffee cup in center of 12-inch plate. Tap lightly to remove rice. Repeat for second plate. Slice chicken on bias and layer around rice. Spoon remainder of the salsa in and around chicken. Serve immediately.

Tangerine Salsa

3-4 tangerines, peeled, sectioned, keep
   juice (about $^3/_4$ cup)
2 ripe tomatoes, peeled, seeded, diced
   medium (about $^3/_4$ cup)
$^1/_4$ cup red onion, diced
$^1/_4$ cup poblano pepper, diced
$^1/_4$ cup red pepper, diced

1 Tbsp. lime juice
1 Tbsp. peanut oil
1 tsp. ground coriander
$^1/_2$ tsp. black ground pepper
$^1/_4$ tsp. kosher salt
2 Tbsp. chopped cilantro

Combine all ingredients and let set at room temperature for 1 hour. Then serve or refrigerate.

Gingered Sticky Rice

$^3/_4$ cup sushi rice
1 tsp. salt
2 Tbsp. chopped fresh ginger
$1^1/_2$ cups water

Rinse rice under cold water till water runs clear. Combine salt, ginger and water. Bring to a boil. Add rice. Reduce heat, cover and cook for 20-22 minutes. Remove from heat and keep warm till ready for use. Remember - rice will be sticky.

Coat raisins with flour to keep them from sinking to the bottom of cake batters.

CHEF ALLEN'S

19088 N.E. 29th Avenue • Aventura, Florida 33180 • (305) 935-2900

Chef Allen Susser is to New World Cuisine what Bill Gates is to computer software..innovative, high profile and extremely good at what he does. When people discuss "who's who" and "what's what" in the exciting Florida culinary scene, Chef Allen's is normally the center of conversation. With training that includes Le Bristol Hotel in Paris and Le Cirque Restaurant in New York, Chef Allen selected Miami as the location for his restaurant where he would develope a stimulating new Florida Cuisine.

Simply put, Chef Allen's defines quality dining with a menu that is drawn up daily to feature the freshest of ingredients South Florida provides at any given time. As one would expect, New World Cuisine is the specialty, with emphasis on fresh seafood and delightful desserts. Everything in the restaurant is exciting, from the region's finest exhibition kitchen to the wonderful flavors resulting from unique culinary combinations. It's easy to see why Chef Allen's is regarded as one of the finest restaurants in Florida and the United States.

Food and Wine magazine named Allen Susser as the Best New Chef in America shortly after Chef Allen's opened in 1992. *Time Magazine* calls Allen's Florida Cuisine "a New World marvel." Additionally, *The James Beard Foundation* bestowed Allen with it's Best Chef in America Award for the Southeast Region.

A special tip of the hat to Allen Susser for his personal involvement in the challenge of helping to feed the homeless and homebound elderly. Chef Allen's philosophy is straightforward, "I love to cook, so food is my life, my profession, my charity and my diversion."

SHRIMP ESCABICHE WITH GRILLED GINGER PINEAPPLE
Serves 4

12 large shrimp, peeled, deveined
1 tsp. sea salt
$^1/_2$ tsp. freshly ground pepper
1 tsp. olive oil
1 medium onion, diced
$^1/_2$ tsp. minced garlic

2 Tbsp. fresh lime juice
$^1/_2$ cup fresh orange juice
2 Tbsp. scallions, chopped
2 Tbsp. cilantro leaves, chopped
Ginger Grilled Pineapple

Season the cleaned shrimp with salt and pepper. Heat a large non-stick pan with the olive oil. Add the shrimp and sauté for one minute. Add the onion and garlic, and continue to sauté until the shrimp are pink. Stir in the lime juice, orange juice, onion and cilantro. Remove the pan from the heat and allow the mixture to cool to room temperature.

Arrange the ginger grilled pineapple slices around the edge of a large platter. Place the shrimp in the center and pour the pan juices over them.

GRILLED GINGER PINEAPPLE

1 large, ripe pineapple
1 Tbsp. sesame oil
4 Tbsp. fresh ginger, minced
$^1/_2$ tsp. Kosher salt

$^1/_4$ tsp. freshly ground pepper
2 Tbsp. fresh lime juice
1 tsp. toasted sesame seeds

Peel the pineapple, reserving several of the long green stems for a garnish. Lay the pineapple horizontally on a cutting board and cut into quarters. In a small bowl, combine the sesame oil, ginger, salt, pepper and lime juice. Brush the pineapple with this mixture and let it set for $^1/_2$ hour.

Preheat your grill to very hot. Grill the pineapple quarters for approximately 2 to 3 minutes on each side, until slightly browning the pineapple. Remove the pineapple from the heat.

To serve, cut each pineapple section into 6 or 7 thin slices. Arrange the slices attractively on plates and use the green stems and the toasted sesame seeds as garnish.

LEMON RED SNAPPER
WITH SPICY GREEN COCONUT RICE

Serves 4

2 2-lb. whole red snappers, scaled & cleaned
2 large lemons, zested, juiced
$^1/_2$ cup dry sherry
$^1/_2$ cup Spanish onion, fine dice
4 Tbsp. olive oil

$^1/_2$ tsp. Kosher salt
$^1/_2$ tsp. coarse ground pepper
$^1/_4$ cup pine nuts
2 tsp. diced chives
Spicy Green Coconut Rice

Wash the snappers in cold water and drain well. Score the flesh 3 times on each side, approximately $^1/_2$-inch deep and 3-inches long. In a stainless steel or glass bowl, combine the lemon juice, sherry, onion, 3 Tbsp. of the olive oil, salt and pepper. Rub this mixture over the snapper and marinate for 30 minutes.

Preheat your oven to 400°F. Place the fish into an oven proof pan with the marinade and bake for approximately 10 to 12 minutes, or until the fish flakes to the bone when tested. For a moist fish, baste with the marinade every 3 minutes, making sure to fill the scored areas in the flesh with the marinade. Remove fish from oven when done and set aside.

In a small bowl combine the lemon zest and pine nuts with the remaining 1 Tbsp. of olive oil. In a small oven proof pan, bake this mixture for 2 to 3 minutes until lightly colored and aromatic.

Remove the snapper to colorful, oversized dish. Garnish the fish with the pine nut mixture and the marinade. Add chives for an additional garnish. Arrange the Spicy Coconut Green Rice attractively on the plate around the snapper.

RED BANANA BRULEE WITH CLEMENTINE FRUIT SALSA

Many varieties of bananas are now finding their way to our neighborhood supermarkets. These "new" banana choices are wonderfully flavorful. The red skinned, red banana has more aromatic vanilla flavor than its yellow cousin. When we tested this dessert everyone fell in love with it. We had to go back to the store for more ingredients since everyone wanted seconds!

Serves 6

6 ripe medium red bananas
1 Tbsp. fresh lime juice
1/4 tsp. pure vanilla extract

3 Tbsp. light brown sugar
2 cups Clementine and Fruit Salsa
4 sprigs fresh mint for garnish

Peel the red bananas. Note that the skin is just a little thicker than a yellow banana, so take care not to break the bananas when peeling them. Split the bananas in half lengthwise and place them cut side up in a flat, ovenproof glass dish. Combine the lime juice and vanilla, then brush the bananas with this mixture. Generously spoon the brown sugar on the bananas.

Preheat your broiler to hot and place the sugar topped bananas under the broiler for 2 to 3 minutes, or until they are well caramelized. Remove from the broiler and let them cool for 1 minute before removing from the pan.

To serve, divide the Clementine and Fruit Salsa into 6 bowls. Place 2 halves of the banana brulee in each bowl and garnish with fresh mint.

CLEMENTINE AND FRUIT SALSA

Tea and citrus are naturally complementary.
The tea adds a depth of flavor and richness.

3 large clementines or tangerines
1 medium ruby red grapefruit
1 medium mango

2 Tbsp. honey
3 Tbsp. brewed orange pekoe tea
2 Tbsp. toasted almonds

Peel the tangerines and the grapefruit. Cut between the membranes with a sharp knife to remove the segments and any seeds. Cut the segments into thirds and place them in a stainless steel or glass bowl. Peel, seed and dice the mango, then add the honey, tea and almonds. Mix well and chill.

DOMINIQUE'S

Alexander Hotel
5225 Collins Avenue • Miami Beach, Florida 33140 • (305) 861-5252

The two things you remember after a meal at Dominique's are the excellent cuisine and equally outstanding setting. Situated in the famous Alexander Hotel, Dominique's provides stunning views of the Atlantic Ocean for its guests, while the rich wood paneling evokes the warmth of a turn-of-the-century men's club. It is no wonder that Dominique's was voted the "Most Romantic" restaurant by South Florida Magazine.

The cuisine of Executive Chef Jean-Claude Plihon is the perfect complement to the romantic setting. Chef Plihon combines a light-handed French technique with a distinctive Florida flair, emphasizing the area's abundance of produce and seafood. In 1992, Chef Plihon was named by food critics as one of the top twelve Chefs in America.

CRUSTED YELLOWFIN TUNA
WITH SZECHUAN PEPPERCORNS & GINGER VINAIGRETTE

An exciting method for tuna - the ginger vinaigrette is a winner.
Serves 4

GINGER VINAIGRETTE

2 lb. sushi quality yellowfin tuna
4 Tbsp. Szechuan peppercorns
2 Tbsp. peanut oil
2 Tbsp. sesame oil
salt and pepper

$^1/_4$ cup honey
$^1/_2$ cup sherry vinegar (xeres)
4 Tbsp. finely chopped shallots
4 Tbsp. finely chopped ginger
2 Tbsp. finely chopped garlic
$^1/_2$ cup soy sauce
$^1/_2$ cup sesame oil
1 cup salad oil
$^1/_2$ cup olive oil

Whisk all ingredients to make the Ginger Vinaigrette and set aside
Cut tuna loin in $^1/_4$ (length) to obtain 4 long loins. Season with salt and pepper and coat them with Szechuan peppercorns. Sear quickly in oil (mix sesame oil and peanut oil) in a very hot pan. Slice loin and serve with ginger vinaigrette.

BLUE CRAB TIMBALE WITH CITRUS SAUCE

Serves 4

8 oz. blue crab (jumbo lump)
8 oz. shrimp, peeled and deveined
$^{1}/_{2}$ cup egg whites
$^{1}/_{2}$ cup heavy cream

3 lemons, juice only
5 oranges, juice only
8 oz. butter
salt & pepper to taste

Place shrimp and egg whites in a food processor and blend until smooth. Place mixture in a mixing bowl over ice and add cream (lightly whipped) slowly. Season with salt and pepper, then add jumbo lump crab meat carefully.

Butter four 4-oz. cups and pour mixture into these cups. Bake in a preheated 350°F. oven for 15 minutes. Meanwhile, reduce the lemon and orange juice by half. Add soft butter bit by bit. Place the crab timbale in the middle of a plate with the sauce around it.

KAHLUA® CHARLOTTE

This is so easy to make, I've been tempted to keep one in the refrigerator at all times.
Yields: one 12" cake

1 cup milk
$^{1}/_{2}$ cup espresso, brewed
3 egg yolks
2 Tbsp. sugar
$1^{1}/_{2}$ cups Kahlua®

3 gelatin leaves (gourmet store)
$^{1}/_{2}$ cup sugar
3 egg whites
1 pt. whipped cream

Make an anglaise with milk, espresso, egg yolks, 1 cup Kahlua and 2 Tbsp. of sugar. When anglaise is cooked and still hot, add soft gelatin leaves, stir well and let cool.

Make meringue with egg whites and $^{1}/_{2}$ cup of sugar. Fold meringue into cold Kahlua anglaise, and fold in whipped cream last. Add $^{1}/_{2}$ cup of Kahlua at the end. Pour this mousse into a 12" cake mold with sponge cake on the bottom and refrigerate.

CHOCOLATE SOUFFLÉ

A classic dessert best enjoyed in a romantic setting like Dominique's.
Serves 3

1 cup milk
¹/₄ lb. sweet chocolate
1¹/₂ Tbsp. sugar
3 Tbsp. flour

6 eggs separated
¹/₂ tsp. vanilla extract
1 tsp. butter

Butter well and sprinkle a 1-quart soufflé dish with sugar. Preheat oven to 350°F. Heat milk and chocolate together on low heat stirring until the chocolate melts. Remove the pan from the heat. Mix the sugar and flour in a bowl, add egg yolks and beat with a whisk until the mixture is very creamy. Slowly stir in the hot chocolate and milk. Return this mixture to the saucepan and cook, stirring until the sauce is smooth and thick. Add vanilla and butter. Fold in the egg whites, beaten stiff, then turn the mixture into the soufflé dish. Bake in a moderate oven (350°F.) from 20 to 30 minutes, until the soufflé is well puffed and browned. Serve at once.

"The only carrots that interest me are the number you get in a diamond."

Mae West

GRAND CAFÉ

Grand Bay Hotel
2669 South Bayshore Dr. • Coconut Grove, Florida 33133 • (305) 858-9600

For the eighth consecutive year, the Grand Bay Hotel in Coconut Grove has earned the Five-Star Award from the Mobil Travel Guide. The Grand Bay is one of only 11 hotels in the U.S. to earn the hospitality industry's most coveted honor for 1995. According to Mobil, "They were already spectacular, but they've become more refined, the service got better and the staff is more knowledgeable."

The signature restaurant for Grand Bay Hotel is the Grand Café, whose Executive Chef is Pascal Oudin. Chef Oudin received his training in the great kitchens of France and came to Miami in 1984 to become the Executive Chef at Dominique's. In 1989 he won the Florida Chef of the Year Award. Chef Oudin has introduced a highly interesting menu of regional American Cuisine, with signature dishes which include Pan-Seared Crabcakes with a Mild Wasabi Sauce and Grilled Double Lamb Chops with Florida Sundried Yellow Tomato and a Red Pepper Lamb Sauce.

PAN SEARED JUMBO LUMP FLORIDA BLUE CRAB CAKES
WITH FRIED SWEET POTATO & WARM CITRUS VINAIGRETTE

Outstanding crab cakes.
Serves 4

SHRIMP MOUSSELINE

4 oz. peeled and deveined tiger shrimp
1 cup heavy cream
2 whole eggs

1 egg yolk
Old Bay Seasoning® to taste

CRAB CAKES

1/2 cup of shrimp mousseline
1/2 lb. jumbo lump crab meat
1 Tbsp. very finely sliced chives
fine sea salt and freshly ground pepper

2 cups of peeled and julienne sweet potato
4 bunches organic baby greens

CITRUS VINAIGRETTE

2 cups orange juice, reduced to 1/2 cup
1/4 cup lime juice
2 tbsp. shallot finely chopped
2 cups olive oil

fine sea salt and finely ground black
pepper to taste
cayenne pepper to taste

Process the shrimp meat in a food processor with the salt and pepper and the Old Bay Seasoning until smooth, add the egg and continue processing just a few seconds, add the cream, process until well blended, set aside.

The Vinaigrette

Combine all ingredients in a medium size bowl, whisking until thoroughly blended, set aside.

The Crab Cake

Heat oven to 350°F., place the shrimp mousseline in a medium size bowl, add the crabmeat, and chive, mixing gently to keep lumps of crab meat intact. Season to taste with salt and pepper, set aside. In a teflon pan with 1 tsp. of oil, divide the crab cake mix into four equal portions and form each portion with a cookie cutter ring of $2^1/_2$ x $2^1/_2$ inches, remove ring and bake uncovered just until heated through, about 10 minutes.

Meanwhile, fry the julienne of sweet potato as follows, heat the oil in the deep fryer to 275°F. Fry the sweet potato in the hot oil just until crisp and barely brown, about 1 minute. Drain on paper towel, set aside.

To serve, place a heated crab cake on each serving plate and place a few baby leaves on the side of the crab cake, with the fried julienne of sweet potato, warm up the vinaigrette and put around the edges of the crab cake.

Beef and Stone Crab Carpaccio

Surf and turf on a different plane.
Serves 4

4 oz. of beef tenderloin	salt and pepper to taste
2 cups olive oil	1 lotus root, sliced
4 Tbsp. of lime juice	8 large yellow peppers
8 oz. of stone crab meat	1 Tbsp. of flour

Place plastic film inside timbale molds, set aside. Place thin slices of raw filet between lightly oiled parchment paper and pound with flat-sided mallet. Remove beef and arrange the thin slices on the bottom and side of the mold. Toss stone crabmeat lightly with lime juice and olive oil, season to taste. Fill center of mold with mixture and press it down. Chill until ready to use.

In a processor, liquify the cleaned and seeded peppers. In saucepan over medium heat, slowly reduce 2 cups of pepper juice to $^1/_2$ a cup, strain through a fine mesh strainer and return to saucepan. Reduce until a syrup no more than $^1/_4$ cup. Add 4 Tbsp. olive oil and mix. Oil will be thick and sweet. Store in the refrigerator. Clean and cut lotus root into slices, dust with flour and fry lightly in olive oil. Season with salt and pepper. Unmold carpaccio timbale, top with lotus chips. Sprinkle the yellow pepper oil around the plate and serve cold.

MANGO CREME BRULÉE
IN PECAN AND COGNAC CRUST
Serves 4

1¹/₂ cups heavy cream
2 cups mango juice reduced to ¹/₂ cup
3 egg yolks

¹/₄ cup granulated sugar
¹/₄ cup dark brown sugar
4 small mint sprigs for garnish

Place the cream in a small pot, bring to a boil, then remove from heat and let set. Meanwhile, combine the egg yolks and the granulated sugar in a medium-size bowl, whisking vigorously until thick and pale yellow (about 2 minutes). Reduce mango juice to ¹/₂ cup to syrup consistency and set aside.

Return cream to a boil, then remove from heat and gradually add the egg yolk mixture, whisking constantly, continue whisking about 1 minute more, strain through a chinois, then add the reduced mango juice and set aside.

PECAN & COGNAC CRUST

¹/₄ cup sugar
¹/₂ tsp. grated lemon zest
8 Tbsp. unsalted butter
¹/₂ large beaten egg

4 tsp. Cognac
pinch of salt
²/₃ cup of all purpose four, sifted
¹/₃ cup of pecan flour

On a cutting board, combine 1 tsp. of the sugar with the lemon zest, kneading with the back of a spoon until it becomes a paste. Place the paste in the medium-size bowl of an electric mixer. Add the butter, the remaining sugar, the ¹/₂ beaten egg, Cognac and salt. Beat at medium speed until light and creamy, 1-2 minutes. Turn speed to low and gradually add the flour and pecan flour, beating just until well blended.

Form dough into a ball and cover with plastic wrap, refrigerate for at least 2 hours or overnight before rolling out. Lightly butter the molds; set aside.

Place dough in the center of the table and roll out to a ¹/₈-inch thickness. Next, quickly place dough on top of four 3-inch diameter cookie ring (or flan ring) molds and line each mold evenly with the dough pressing it gently into place. Trim edges, refrigerate for at least 30 minutes. Heat oven to 300°F. Place molds on a cookie sheet and bake until crusts are golden brown, about 5 minutes. Let cool to room temperature.

Place rings with pre-cooked dough in a baking pan and fill them with the Créme Brulée mixture. Transfer pan to the preheated oven and bake uncovered in a 300°F. oven until custard is done - about 45 minutes to 1 hour. When done, the custard will only jiggle a tiny bit if mold is gently shaken. Let mold cool on a wire rack, then refrigerate until well chilled.

Meanwhile, spread the brown sugar evenly over the bottom of a small baking pan and bake in oven at 450°F., until dry but not caramelized (about 4 minutes), shaking at least once. Process the sugar a few seconds in a blender, then sift through the strainer.

Sprinkle baked brown sugar on top of each Crème Brulée evenly.

Preheat broiler and broil about 4 inches from the top just until sugar melts and starts to caramelize. Remove from broiler and top each custard with a mint sprig.

Serve immediately.

WHITE CHOCOLATE TERRINE

Not in the least bit difficult to make, this is an incredible dessert treat.

FOR THE WHITE CHOCOLATE MOUSSE

$^1/_2$ lb. white chocolate
$^5/_8$ cup heavy cream
$^1/_4$ lb. pastry cream

FOR THE SYRUP

$^1/_2$ cup water
$^1/_2$ cup sugar
4 Tbsp. Frangelico Liqueur®

FOR THE PASTRY CREAM

$^1/_2$ cup sugar
6 Tbsp. cornstarch
4 egg yolks
2 cups whole milk
$^1/_2$ vanilla bean

FOR THE CAKE

1 medium box sponge cake
(follow directions)

SYRUP

Boil the water & sugar for 2 minutes, add Frangelico and cool.

PASTRY CREAM

Put the cornstarch and half of the sugar into a small bowl, add the egg yolks and $^1/_2$ cup milk, blend well.

Bring the rest of the milk and sugar to a boil in a small sauce pan. Pour it slowly into the corn starch mixture, and then back into the sauce pan, at the same time whisking in over a constant heat. Cook the cream for 5 minutes while stirring. Pour into a bowl and let cool.

WHITE CHOCOLATE MOUSSE

Break up the chocolate and melt it over a waterbath in a mixing bowl. Whip the heavy cream into soft peaks and refrigerate.

When chocolate is completely melted, add pastry cream and place in an electric mixer at medium speed for about 5 minutes until rising, then remove and carefully fold in the refrigerated whipped cream.

TO ASSEMBLE

Cut 2 pieces of sponge cake in the shape of the terrine mold. With a paint brush, moisten heavily with Frangelico syrup. Spoon in mousse halfway up terrine, tapping mold to remove air. Add first piece of sponge cake and repeat for 2nd layer, finishing off with the second piece of sponge cake. Cover and freeze overnight.

TO UNMOLD

Place in warm water $^{3}/_{4}$ the height of the terrine for 1 or 2 minutes, then turn the mold upside down, tapping until unmolded.

TO SERVE

Remove a Granache from the refrigerator and heat $^{3}/_{4}$ cup in a sauce pan over a water bath. When liquid is consistent, pour over terrine, then refrigerate terrine for 20 minutes. Serve at the table cold.

GRANACHE CHOCOLATE COATING

A great treat when served with ice cream!

$^{1}/_{4}$ lb. semi-sweet chocolate
$^{3}/_{4}$ cup heavy cream
1 oz. Frangelico Liqueur®

Cut chocolate into small pieces, place in bowl. In another bowl bring heavy cream to a boil and pour over the chocolate, beating until it is completely dissolved. Add liqueur and refrigerate.

To store fresh ginger, place it in a tightly closed plastic bag with a piece of paper towel to absorb any moisture.

IL RISTORANTE

The Miami Biltmore
1200 Anastasia Ave. • Coral Gables, Florida 33134 • (305) 445-1926

As the Biltmore's signature restaurant, Il Ristorante opened its doors in the late 1980's and has consistently served Italian-Mediterranean cuisine with an innovative flair. Il Ristorante's richness of decor provides an elegant and romantic atmosphere that blends nicely with the hotel's Old World charm. The combination gives guests the feeling they have stepped back in time when dining at Il Ristorante.

Chef de Cuisine for Il Ristorante over the past two years, Donna Wynter specializes in the food of Northern Italy. Her interpretation of these traditional dishes is precisely what we expected and looked forward to in this grand setting. Additionally, the Sunday Champagne Brunch is considered one of the finest in South Florida, served both inside the restaurant and on the outdoor courtyard.

CALAMARI MEDITERRANEO

With authentic Mediterranean flavor, this is one of the best ways to prepare calamari.
Serves 2

2 Tbsp. roasted garlic oil*
2 Tbsp. roasted garlic cloves
2 cups sliced calamari
2 Tbsp. capers
$1/2$ tsp. cumin
$1/2$ tsp. red pepper flakes
$1/2$ tsp. chopped ancho chili

2 medium size diced plum tomatoes
$1/4$ cup white wine
3 Tbsp. fresh lime juice
1 Tbsp. Italian parsley
salt to taste, pepper is optional
1 tsp. unsalted butter (optional)

* For the roasted garlic oil, combine 1 cup of good quality olive oil with $3/4$ cup of peeled garlic cloves and cover with aluminum foil. Bake in the oven at 300°F. for 10 to 15 minutes, or until the cloves are soft.

In a hot sauté pan, add the garlic oil, garlic cloves and calamari. Sauté for 1 minute, then add the capers, cumin, red pepper flakes, chopped ancho chili and diced tomatoes, and cook for another minute. Add the white wine and lime juice, then simmer for a few minutes. Finish with parsley, salt, pepper and butter. Reduce until sauce thickens.

Mixed Berries With Zabaglione

This recipe is excellent by itself. It is also an ideal accompaniment to the "Lace Baskets" recipe by Dux Restaurant in the Orlando Peabody.

Serves 6

¹/₂ pint blueberries
¹/₂ pint raspberries
¹/₂ pint blackberries
3 large strawberries, cut into halves

Wash and mix the berries. Place the berries into 6 serving cups and top with the zabaglione sauce.

Zabaglione Sauce

6 egg yolks
¹/₂ cup sugar
3 Tbsp. water

¹/₄ cup Marsala sweet wine (or the liqueur of your choice)
1 cup heavy cream
2 Tbsp. sugar

Place the egg yolks in a double boiler and add the ¹/₂ cup sugar and the water, then beat vigorously until the mixture is quite foamy and has thickened.

Gradually beat in the Marsala and continue beating for another minute, then remove from heat.

In another bowl, whip the heavy cream until almost thick. Add the 2 Tbsp. of sugar and continue whipping until thick. Fold the whipped cream into the egg yolk mixture. Chill or serve at room temperature over the mixed berries.

Capellini D'Angelo

Serves 2

1 lb. angel hair pasta
3 cups canned whole, peeled tomatoes, chopped
4 Tbsp. good quality olive oil

1 garlic clove
salt and pepper to taste
3 Tbsp. fresh basil chiffonade
4 Tbsp. Parmesan cheese, freshly grated

Put the tomatoes, olive oil and garlic in a sauté pan and simmer for 20 minutes. Add the fresh basil and salt and pepper to taste, then simmer for 5 more minutes.

Serve with cappellini which has been cooked al dente, and top with freshly grated Parmesan.

Pollo Alla Tuscany

Serves 2

2¹/₂ lb. chicken, boned
salt and pepper
¹/₄ cup olive oil
3 Tbsp. shallots, sliced
1 garlic clove, chopped
³/₄ lb. small button mushrooms
³/₄ lb. pearl onions
¹/₂ tsp. fresh oregano

1 bay leaf
1 Tbsp. tomato paste
¹/₂ lb. pancetta, diced
1 cup red wine
3 plum tomatoes, peeled & seeded, diced
1 cup chicken stock
3 Tbsp. Italian parsley

In a hot sauté pan, add the olive oil and pancetta, and sauté for a couple minutes. Then add the garlic, mushrooms, pearl onions, sliced shallots, fresh oregano, bay leaf and the tomato paste.

Sauté for 10 minutes, then add the red wine and simmer for 10 minutes. Add the stock and reduce. Sauté the boned chicken and finish in a 350°F. oven for 15 minutes. Remove from heat and place into the sauce mixture to finish cooking until tender. Garnish with chopped parsley.

Deglaze the pan with red wine and simmer for 10 minutes.

Penne With Florida Lobster Tail

¹/₂ lb. penne rigate pasta
¹/₃ cup olive oil
2 Florida lobster tails
¹/₂ tsp. garlic, chopped fine

3 cups canned whole plum tomatoes with
    juice, coarsely chopped
¹/₄ tsp. red pepper flakes
salt to taste
4 basil leaves, chiffonade

Put the olive oil in a hot sauté pan and add the garlic. Cook until it sizzles, but do not allow it to brown. Add the lobster tails, the plum tomatoes, red pepper flakes and salt to taste. Simmer for 6 to 8 minutes. Add the fresh basil and simmer for another minute. Serve with the cooked penne.

LE FESTIVAL

2120 Salzedo Street • Coral Gables, Florida 33134 • (305) 442-8545

In a city noted for its rich landscape of outstanding restaurants, one Coral Gables' favorite continues to offer an exquisite dining experience - Le Festival French Restaurant. The Sun Sentinel's Robert Tolf described Le Festival as "a festival of fine service, fresh flowers, sophisticated settings and fine food," and South Florida Magazine continues to hail Le Festival as "the best French restaurant in Dade County."

Each new season at Le Festival brings small, but exciting changes to Le Festival's presentation of classic French cuisine. Chefs Benito del Cueto and Jackie Kapala have lightened the sauces and brought classic French dining into the 90's with dishes like Buffalo Carpaccio, Baby Lamb Rack with Pesto Cilantro Sauce and Tuna Oriental, while retaining such perennial favorites as Homard en Croute and Veal Gourmet.

With the addition of exciting new seafood and wild game entrées to its menu, plus the tradition of providing a complimentary soufflé to each guest on Monday nights, it is no wonder that Le Festival has once again been awarded Florida Trend's Golden Spoon Award as one of the top 20 restaurants in Florida.

BUFFALO CARPACCIO WITH CILANTRO PESTO

Many butchers either provide buffalo regularly or make it available as a special order item. This recipe also works well with extremely fresh beef tenderloin.
Serves 4 as an appetizer

1 lb. buffalo sirloin, very clean
2 bunches fresh cilantro (8 oz.)
1 head of garlic, peeled
3/8 cup white vinegar
3/4 cup toasted pine nuts

1 bunch fresh basil (3 oz.)
1/2 cup Parmesan cheese
1/4 cup virgin olive oil
salt and pepper to taste
radicchio and endive for garnish

To make the pesto, place the cilantro, garlic, vinegar, pine nuts, basil and cheese in a blender or processor. Blend and add the oil slowly, until the consistency of a loose paste.

Take 1/2 of the pesto for a marinade. Cut the sirloin into 4 pieces, dip into the pesto to coat well, then wrap tightly in a plastic wrap. Marinate for 4 hours in the refrigerator.

When ready to serve, cut the sirloin into thin slices and arrange it around a large plate.

Sprinkle with the extra cilantro pesto, some olive oil and pine nuts. Arrange some radicchio and endive on the edge of the plate for decoration.

African Pheasant
with Lingonberry Sauce & Chestnut Purée

We tried this with both lingonberries and raspberries with great success.
Serves 2

1 African pheasant (2½ to 3 lbs.)
3 cups of lingonberry preserves, or fresh
   purée
4 cups of brown pheasant stock (substitute
   chicken)

2 cups of Port wine
3 cans of whole, peeled chestnuts
2 Tbsp. unsalted butter
½ cup heavy cream
½ cup red wine vinegar

To make the sauce, combine the preserves and vinegar and reduce to a syrup consistency. Add the Port wine and reduce ½ of the volume. Add the brown pheasant stock and reduce to a sauce consistency.

To make the chestnut purée, boil the chestnuts in their liquid, then process in a blender or a food processor, adding the heavy cream and butter. Place the purée in a pastry bag with a star tip.

Have your butcher bone the pheasant and separate the breasts, thighs and the bottom legs. Sauté these pieces skin side down first, then turn and finish.

For the presentation, cover the plate with sauce. Slice the breasts and thigh meat and fan over the sauce. Place a floweret of chestnut purée in the middle of the fan and place the bottom leg resting on the purée. Garnish with a sprig of fresh thyme.

Caramelized Mango Over Puff Pastry
With Raspberry Coulis and Port Macerated Fruit Salad

*This dessert is a sheer delight. Though the preparation is not difficult, it certainly makes sense
to increase the recipe and share this delight with friends.*
Serves 2

1 ripe mango, peeled, sliced ¼-inch thick
   sheets
2 pieces of 3 x 3-inch puff pastry, baked
½ cup whipped cream
¼ cup pastry cream
½ raspberry purée

1 pint mixed berries (raspberry, blueberry,
   strawberry, blackberry)
½ cup Port wine
2 Tbsp sugar
2 Tbsp. cassis syrup

Allow the cleaned, mixed berries to marinate in a mixture of the Port wine, 2 Tbsp. sugar and cassis for an hour.

Stuff the puff pastry squares with whipped cream by punching a hole with the pastry bag and fill.

Turn the puff pastry squares over and place some of the pastry cream on the puff pastry square bottoms and place two slices of the mango over this. Sprinkle with sugar on top of the mango and caramelize with a butane torch or under a broiler.

Add some of the raspberry purée to cover ¹/₂ of the plates. Place the mango covered puff pastry on the bottom dry corner of each plate. Add 1 spoon full of the macerated berry salad next to the puff pastry squares and garnish with a mint sprig.

For fullest flavors in salad dressings, mix seasoning with vinegar before adding the oil. Oil coats the herbs and traps the flavor.

JOE'S STONE CRAB RESTAURANT

227 Biscayne Street • Miami Beach, Florida 33139 • (305) 673-0365

Eighty-two years ago, the legendary Joe's Stone Crab Restaurant was founded on Miami Beach. Over the years its Old World atmosphere and delicious entrées have become the favorite among presidents, celebrities and anyone appreciating fine food. In the 90's it continues to be a premier dining experience and Florida's most famous restaurant.

The venerable restaurant's fame centers on its succulent stone crab claws, which are brought in daily from the Florida keys by their own fishing fleet. In fact, Joe's serves an average of one ton of crab claws per day. When you add in the excellent side dishes and desserts, it is no wonder Joe's 400 seats are always filled.

JOE'S VINAIGRETTE DRESSING

Makes about 1³/₄ cups

¹/₄ cup chopped onion or scallion	1 tsp. salt
3 Tbsp. minced fresh parsley	¹/₂ tsp. cayenne pepper
2 Tbsp. chopped pimento	¹/₂ cup drained capers (optional)
1 chopped hard-cooked egg	¹/₃ cup wine or cider vinegar
2 Tbsp. minced chives	³/₄ cup olive oil
1¹/₂ tsp. sugar	

Whisk together all the ingredients. Store in refrigerator.

ROQUEFORT DRESSING

An excellent Roquefort dressing.
Makes about 1¹/₃ cups

¹/₂ pound Roquefort, crumbled	¹/₄ cup plus 2 Tbsp. light cream (or 3 Tbsp. each heavy cream and milk)
³/₄ tsp. Worcestershire® sauce, or to taste	1¹/₂ Tbsp. cider vinegar
³/₄ tsp. A-1 Sauce®, or to taste	¹/₂ tsp. corn or vegetable oil
pinch of Coleman's® dry mustard	³/₄ tsp. sugar

Chop or crumble the cheese into small pieces. Place in a mixing bowl and add the Worcestershire, A-1, mustard, ¹/₄ cup cream, and the vinegar. Mix gently until well combined; then add the oil and sugar. Thin, if necessary, with the remaining cream. Chill until serving.

Joe's Creamed Spinach

Serves 4

2 10-ounce boxes frozen, chopped spinach,
thawed
1½ cups light cream (or ¾ cup each heavy
cream and milk)

1 tsp. salt
¼ tsp. nutmeg, or to taste
2 Tbsp. unsalted butter
2 Tbsp. all-purpose flour

Gently squeeze the spinach, discarding excess water. Place spinach in a non-aluminum saucepan and cook over low heat, stirring constantly, for 5 minutes, until it just begins to become tender, but still bright green.

Add the cream, salt, and nutmeg and simmer for 5 minutes, until the cream has bubbled and reduced slightly.

Meanwhile, melt the butter in a small skillet; add the flour and cook over low heat, stirring for 3 to 4 minutes, until creamy and smooth but still bright green. Correct the seasoning and serve hot.

Variation: Joe's Creamed Garlic Spinach

1 garlic clove, minced
1 tsp. unsalted butter

Cook the garlic in the butter over medium-low heat until fragrant and softened but not browned, about 3 minutes. Add to the spinach with the roux; then proceed as directed above.

Joe's Apple Pie

This is an extraordinary pie, developed by owner Jo Ann Bass. It's piled high with apples and topped with a brown sugar streusel. At Joe's, these are baked every day by Esther Salinas; on weekends, she bakes about two dozen pies, plus more for the Take Away.
Makes one 9½ - or 10 inch pie

Pie Pastry

2 cups all-purpose flour
1 Tbsp. plus 1 tsp. sugar
½ tsp. salt
½ cup cold unsalted butter, cut into pieces

¼ cup plus 3 Tbsp. solid vegetable shortening
1 Tbsp. white vinegar
1 Tbsp. cold water, or more as needed

FILLING

3 red apples (Northern Spy, Jonathan)
juice of ¹/₂ lemon
¹/₂ cup sugar, or more to taste, depending
  on sweetness of apples
3 Tbsp. flour

1¹/₂ tsp. cinnamon
¹/₂ tsp. cloves
¹/₂ tsp. nutmeg
¹/₂ tsp. salt

TOPPING

1 cup plus 3 Tbsp. flour
1 stick plus 1¹/₂ Tbsp. cold unsalted butter,
  cut into chunks

²/₃ cup dark brown sugar
¹/₂ cup pecans, broken up coarsely

For the pastry, in a food processor or medium bowl, mix the flour, sugar, and salt briefly. Add the butter and shortening and cut the ingredients together until crumbly. Combine the vinegar and water; add to the mixture, mixing briefly. If necessary, add just enough cold water for the dough to come together. Gather it into a ball; then wrap in plastic wrap and chill for at least ¹/₂ hour.

On a lightly floured surface, roll the dough out fairly thin into a neat circle. Fit it, without stretching, into a buttered deep 9¹/₂- or 10-inch pie pan. Form a high fluted border. Chill the pie shell.

For the filling, peel, quarter, and core the apples and slice them into a large mixing bowl, tossing them with the lemon juice to prevent darkening. In a small bowl, stir together the sugar, flour, cinnamon, cloves, nutmeg, and salt. Sprinkle this mixture over the apples and toss to coat. Preheat the oven to 375° F.

For the topping, in a food processor, or using two knives or your fingers, cut together the flour and butter, leaving the butter in pieces about the size of a nickel. Mix in the brown sugar, then the pecans. Refrigerate the mixture.

Scatter the apple mixture into the crust, mounding it in the center. Place in the oven; place a sheet of aluminum foil on the rack below to catch any drips. Bake for 25 minutes. Raise the oven heat to 400°F. Scatter the topping over the apples, covering them completely and pressing gently to adhere. Bake until the topping is nicely browned, 25 to 30 minutes longer. Cool the pie on a wire rack; serve at room temperature or lukewarm.

Shave chocolate with a potato peeler.

THE STRAND

671 Washington Ave. • Miami Beach, Florida 33139 • (305) 532-2340

Esquire Magazine refers to The Strand as "the leader of café society on South Miami Beach, with a hip crowd of directors, playwrights, models and celebrities." This is all true, but the primary reason for all the activity and appeal is first and foremost the culinary integrity of The Strand. The cuisine of The Strand combines many cultures, primarily those of Thailand and the Mediterranean, with an emphasis on the less heavy foods.

The candlelit tables and large, open-room layout with impressive archways are conducive to both intimate dining and table-hopping. And, in addition to the outstanding food, this is still a good place to "see and be seen."

SPICY GRILLED SHRIMP WITH LEEK HAY

A wonderful seafood presentation.
Serves 4 as an appetizer

16 medium to large shrimp, cleaned and deveined
1 or 2 tsp. cayenne red pepper, according to taste
1 tsp. Hungarian or Spanish paprika
2 tsp. fresh minced garlic
2 tsp. dry onion powder
1/2 tsp. fresh or dry basil
1/2 tsp. fresh or dry thyme
1/2 tsp. fresh or dry oregano
1 tsp. salt

1/2 tsp. ground white pepper
juice of one lemon
1/4 cup extra virgin olive oil
6 large leeks

SAUCE (OPTIONAL)

1 tsp. lemon grass powder
1 tsp. chopped shallots or red onion
1/2 cup white wine
1/4 cup heavy whipping cream
1/4 lb. unsalted butter, cut in small chunks

Combine shrimp with all the spices, lemon juice and olive oil, and marinate for one hour. Cut leeks so that only one inch of the green tops portion remains, then cut in half lengthwise, then in strips 3-inches long and 1/4-inch thick.

In a saucepan, combine the shallots, lemon grass powder and wine, reduce by half, and then add cream until reduction has thickened. Add the butter in small chunks, rotating the pan so as not to melt it too rapidly. Strain, salt and pepper to taste.

Grill, bake or sauté shrimp 2 minutes on each side. Put aside and keep warm. Deep fry leeks in oil until golden brown, drain excess oil, twist leeks to curl and place in center of round appetizer plate.

Pour lemon grass butter sauce around leeks. Place four shrimp on each side of plate. Garnish with fresh, seedless, diced tomatoes and chopped chives, if desired.

Charred Rare Tuna

with Mixed Greens and Miso Dressing

Excellent! This miso dressing is a natural with the tuna!
Serves 4

4-6 oz. fresh tuna steaks, very thick
$^1/_4$ cup extra virgin olive oil
$^1/_2$ tsp. fresh oregano
$^1/_2$ tsp. fresh basil
$^1/_2$ tsp. fresh thyme
$^1/_2$ tsp. fresh parsley
$^1/_2$ tsp. fresh chervil
$^1/_2$ tsp. tarragon
      (Mix above spices together)
1 Tbsp. salt
$^1/_2$ Tbsp. white pepper

Mixed Greens

2 heads radicchio
2 heads bibb lettuce
2 heads frisee or any available baby
      lettuce
1 cup extra virgin olive oil
$^1/_3$ cups balsamic vinegar
salt and pepper to taste

Miso Dressing

1 whole egg
1 Tbsp. white miso
1 Tbsp. yellow miso
1 cup rice vinegar
$^1/_2$ cup mirin
2 cups peanut oil
salt and pepper to taste

Marinate tuna in oil and fresh herbs, sprinkle with salt and pepper.

In a very hot skillet, preferably iron cast, sear tuna at least one minute on each side for rare. The longer cooked, the firmer the fish will be.

Set aside for 2 minutes before slicing.

Toss all mixed greens together with oil, vinegar, a pinch of garlic if desired, salt and pepper to taste.

In blender or food processor, mix egg, miso, mirin and vinegar, blending together to create an emulsion.

Start adding oil little by little to desired thickness, salt and pepper to taste.

Place mixed greens on one side of dinner plate and pour 3 Tbsp. of miso on bottom of plate opposite mixed greens.

Slice tuna in five thin pieces and serve fanned around greens on miso dressing.

GRILLED MAHI-MAHI
WITH A MANGO-BLACK BEAN RELISH & SWEET PLANTAINS

Serves 4

4-6 oz. filets of mahi-mahi or red snapper
    seasoned with salt and pepper

2 whole ripe plantains, peeled and sliced
    on a bias

FOR RELISH

1 cup black beans cooked in water, salt,
    pepper and a bay leaf. Make sure the
    beans are not overcooked. Drain and
    cool after cooked.
1 cup sliced mango
1 cup diced red onion
1 cup diced green pepper
1 cup diced red pepper

3 cups white vinegar
2 cups sugar
1 Tbsp. salt
$1/2$ Tbsp. white pepper
$1/2$ Tbsp. ground ginger
$1/2$ Tbsp. cinnamon
$1/2$ Tbsp. allspice
$1/2$ Tbsp. cayenne pepper

    Fish may be grilled, sautéed or baked. Make sure it is not overcooked. It should not take more than five minutes. Set aside and keep warm.

    Sauté or deep-fry sweet plantains in peanut oil, drain excess fat and set aside and keep warm. Mix all relish ingredients. Let sit at room temperature one hour before cooking fish and plantains.

    Place sweet plantains on dinner plate in star design. Place fish in center and top with the mango-black bean relish.

MIXED SEAFOOD
WITH THIN NOODLES & LIGHT PESTO CREAM SAUCE

Serves 4

PASTA

8 oz. vermicelli or fresh angel hair
1 gal. boiling water
1 Tbsp. oil
1 Tbsp. salt

2 cups whipping cream
8 medium to large shrimp, cleaned and
    deveined
8 sea scallops
10 oz. fish filet cut in chunks
8 fresh mussels
$1/2$ lb. cleaned calamari
4 garlic cloves, crushed
$1/2$ cup chopped shallots or red onions
$1/2$ cup white wine

PESTO

3 bunches fresh basil
$1/2$ cup roasted pine nuts
$1/4$ cup Parmesan cheese
2 cloves garlic
$1/4$ cup extra virgin olive oil

Mix pesto ingredients together in food processor until a paste is formed.

In sauce pan, reduce 2 cups of whipping cream until thickened, add pesto to taste, (about 3 Tbsp.) salt and pepper to taste.

Pour a tsp. olive oil in hot skillet, fry garlic until golden brown, add shallots and mussels.

When mussels open, add the rest of the seafood.

Add white wine and cook for 3 more minutes. Add fresh chopped herbs, if desired.

Boil water with salt and oil in large pot, add pasta and cook for 9 minutes. Pasta should be al dente, and have a bite to it.

Pour cream sauce over a dinner plate, covering the bottom. Twist 2 oz. of pasta on each plate and surround with 2 pieces of each type of seafood. Top pasta with more sauce. Garnish with seedless, diced tomatoes and chopped chives.

Put a bay leaf in flour and cereal canisters to discourage weevils.

THE VERANDA

Turnberry Isle Resort & Club
19999 West Country Club Drive • Aventura, Florida 33180 • (305) 932-6200

As the signature restaurant at Turnberry Isle Resort & Club, The Veranda has been long established as one of the finest restaurants in the Miami region. Turnberry Isle is the flagship resort of the prestigious Rafael Group. It is rated by The Zagat Hotel, Resort and Spa Survey as "Miami's Best Gourmet Dining Experience."

Executive Chef Todd Weisz received much of his training at Aspen's Copper Kettle Restaurant and Ernie's in San Francisco. His background is an intriguing blend of classical French techniques and fabulous spa cuisine. Chef Weisz is especially adept at achieving the silky textures and hearty flavors of Continental cuisine with a low-fat approach that does not rely on butter or heavy creams.

The Veranda's total commitment to freshness results in a menu that changes daily to incorporate the freshest of seafood, and fruits and vegetables that are at their peak. Much of the produce and most of the herbs used are grown in Turnberry's own tropical gardens. Breads are baked continuously through the day in Turnberry's own ovens. On any given day the options may include pumpkin sunflower bread, saffron raisin bread, mango and chocolate croissants, country sourdough bread, cheese bread, French baguettes and an endless variety of muffins and sweet rolls.

MARINATED HEARTS OF PALM & ASPARAGUS SALAD
WITH CHUNKY MANGO VINAIGRETTE

Serves 4

2 cups hearts of palm, sliced thin	1/4 cup fresh lime juice
1 bunch fresh green asparagus	1 Tbsp. pink peppercorns
4 cups mixed baby greens	2 Tbsp. Dijon mustard
1/4 cup fresh orange juice	salt & fresh pepper to taste
1/4 cup fresh lime juice	

Cook the asparagus in boiling water and chill. Combine the remaining ingredients except for the baby greens, and allow to marinate for at least 4 hours in the refrigerator.

Arrange the baby greens on plates. Stack the asparagus in the center of each plate, forming a box shape. Place 1/4 of the marinated hearts of palm on each plate on top of the asparagus. Spoon 1/4 of the Chunky Mango Vinaigrette around each plate and garnish with freshly snipped chives.

Chunky Mango Vinaigrette

¹/₂ cup olive oil
¹/₄ cup extra virgin olive oil
¹/₄ cup rice wine vinegar
2 Tbsp. sherry wine vinegar

¹/₂ tsp. fresh ground pepper
Kosher salt to taste
1 cup mango, ¹/₄-inch dice

Combine oils and vinegars in a bowl and whisk thoroughly. Add the seasoning and whisk again. Add the diced mango just prior to serving.

Roast Chicken & Oriental Marinade

The delicious Oriental marinade is used for only the last 5 minutes of cooking. We also tried it with salmon with excellent results.
Serves 4

6 5-oz. chicken breasts, skinless, boneless
2 cups cooked brown rice
1 cup snow peas, steamed

4 Tbsp. scallions, sliced on bias
2 Tbsp. olive oil

Combine ingredients for the Oriental Marinade (below) and allow to set for 1 hour.
Preheat oven to 400°F. Brush each breast with olive oil, place in a roasting pan and bake until slightly brown, being careful not to overcook. Pour marinade over the chicken and continue to cook for an additional 5 minutes.

Arrange each plate with ¹/₂ cup brown rice, the steamed snow peas and the chicken breasts. Spoon the remaining marinade over the chicken and rice. Garnish with the scallions.

Oriental Marinade

1 cup rice wine vinegar
¹/₄ cup low sodium soy sauce
2 Tbsp. Dijon mustard
2 Tbsp. honey
1 Tbsp. sake
1/4 tsp. fresh ground pepper

¹/₂ tsp. dry thyme
1 tsp. ginger, minced
1 Tbsp. cilantro, chopped
1 Tbsp. mint, chopped
1 tsp. sesame oil

Whisk all ingredients together and allow to set 1 hour for flavors to marry.

STACKED PORTOBELLO MUSHROOMS
WITH TOMATOES, MOZZARELLA CHEESE & BALSAMIC VINAIGRETTE

We were surprised at the number of calls from readers of our first edition who wanted to see more recipes featuring portobello mushrooms. Executive Chef Todd Weisz provided us with one that was a smash hit with our test group.

Serves 4

8 portobello mushrooms, medium size
1 large red tomato
1 large yellow tomato
1/2 lb. mozzarella cheese, sliced
1/4 cup olive oil

8 basil leaves
salt & fresh ground pepper to taste
1/4 cup chicken broth
4 cups mixed organic greens
1 bunch chives

Preheat oven to 350°F. Trim stems and remove dark gills under the mushroom caps. Brush the caps lightly with olive oil. Salt and pepper to taste. Grill the mushrooms for 2 to 3 minutes on each side. Transfer to a baking dish and add the broth (may substitute vegetable broth). Place the baking dish into the oven for 2 to 3 minutes, or until the mushrooms are tender, remove from baking dish and set aside.

Meanwhile, slice both tomatoes so you have 4 slices from each. Season with salt and pepper, and brush lightly with olive oil. Quickly grill on both sides to heat tomato slices through.

To assemble, first layer a mushroom cap, then tomatoes, basil leaves and cheese, and finish off with a mushroom cap. A toothpick works well to keep all in place. Place the finished mushroom stack in the oven for 3 or 4 minutes, or until the cheese starts to melt. Remove from the oven and cut each stack in half with a sharp knife, exposing the layers.

Toss the greens with balsamic vinaigrette and arrange on the plates. Drizzle 1 Tbsp. of vinaigrette on each stack and garnish with snipped chives and freshly ground pepper.

BALSAMIC VINAIGRETTE

1/3 cup aged balsamic vinegar
1 cup extra virgin olive oil
1 Tbsp. chopped shallot

1 Tbsp. chopped garlic
salt & fresh ground pepper to taste

Whisk all ingredients together.

UNICORN VILLAGE

3565 N.E. 207th Street • Aventura, Florida 33180 • (305) 933-8829

We were amazed at the number of calls we received from readers of our first edition who requested more vegetarian recipes. It just so happens that one of my wife's favorite restaurants is Unicorn Village, a natural food restaurant considered by many to be the finest of its kind in Florida. Over the years Unicorn Village has developed a tremendous following, attracting as many as 1,200 people on a given day. Unicorn Village is billed by owner Terry Dalton as a health food restaurant, emphasizing organically grown products and light, healthful cooking.

The views from the restaurant are enhanced by the floor to ceiling windows overlooking the waterfront dining terrace. In addition to outstanding vegetarian cuisine, Unicorn Village offers some of the areas finest seafood, delivered fresh to the restaurant docks each day by local fishermen. Many of the delicious recipes at Unicorn Village are created by Steven Petusevsky, owner of Cooking… Naturally, a natural foods consulting company, and contributing editor for *Cooking Light* magazine.

BAKED, STUFFED ACORN SQUASH
WITH WEHANI RICE AND WALNUTS

2 acorn squash, halved, seeded
1 12-oz. package wehani rice mixture
2 Tbsp. canola or olive oil
1 cup onions, chopped
¹/₂ cup celery, chopped
¹/₂ cup carrots, chopped

¹/₄ cup walnuts, toasted
¹/₄ cup raisins or sun dried
  cranberries
1 orange, zest and juice
salt and pepper to taste

Preheat the oven to 350°F. Cook the Wehani rice according to package directions, set aside.

Heat oil in a non-stick sauté pan over medium heat and sauté onions, carrots and celery for approximately 5 minutes, or until tender. Add toasted walnuts, raisins, orange zest and orange juice. Season with salt and pepper to taste. Mix with the rice and set aside.

Steam acorn squash halves for approximately 20 minutes, or until just tender. Or, you may microwave on high for 12 minutes. Stuff squash halves with the rice mixture, cover with foil and bake again in a pan with 1-inch of water for 20 minutes until the squash and filling are heated through.

VIETNAMESE SOFT SPRING ROLLS
4 Spring Rolls

$^1/_2$ cup cooked angel hair pasta or
   rice noodles
1 Tbsp. tamari or soy sauce
1 Tbsp. roasted sesame oil
$^1/_2$ Tbsp minced ginger
$^1/_2$ Tbsp. minced garlic
1 Tbsp. hot chili paste

4 rice paper wrappers, dampened
$^1/_2$ cup shredded carrott
$^1/_2$ cup shredded lettuce
4 fresh basil leaves
2 sprigs fresh mint
2 sprigs fresh cilantro

Toss the cooked pasta with soy sauce, sesame oil, ginger, garlic and chili paste.
   Moisten the rice paper wrappers with a pastry brush or damp towel. Divide the pasta mixture into the center of the four wrappers. Top each with $^1/_4$ of the shredded carrots and lettuce. Top with a basil leaf, cilantro and mint. Fold the two opposite ends of each wrapper over the filling and roll. This spring roll is not fried or baked.

SHITAKE, BROCCOLI AND BLACK BEAN SOFT TACO
Serves 6 Large Tacos

1 package 9-inch whole wheat soft taco shells
1 15-oz. can black beans, drained, rinsed
1 Tbsp. olive oil
1 cup red onions, sliced
1 cup green bell pepper, sliced
$^1/_2$ cup red bell pepper, sliced
2 cups broccoli florets, coarsely chopped
1 cup button mushrooms, sliced
1 cup shiitake mushrooms, sliced

1 Anaheim or poblano pepper, seeded,
   minced
$^1/_2$ tsp. ground cumin
$^1/_2$ tsp. ground chili powder
1 cup tomato juice
1 Tbsp. fresh cilantro, minced
2 Tbsp. fresh lime juice
6 oz. Monterey Jack cheese, shredded

Heat the olive oil over medium high heat in a large, non-stick pan. Add red onion, green and red pepper and broccoli. Sauté for 2 minutes, stirring occasionally. Add both mushrooms, minced chili and the spices, continue to sauté. Add the tomato juice and continue to cook for another minute until the vegetables are just tender and the juice thickens. Remove from the heat and add the cilantro and lime juice.
   To assemble, spread a thin layer of black beans on half of each taco shell. Top with enough of the mushroom filling to make an even layer over the beans. Sprinkle with the shredded cheese and fold the top over, forming a taco. Place on cookie sheets and warm in a 375°F. oven for 5 minutes, until the cheese melts and the taco is warmed through. Serve with shredded lettuce, salsa and fat free sour cream or plain yogurt as a garnish.

YUCA RESTAURANT

177 Giralda Avenue • Coral Gables, Florida 33134 • (305) 444-4448

Since its inception in 1989, YUCA has blended the quintessential elements of traditional Cuban and Latin American cooking with the freshest of Miami's Modern Cuban Cuisine. YUCA blends bold and exotic spices to create a world of sumptuous flavors to delight every culinary taste. The juxtaposition of distinct textures and styles results in an irresistible dining experience.

Among YUCA's signature dishes is a tender Dolphin Filet Coated in Plantain Chips, Garnished with Fufú, a Plantain Purée with Bacon and Red Onion and complemented by a Tamarind Tartar Sauce. The chef, Guillermo Veloso, fashions daily specials ranging from a succulent Loin of Venison drizzled with a Godiva Liquer reduction sauce with a mélange of berries and wild mushrooms to a delicate Flounder Stuffed with Black Olive Picadillo, accompanied by Coconut Vegetable Rice and Avocado Vinaigrette. The desserts are exquisite and beautifully sculptured; try the Trés Leches which is sure to intoxicate even the most avid chocolate fanatic.

Baby Back Ribs with Guava Barbeque Sauce

A delicious barbecue twist - absolutely out of this world!
Serves 4

Guava Barbecue Sauce

1 9-oz. jar guava marmalade
2 Tbsp. each tomato paste, corn syrup and
   molasses
3 Tbsp. vinegar

1 tsp. each, dry mustard, cumin, minced
   onion and garlic
1/4 cup dry sherry

Blend all ingredients in a pot and simmer for 1 hour.

Ribs and Their Marinade

4 racks of baby back ribs
1/2 onion, diced
2 Tbsp. each, chopped fresh cilantro and
   oregano, stems removed
1 tsp. each cumin and freshly ground black
   pepper

1/2 cup red wine vinegar
5-6 cloves garlic, minced
salt to taste
2 cups water
2 bay leaves

Combine all ingredients except ribs, water and bay leaves and purée in blender or food processor. When mushy, pour into a container, add water and bay leaves and stir well.

Pour mixture over ribs and leave overnight in refrigerator. The next day, place ribs, still covered with marinade, in oven preheated to 550°F. Cook for 20 minutes. Remove pan from oven and pull ribs out of marinade. Dispose of liquid. Let ribs cool at room temperature and make incisions down the side of each bone, being careful not to cut all the way through. Brush ribs with guava sauce and either put back in oven for 10 minutes or barbecue for the same amount of time, turning rib racks over often and basting with guava sauce several times before serving.

PLANTAIN-COATED FILET OF DOLPHIN

If you are within 100 miles of fresh dolphin and plantains, you MUST make this.
Serves 6

6 8-oz. dolphin filets
1 qt. (approx.) vegetable oil for deep
　frying (350-360°F.)
4 green plantains, peeled, thinly sliced

5 eggs
1 cup flour
salt and pepper to taste

Deep fry green plantain slices until light brown - about 3 three minutes. Grind the slices in a food processor until they are the size of whole peppercorns.

Cut fish into 8 oz. portions. Dust with flour seasoned with salt and pepper. Dip in beaten eggs, then coat with the plantain mixture. Deep fry until golden brown.

KEY LARGO POMPANO COOKED IN A PLANTAIN LEAF
WITH HEARTS OF PALM, SWEET PLANTAINS AND SAFFRON-GARLIC BUTTER

Chef Guillermo indeed has a special way with fish - this is just one delicious example.
Serves 6

6 filets of pompano, 6 to 8-oz. each
$^1/_2$ cup flour (approximately)
salt and pepper to taste
1 Tbsp. chopped fresh parsley
1 Tbsp. chopped fresh oregano
4 Tbsp. extra virgin olive oil.
6 cloves garlic

pinch of saffron
$^1/_2$ cup white wine
$^1/_4$ lb. butter
2 large semi-sweet plantains
1 small can hearts of palm
plantain leaves (available in Latin grocer-
　ies)

Lightly flour the fish filets with mixture of flour, salt and pepper, parsley and oregano.

Heat up a large skillet, add olive oil and cook filets until light browning begins. Be careful not to overcook, since final cooking takes place inside the leaf.

In a small saucepan, bring to a boil the white wine, saffron and 6 cloves of garlic. Reduce by half.

Process in food processor with the butter. Dice the plantains and fry well until golden brown. Cut hearts of palm into slices. Unfold the plantain leaves, placing fish in center. Add a tablespoon of the saffron-garlic mixture, 6 or 7 pieces of plantain and 5 slices of hearts of palm. Fold the leaf over, enclosing the fish and tuck the ends under. Bake at 500°F. for 15 minutes.

TAMALES FILLED WITH CONCH AND SPANISH CHORIZO
The conch and chorizo are a great combination.
Serves

25 ears of corn husked, kernels ground
1 lb. Spanish chorizo, ground
1 lb. conch, ground
2 Tbsp. extra virgin olive oil
4 cloves garlic, chopped
1 green pepper, chopped

1 red pepper, chopped
1 large or 3 medium onions, coarsely chopped
1 small can tomato paste
salt and pepper to taste
corn husks and string

Make a sofrito with the olive oil, two kinds of bell peppers, onions and garlic. Once the onions have wilted and become transparent, add the tomato paste and cook, stirring the mixture. Add ground chorizo and allow to cook about 5 minutes. Add conch, salt and pepper to taste. Using the food processor or blender, liquify the sofrito. Blend with the ground uncooked corn.

Make up the tamales by placing about 4 ounces of the above mixture in the folded husks. To fold the husks, take two together, fold the sides towards the center, fold bottom inward to make a pocket. Fill pocket almost to the rim. Cover and wrap with another husk. Close by folding open end inward. Tie crisscross with string.

Place in a kettle of water for one and a half hours. Allow to cool and freeze if desired. Homemade tamales will keep frozen for at least six months.

To serve: allow to thaw and warm by steaming them or heating them in the microwave for a couple of minutes on high.

Recipe may be halved.

To remove sand from clams, soak for 1½ to 2 hours in salt water,
using ½ cup sea salt per quart of water.

ATLANTIC'S EDGE

The Cheeca Lodge
P.O. Box 527 • Islamorada, Florida 33036 • (305) 664-4651

This is one of the wonderful resorts in Florida which has an interesting history. The Cheeca Lodge was originally built by Clara Mae Downey in 1946, directly on the Atlantic Ocean, 75 miles south of Miami. The next owners were A&P grocery heirs, Carl and Cynthia "Che Che" Twitchell, who rebuilt the resort, and renamed it "Cheeca" by merging their names. Cheeca was purchased by Coca-Cola bottler Carl Navarre in the 1970's, who is now a limited partner of the present owners, Cheeca Associates. In 1987, the resort underwent a $33 million renovation with new accommodations and recreational facilities being added.

The Atlantic's Edge Restaurant is a lovely, semi-circular room with sweeping views of the ocean. It is also one of the most critically acclaimed restaurants in Florida. Executive Chef Dawn Sieber has received numerous accolades and awards, as well as being profiled on *CBS This Morning* and personally selected by Julia Child to prepare a dish for Ms. Child's 80th Birthday Party, televised by PBS. Chef Sieber uses fresh, local products to prepare a variety of dishes with a unique "Keys" flair. She is also environmentally sensitive, choosing not to serve endangered species like conch and swordfish. An avid fan of Atlantic's Edge and Chef Sieber is former President George Bush, a frequent visitor to Cheeca Lodge.

CHEECA LODGE WHITE GAZPACHO

A wonderful variation on a perfect summer dish.

1 red pepper	4 cups buttermilk
1 green pepper	2 cups sour cream
1 yellow pepper	juice of 4 limes
2 English cucumbers	salt and pepper to taste
6 Roma tomatoes	pita croutons

Finely dice peppers, cucumbers and tomatoes. Reserve a little tomato and cucumber for garnish. Mix buttermilk, sour cream, and lime juice. Add vegetables to buttermilk mixture. Season with salt and pepper. Serve with a garnish of chopped cucumber, tomato and pita croutons around edge of soup bowl.

PITA CROUTONS

Cut 6 pieces of pita bread into 8 wedges. Separate, brush with olive oil, toast in oven till crisp.

CRISPY SCALLOP SALAD WITH STRAWBERRY VINAIGRETTE

Serves 4

20 sea scallops
1 cup flour
Assorted mixed baby greens
2 cups vegetable oil
1 tsp. salt

1 tsp. freshly ground pepper
1/2 cup toasted hazelnuts
4 fresh strawberries, julienne
16 orange segments
12 Belgian endive spears

Season the flour with salt and pepper. Dredge the scallops in the flour to coat. Place the oil in a pan over medium high heat, approximately 375° F. Pan fry the scallops until golden brown. Toss the baby greens with Strawberry Vinaigrette to coat.

Arrange the mixed baby greens in the center of each plate. Place the scallops on the mixed greens and garnish with the hazelnuts, strawberries slices, orange segments and Belgian endive.

STRAWBERRY VINAIGRETTE

1 Tbsp. Dijon mustard
1 cup strawberry vinegar
1 orange, zest only
2 oranges, juice only

2 cups vegetable oil
3 Tbsp. hazelnut oil
2 Tbsp. honey
Salt & freshly ground pepper to taste

Mix all the ingredients except the oils, salt and pepper in a bowl. Slowly pour in the oils while whisking to emulsify the vinaigrette. Season to taste with salt and freshly ground pepper.

CHEECA CORN AND CRAB SOUP

8 ears yellow corn, cut off cob
2 bulbs fennel, washed and chopped
1 large onion, chopped

6 stalks celery, washed and chopped
1 jalapeño pepper, seeded and chopped
1/4 cup clarified butter

In a heavy pot over high heat, sauté vegetables in butter. Sauté until vegetables become wilted and clear.

While sautéeing, season with:

1 bay leaf	½ tsp. leaf thyme
1 Tbsp. course grind black pepper	½ tsp. oregano
1 tsp. chili powder	1 Tbsp. salt
¼ tsp. cayenne	1 Tbsp. Old Bay Seasoning®

Deglaze with 2 cups white wine. Reduce, add 1 quart heavy cream and 2 cups half-and-half. Bring to a boil, simmer until reduced by ⅛th volume. Blenderize and strain. Serve in bowls garnished with corn kernels, lump crab and scallions.

THE PRESIDENTIAL SNAPPER

This yellowtail snapper, encrusted in yucca with roasted pepper-orange salsa and sizzling black beans, is absolutely outstanding.

Serves 4

2 lbs. (about four medium) yucca	½ bunch cilantro, chopped
4 7-8 oz. yellowtail (or other type) snapper filets, skin on	1¼ cups extra virgin olive oil
	salt and pepper to taste
4 Florida oranges, peeled and sectioned, no pith	1 eggplant (sliced in eight rounds and grilled or sautéed in olive oil)
1 roasted red bell pepper, diced	1 cup cooked black beans
2 key limes, juiced	

Peel yucca and grate fine. Season fish and grated yucca with salt and pepper. Press and mold grated yucca on to snapper, opposite the skin side.

Heat sauté pan and carefully place snapper, yucca side down, in ½ cup olive oil. Cook until golden brown and then turn and finish cooking skin side down. Place on sliced, grilled eggplant.

FOR SALSA

Mix orange sections and diced, roasted red pepper, lime juice, ½ cup extra virgin olive oil, chopped cilantro, salt and pepper to taste. Place salsa on top of yucca snapper.

FOR SIZZLING BLACK BEANS

Wash and dry black beans. Heat ¼ cup olive oil until very hot and toss dry cooked beans. Just prior to serving, garnish salsa topped fish with sizzling black beans and cilantro sprig.

CHEECA LODGE STONE CRAB FRITTERS

The best we have had.

¹/₄ lb. stone crab meat
3 Tbsp. red bell pepper, diced
3 Tbsp. yellow bell pepper, diced
3 Tbsp. green bell pepper, diced
¹/₄ bunch parsley, chopped

4 Tbsp. all-purpose flour
4 Tbsp. cornmeal
1 Tbsp. Old Bay Seasoning®
1 - 2 whole eggs
2 Tbsp. mayonnaise

Lightly toss wet ingredients. Add dry ingredients and lightly mix with fingertips. It should be loose and wet. Drop by spoonfuls into hot peanut oil and deep fry at 350-360°F. until golden brown. Serve with cocktail sauce.

KEYS SHRIMP SCAMPI

WITH SAUTEED RICE, BLACK BEANS, CHAYOTE SQUASH & RED PEPPER

Serves 4

24 jumbo Key West pink shrimp, peeled, deveined
1 ¹/₂ Tbsp. garlic, minced
1 Tbsp. extra virgin olive oil
1 cup white wine
3 key limes, juice only (substitute Persian)
2 red bell peppers, seeded, cut into triangles
2 chayote squash, green part only, cut into triangles

1 ¹/₂ cups cook black beans, rinsed
4 Tbsp. butter
¹/₄ bunch cilantro, chopped
1 ¹/₂ cup Basmati rice
2 ¹/₄ cups water
Salt & freshly ground pepper to taste
12 slices of Cuban bread with garlic butter, toasted under broiler

Bring the water to boil. Add the Basmati rice and simmer while covered until the rice is done, approximately 20 minutes.

Place a large skillet over high heat. Add the olive oil, shrimp and vegetables and saute for 1 minute. Add the garlic, season with salt and pepper and cook for another minute. Add the white wine and lime juice. Let reduce until the shrimp are cooked through. Add the butter, rinsed black beans and chopped cilantro. Stir until all the butter is melted.

To serve, place the rice on a plate. Spoon the beans and vegetable mixture over the rice. Arrange the shrimp on top of the vegetables. Add toasted Cuban garlic bread and garnish with fresh cilantro and wedges of lime.

❧

FLAGLER'S

Marriott's Casa Marina Resort
1500 Reynolds St. • Key West, Florida 33040 • (305) 296-3535

The setting for Casa Marina Resort is quite simply the finest in Key West. Situated directly on the Atlantic Ocean, Casa Marina is off the beaten path, yet close to everything. The elegant architecture of this historic 1921 resort is conveyed with spectacular palladian windows and the gracious Casa Marina veranda, all overlooking sweeping white beaches and tropical palm trees.

As the sun sets, Flagler's transforms into a spectacular dining experience with the standard Key West "no jacket preferred" theme. Dining may be indoors or al fresco on the magnificent veranda. The menu is primarily fresh seafood, with numerous "lighter" dishes for those seeking alternatives without sacrificing great taste. It's no wonder that so many Floridians join the many Northern visitors who like to "get away from it all" in selecting the Casa Marina Resort for their Florida Keys vacation.

KEY LIME PIE

Key (or West Indian) limes are small, yellow fruits with a sour taste. The large groves of Key Limes were destroyed in hurricanes early in this century. Today they are found primarily in the backyards of residents. The green limes found in supermarkets (Persian Limes) have a different taste. If you cannot find Key Limes, combine the juice of limes and lemons.

2 cups graham cracker crumbs
¹/₄ lb. melted butter
¹/₂ cup granulated sugar
5 egg yolks

15 oz. can of sweetened condensed milk
¹/₂ cup fresh Key Lime juice
2 Tbsp. grated lime peel

Mix the graham cracker crumbs, melted butter and sugar in a mixing bowl. Press evenly into a buttered pie dish. Preheat oven to 350°F. and bake for 10 minutes.

Beat the egg yolks until smooth. Add the condensed milk and beat again until smooth. Stir in the lime juice and grated lime peel. Fill the pie crust with the mixture and chill in the refrigerator for at least one hour. Garnish with a slice of lime or lemon and serve chilled.

YELLOWTAIL SNAPPER MARTINIQUE

One of the most popular items at Flagler's.
Serves 4

2 8-oz. yellowtail snapper filets
½ cup flour seasoned with salt and white
   pepper
4 Tbsp. clarified butter

Martinique sauce
2 plantains, sliced into ¼ inch slices, deep
   fried or sautéed until crispy

Heat the sauté pan, add clarified butter. Lightly dredge the filets in the seasoned flour. Place the filets in the sauté pan and cook for three minutes for color per side. Change pan and bake in a 350°F. oven for three to five minutes, depending on the thickness of the filets. Drain thoroughly. Ladle two to three ounces of the Martinique sauce onto the plate. Top with the snapper and garnish with the crisp, fried plantain slices. Serve with saffron rice and vegetables.

MARTINIQUE SAUCE

2 slices bacon
1 small onion, diced
4 ripe bananas, peeled and sliced
1½ cups clam juice
¾ cup chicken stock

4 Tbsp. flour
1 pint whipping cream
¾ cup white wine
6 Tbsp. dark rum
4 Tbsp. banana liquor

Sauté bacon briefly. Add onion and sauté until clear. Add white wine and reduce. Add the flour to the pan to absorb any bacon grease, and mix well. Add the bananas, clam juice, chicken stock and rum. Bring to a boil and reduce to a simmer for 15 minutes. Add whipping cream and mix well. Continue simmering for 5 to 10 minutes. Strain through a sieve and return to a simmer. Add banana liquor, stir and remove from heat. Serve with sautéed snapper.

SOFT FISH TACO

WITH AVOCADO TEQUILA SAUCE & BLACKBEAN RELISH

I first tried soft fish tacos in San Diego and loved them. The fish tacos in Flagler's were even
better. Both the Avocado Tequila Sauce and the Blackbean Relish are great.
Serves 2

3 oz. grouper filet
2 Tbsp. whipping cream
1 Tbsp. chopped cilantro
½ tsp. ground cumin
⅜ cup avocado tequila sauce (recipe
   follows)
2 Tbsp. salsa

2 Tbsp. blackbean relish
1 Tbsp. diced red pepper
1 Tbsp. diced green pepper
1 wedge lime
1 sprig cilantro leaf
2 6-inch corn tortilla
1 whole jalapeño pepper

Mix cream, cilantro and cumin and heat briefly. Grill grouper fillet and flake into cream mixture. Warm corn tortilla on griddle or small skillet. Place flaked grouper into tortilla and fold in half. Place 3 oz. avocado-tequila sauce on plate. Place folded tortilla onto sauce. Garnish plate with blackbean relish and lime wedge. Sprinkle diced red and green peppers over taco. Garnish with cilantro sprig and jalapeno. Serve salsa on the side.

AVOCADO TEQUILA SAUCE

2 avocados (Haas variety preferred),
   peeled, seeded and chopped
$^3/_4$ cup lime juice
1 small onion, minced
2 Tbsp. chopped cilantro
2 Tbsp. chopped parsley
2 Tbsp. chopped garlic
1 clove garlic, chopped

1 Tbsp. ground black pepper
Dash salt
6 green stuffed olives
$^1/_4$ cup white wine
$^1/_4$ cup orange juice
$^1/_4$ cup tequila
dash Tabasco®

Place avocado, onion, lime juice, parsley, cilantro, garlic, olive, salt and pepper into blender. Purée until smooth. Add wine, tequila, orange juice and stir well. Add Tabasco. (Serve at room temperature. May be kept 2-3 days, refrigerated).

BLACKBEAN RELISH

1 cup cooked black beans
$^1/_4$ cup mixed diced red, green and yellow
   bell peppers and red onion

1 Tbsp. cilantro
1 tsp. ground cumin
3 Tbsp. Italian salad dressing

Mix all ingredients together and serve with soft grouper tacos.

> "Gastronomic perfection can be reached in these combinations:
> - one person dining alone, usually upon a couch or on a hillside;
> - two people, of no matter what age or sex, dining in a good restaurant;
> - six people, of no matter what age or sex, dining in a good home."
>
> M.F.K Fisher

THE SPECIAL TASTE OF FLORIDA

THE DINING ROOM

Little Palm Island
Rt. 4, Box 1036 • Little Torch Key, Florida 33042 • (305) 872-2524

Little Palm Island is an exquisite private luxury resort which occupies a small tropical island just three miles offshore, in the turquoise waters of the lower Florida Keys. The joy of dining at Little Palm Island is not a well kept secret since The Dining Room has been hailed as one of the very best in Florida by such noted publications as Zagat's Restaurant Survey, Gourmet Magazine, Travel & Leisure, Bon Appetit and Condé Nast.

The Dining Room serves the outstanding gourmet cuisine of Swiss-born Executive Chef Michel Reymond, named one of America's Outstanding Chefs by the prestigious Chefs of America organization. Highly innovative, the cuisine offers an exciting blending of classic nouvelle French cooking with the new American style, often embellished with the flavors of the Caribbean and the Orient. The Dining Room is open to dining guests on a reservation-only basis, with guests having the option to dine indoors, outdoors on its spacious terrace, or a few steps below, directly on the resort's sandy beach.

Little Palm Island is one of only 23 U. S. hospitality establishments affiliated with the prestigious Paris-based Relais & Chateaux, which represents 411 elegant small hotels, resorts and gourmet restaurants in 40 countries around the world.

Vanilla-Infused Grilled Shrimp

The vanilla-infused beurre blanc caught our interest;
the taste combination is exquisite.
Serves 4

20 large shrimp, peeled & deveined
$^1/_4$ cup dry white wine
$^1/_2$ vanilla bean
1 cup beurre blanc (see recipe below)

3 Tbsp. olive oil
1 Tbsp. butter
3 bunches of watercress
salt and pepper to taste

Cut the $^1/_2$ vanilla bean lengthwise, scrape the seeds into a small sauce pan and warm up the seeds and the bean with the white wine, then whisk the wine & bean into the beurre blanc and keep warm.

Lightly cook the shrimp with olive oil and season with salt and pepper, grilling each side until cooked.

In a small sauté pan, heat up a tablespoon of butter and quickly sauté the watercress, season with salt and pepper. Spoon a generous amount of the vanilla beurre blanc on the plate, place the wilted watercress in the middle and arrange the shrimp around it. Garnish with a fanned out vanilla bean.

BEURRE BLANC

9 Tbsp. cold, unsalted butter
1/4 cup finely chopped shallots
3 Tbsp. white vinegar

2 Tbsp. dry white wine
1/2 cup cream
  salt and freshly ground white pepper

Heat 1 tablespoon of butter in a saucepan and add the shallots. Cook briefly while stirring. Add the vinegar and wine and simmer until the liquid is reduced by half. Pour in cream and simmer. Continue to simmer while adding remaining butter, one tablespoon at a time. Salt and pepper to taste.

GRILLED RADICCHIO AND BELGIAN ENDIVE
WITH TOMATO BASIL VINAIGRETTE

Serves 4

1 head radicchio, quartered through the
  base
1 large head, or 2 small heads, Belgian
  endive, quartered or halved through
  base

1/2 lemon, juice only
1/2 lb. young, fresh spinach, stemmed
2 oz. roasted walnuts
4 oz. fresh goat cheese

Squeeze lemon over radicchio and endive, place on a medium heat grill and turn several times, marking all sides, a total of roughly 3 minutes.

Place spinach in medium bowl and add some of the vinaigrette, toss very carefully and place on plates. Arrange radicchio and endive over the spinach, and sprinkle with goat cheese and walnuts. Serve additional vinaigrette on the side.

TOMATO BASIL VINAIGRETTE

1/2 red onion, chopped
1 ripe tomato, seeded, peeled, chopped
1 Tbsp. fresh basil

1 clove of fresh garlic, chopped
1/3 cup balsamic vinegar
1 cup extra virgin olive oil

Mix all ingredients in order, allow flavors to marry for 1/2 hour. Serve immediately or refrigerate.

Fresh Lobster Ravioli
with Lobster Bouillon, Tomato Concasse

You will get a kick out of making your own Ravioli - it is both easy and fun, and you can't beat the flavor.
Serves 2

Ravioli

2 cups all purpose flour
2 eggs
1/2 tsp. oil
salt and white pepper to taste
egg white (to seal the ravioli seams)
Water

Lobster Filling

5 oz. Maine lobster tail, steamed, shelled, chopped
1 Tbsp. chopped celery
1 Tbsp. chopped leeks
1 egg yolk
salt and white pepper to taste

Fish Broth

1/2 lb. fish bones
4 stalks celery
2 leeks
1/4 onion
1 bay leaf
3 cloves

Garnish

1 Tbsp. chopped carrots
1 Tbsp. shopped celery
1 Tbsp. chopped leeks
1 pinch fresh garlic
1 pinch of saffron
1 Tbsp. fresh chopped basil
1 cup tomato, peeled, seeded, chopped

To make the ravioli, combine the flour, eggs, oil, salt and pepper in a bowl. Add water a little at a time to make a soft, but firm dough. Let stand for 30 minutes.

To make the lobster filling, simply combine all of the shown ingredients.

To assemble the ravioli, take one half of the dough and roll to a thin layer, cut into 8 squares of the same size (roughly 3-in. x 3-in.). Wet the edges with egg white.

Spoon the lobster filling in the middle of the ravioli squares. Roll the second half of the dough as the first, and again cut the 8 squares. Place these squares over the ones with the filling, and with your fingers press along the edges to seal.

To make the broth, bring the fish bones and 2 quarts of water to a simmer. Add all the other broth ingredients and continue simmering for 30 minutes while uncovered. Strain 1/2 quart of broth into a small sauce pan, add the carrots, celery, leeks, garlic and saffron. Keep warm, salt and pepper to taste.

Put the ravioli in the original broth and simmer for 8 minutes over low heat. Take the cooked ravioli out of the broth and place two in each soup bowl. Pour some of the strained bouillon over the ravioli.

Combine the basil and tomatoes, and spoon one tablespoon of this mixture over the ravioli. Serve immediately.

Maine Lobster, Scallops, Shrimp & Oysters
With Chive Sauce & Puff Pastry

Very elegant, very easy.
Serves 4

1¹/₂ lb. Maine lobster steamed, shelled
8 large sea scallops
8 medium shrimp, peeled & deveined
8 oysters out of shell

1 Tbsp. butter
4 sheets puff pastry
2 heads, Belgian endive
salt and pepper to taste

Sauté scallops, shrimp and oysters in butter.

Cut pieces of rolled puff pastry into rounds. Brush with an egg wash and bake at 350°F. for 8 minutes, or until golden brown.

Cut Belgian endive into julienne and sauté in 1 Tbsp. butter until translucent. Salt and pepper to taste.

Slice the puff pastry round horizontally. Place the bottom half on the center of the plate, fill with endive and replace top. Arrange the seafood around the puff pastry and cover with chive sauce.

Chive Sauce

1 Tbsp. chopped shallots
2 cups Champagne
1 cup heavy cream
1 stick butter
¹/₂ cup chopped chive

In a medium sauce pan, add shallots and sauté for 1 minute. Add Champagne. Let reduce until a syrup consistency and then add 1 cup heavy cream, then reduce the sauce by half.

Add butter 1 Tbsp. at a time, whisk well, salt and pepper to taste, add chives, serve.

To prevent whole onions from breaking apart as they cook, peel them and make an incision in the form of a cross in the root end.

LOUIE'S BACKYARD

700 Waddell Street • Key West, Florida 33040 • (305) 294-1061

Key West in the early 1900's was a wealthy, rowdy town. A place where a brave man with a fast boat could easily make a fortune salvaging goods from ships wrecked by the whims of wind and wave.

Capt. James Adams was one such wrecker. Having made his fortune, he ordered the construction of a gracious revival home on Waddell Street—the building now known as Louie's Backyard. Capt. Adams was fond of boasting that everything in his home, with its unusual two story side porch and doric columns, was salvaged merchandise.

Louie's Backyard not only has a great history, it also has great food, with a dining excellence known to local residents and visitors from around the country. In addition to being designated a place in the National Register of Historic Places, Louie's Backyard has been listed by Florida Trend as one of Florida's finest restaurants for 10 consecutive years.

HOT-FRIED CHICKEN SALAD

This recipe is a study in contrasts: Hot and Cold, Spicy and Sweet, Raw and Cooked, Crunchy and Smooth. It needs to be served immediately after preparation.
Serves 4

4 boneless, skinless chicken breasts, cut into small finger size pieces

MARINADE

Combine all ingredients and mix well.
2 jalapeño peppers, stems and seeds
   removed, sliced thin
1¹/₂ Tbsp. crushed red pepper flakes
1¹/₂ Tbsp. cayenne pepper
salt and ground black pepper to taste
2 cups heavy cream
6 whole eggs
1¹/₂ Tbsp. hot paprika

FLOUR

1¹/₂ cups all-purpose flour
1 Tbsp. salt
2 Tbsp. black pepper
3 Tbsp. crushed red pepper flakes

SALAD DRESSING

3 egg yolks
1¹/₂ Tbsp. honey
3 oz. Creole mustard
¹/₂ cup (slightly less) balsamic vinegar
1¹/₂ cups safflower oil
¹/₂ cup olive oil
¹/₈ cup roasted sesame oil

LETTUCES

1 head of romaine, outer leaves removed,
   washed and torn
1 head of red leaf lettuce, outer leaves
   removed, washed and torn
1 red onion, cut into rings

The dressing can be made 1 or 2 days ahead. The chicken is best marinated 12 hours in advance. The lettuces can be prepared a few hours ahead and left in paper towels in a bowl in the refrigerator. At Louie's, they deep-fry their chicken in peanut oil, but you can pan fry this in a deep-skillet, taking normal safety precautions.

Make the dressing by beating the egg yolks until thick and lemon colored. Slowly beat in the remaining ingredients. The dressing should by creamy with a sweet, tart taste. Refrigerate.

Add the chicken strips to the marinade and refrigerate until ready to cook and serve. Prepare lettuces.

When ready to serve, heat the oil to approximately 350°F. Remove the chicken meat allowing excess marinade to drip off. (You can simply strain the marinade off into a sink, since you'll be cooking all the chicken at once.)

Roll the chicken "fingers" in the seasoned flour.

Fry the chicken — turning it from time to time until it is light brown.

Put the salad greens into a bowl and add just enough dressing to lightly coat the leaves. Mound the leaves in large chilled bowls.

Remove the hot chicken to toweling and cut up into bite-size chunks. Arrange them over the greens and top the salad with 4 or 5 rings of red onion.

PAN-COOKED WHOLE YELLOWTAIL
WRAPPED IN LEEKS
WITH A WARM BALSAMIC VINAIGRETTE

Serves 4

FOR FISH

4 1¹/₄ - 1¹/₂ *lb. yellowtail snapper, cleaned
and scaled, head & tail on*
4 *tsp. sea salt*
4 *tsp. freshly cracked black pepper*
¹/₄ *cup flour*
¹/₂ *cup clarified butter*
4 *large bunches leeks, cleaned and cooked
in water until soft. Drain, then ice and
reserve*

FOR SAUCE

¹/₄ *cup balsamic vinegar*
1 *cup olive oil, steeped with crushed red
pepper*

Cut a shallow diagonal slash into the sides of each fish. Season the yellowtail with the salt & pepper. Heat a pan large enough to hold a single yellowtail, flat.

Dredge the fish lightly in flour. "Spank" off any excess.

Heat enough clarified butter to coat the bottom of the pan, then sear the fish. You can do more than one fish at a time if you have a large enough pan. Sear the fish on each side and remove to a work surface.

Lightly oil the leeks and lay them out carefully. Now, completely wrap the fish with the leeks - except the head and tail - alternating them and over-lapping them in an attractive fashion. Brush a bit more of the oil on the leeks that are wrapped around the fish.

Transfer the fish to a baking pan that will hold them flat. Put into a 400°F. oven and bake for 15-18 minutes. Serve immediately with Warm Balsamic Vinaigrette.

CHOCOLATE BROWNIE CRÈME BRULÉE
Serves 8

4 1/2 oz. bittersweet chocolate, chopped	*5/8 cup sugar*
6 Tbsp. cubed butter	*1/2 tsp. vanilla*
3/4 chopped pecans	*1/4 tsp. salt*
	1 large egg
	4 Tbsp. flour

Melt the chocolate and butter in the top of a double boiler and whisk together until blended. Whisk in the sugar, vanilla, salt, egg and flour in the order shown above. Fold in 3/4 cup chopped pecans. Spread in buttered, floured 8 x 8 inch pan.

Bake at 350°F. until sides slightly pull away from pan (about 15-18 minutes). Allow brownies to cool, then cut into nine equal squares. (Yes, when recipe is completed, you will have one square remaining - enjoy!)

CRÈME BRULÉE

Scald: 3 7/8 cups cream	*8 large egg yolks*
2 vanilla beans, split open, seeds scraped into cream	*3/8 cup sugar*

Scald the cream and vanilla, then slowly whisk in the egg yolks mixed with the sugar. Do not beat eggs too much. Cook the cream with the eggs over medium heat until it coats the back of a wooden spoon. Strain immediately.

Press a small brownie into the bottom of eight 6 ounce custard cups. Pour brulée mixture into cup to the rim. Put cups in large baking dish, then fill dish with water to halfway up the cups.

Cover with foil and and bake at 325°F. approximately 40 minutes, or until your finger leaves a slight mark. The custard will move a little. Cool, then chill.

Before serving, sprinkle with 1 Tbsp. of sugar and broil until caramelized. Brownies and brulée can be made one day ahead of time.

THE PIER HOUSE RESTAURANT

The Pier House Resort & Caribbean Spa
1 Duval Street • Key West, Florida 33040 • (305) 296-4600

The *New York Times* refers to The Pier House Restaurant as, "Key West's premier restaurant." Overlooking the water at the foot of Duval Street, this AAA Four-Diamond restaurant is located in the famous Pier House Resort. Over the years, The Pier House has become an intimate resort that attracts guests from throughout the world to its unique, village-like setting.

The cuisine of The Pier House Restaurant is a delightful fusion of Floridian and Caribbean styles that perfectly complements the resort's elegant, yet tropical ambiance. Executive Chef Phil Heimer makes annual summer trips to various kitchens in the Caribbean to stay abreast of the latest ingredients and techniques used in his special cuisine. The Pier House Restaurant's creative seafood and conch dishes are superb, and the ceviche is the best in Florida.

The "Conch Republic" of Key West has a special, laid back approach to the good things in life. Among the visitors and those who call Key West home, you will find many many who feel quite strongly that a good beer and conch fritters at sunset is indeed a positive thing for one's outlook on life. I would have to agree with this, and The Pier House provides the perfect location.

Stone Crab Salad
with Hibiscus Vinaigrette

Serves 4

$^1/_4$ *cup vegetable oil*
$^1/_4$ *cup extra virgin olive oil*
$^3/_8$ *cup raspberry vinegar*
1 orange, zest only
assorted field greens

$^1/_4$ *cup hibiscus tea*
$^1/_4$ *cup pureed raspberries*
salt & freshly ground pepper to taste
12 stone crab claws

Place washed and dried field greens in the center of chilled plates. Arrange the meat from the crab claws on top.

Place the remaining ingredients into a blender and blend for about 10 seconds. Drizzle the vinaigrette over the salad and garnish with hibiscus flower petals.

GROUPER PHILIPE

This dish has a true Caribbean accent. The Mango-Almond Chutney
is pure heaven and breeze to prepare, with a number of uses.
Serves 2

2 7-oz. grouper filets
4 thin slices of Pancetta or regular bacon
2 cups fresh spinach
1 clove garlic, minced
1 tsp. olive oil

3 Tbsp. fresh lemon juice
8 thin slices of ripe plantain
salt & fresh ground pepper to taste
6 Tbsp. Mango-Almond Chutney

Heat a non-stick pan with the olive oil and add the garlic. Cook for 30 seconds. Add the lemon juice and fresh spinach. Turn to coat the spinach with the mixture while heating until just slightly wilted.

Lay the grouper filets on a flat surface and with a sharp knife parallel to the surface, butterfly the grouper filets so the bottom and top portion are each about $1/4$-inch thick. Place half of the Mango-Almond Chutney on the lower pieces of each filet, then fold the upper pieces over the chutney to cover it. Salt and pepper the grouper to taste.

Place the grouper into a baking dish that has been lightly oiled. Layer with the spinach, plantains and bacon. Bake at 400°F. for 20 minutes. If browning too much, cover with foil. Serve with Mango-Almond Chutney and rice.

MANGO-ALMOND CHUTNEY

1 small onion, diced
6 Tbsp. fresh ginger, peeled, minced
1 Tbsp. chili powder
$3/4$ tsp. cinnamon
$1/8$ tsp. mace
$1/8$ tsp. alspice
$1/8$ tsp. ground clove
1 Tbsp. Coleman's Dry Mustard
$1/2$ Tbsp. ground coriander

$1^1/2$ cups rice vinegar
$1^1/2$ lb. light brown sugar
1 cup white wine
$2^1/2$ lb. fresh, diced mango
1 fresh pineapple, peeled, diced
$1/2$ cup seedless raisins, or to taste
$1^1/2$ cups toasted almonds
1 cup plain bread crumbs

Mist a large pan with canola oil and sauté the onions and ginger. Add the spices, white wine, mango, pineapple, vinegar and brown sugar. Simmer over a low heat until the mixture develops the consistency of a light syrup. Remove from heat, add raisins and almonds. Cool, then mix in bread crumbs. Store in refrigerator.

Frozen Key Lime Pie with Meringue

An interesting variation on this venerable classic from the Florida Keys.
One 8-inch pie

3 egg yolks
14 oz. sweetened condensed milk
1/2 cup fresh lime juice

1 tsp. cream of tartar
1 prepared graham cracker crust

Whip yolks until thick and light in color. Add sweetened condensed milk and mix on low speed for a minute, then add lime juice, cream of tarter and mix until blended. Ladle mixture into the prepared graham craker cust. Bake at 300°F. until set, around 15 minutes or until filling doesn't stick to fingers when touched. Freeze for 3 1/2 hours before topping with meringue.

Meringue

1 cup egg whites
1 cup fine granulated sugar

1/2 tsp. cream of tartar

Preheat oven to 400°F. Place all ingredients into a clean, dry mixing bowl. A copper bowl is best.

Whip until you can form stiff peaks. Remove pie from freezer. Form a mountain on top of the pie. Pick at this with a spatula to form peaks. Bake the pie until the peaks have browned slightly, about 10 minutes. Return to freezer until ready to serve.

Note, chef Philipe uses the technique of placing a lighted can of sterno below the mixing bowl while whipping the egg whites to their fluffiest. To serve this frozen pie, dip a knife into hot water before slicing to make clean cuts.

Note: 10 day old eggs at room temperature work best for a fluffy meringue.

INDEX

C

D

Z

Notes

Notes

Notes